Decentralizing
City Government

Walter G. Farr, Jr.
Lance Liebman
Jeffrey S. Wood

This study was sponsored by
the Bar Association
of the City of New York
in connection with
its Centennial celebration

The Praeger Special Studies program—utilizing the most modern and efficient book production techniques and a selective worldwide distribution network—makes available to the academic, government, and business communities significant, timely research in U.S. and international economic, social, and political development.

Decentralizing City Government

A Practical Study of a Radical Proposal for New York City

PRAEGER SPECIAL STUDIES IN U.S. ECONOMIC, SOCIAL, AND POLITICAL ISSUES

Praeger Publishers   New York   Washington   London

PRAEGER PUBLISHERS
111 Fourth Avenue, New York, N.Y. 10003, U.S.A.
5, Cromwell Place, London S.W.7, England

Published in the United States of America in 1972
by Praeger Publishers, Inc.

Library of Congress Catalog Card Number: 72-83567

Printed in the United States of America

This study of decentralization of city government was sponsored
by the Association of the Bar of the City of New York as a project of
its centennial celebration. The Ford Foundation and the Rockefeller
Foundation made generous financial contributions. The association
appointed a special committee of members with experience in, and
concern for, New York City's government and urban problems. The
committee members, whose names are listed on pages vi and vii, read
and commented on numerous study drafts and met many times to discuss
controversial issues and to suggest ways to improve the study's content and focus. But the authors take full responsibility for the study
itself, particularly the conclusions and the many subsidiary value
judgments in the body of the study. Statements of the individual views
of some of the Committee members are set forth beginning at p. xvi.

As background for the study, the association commissioned
special studies of decentralization of four governmental programs:
elementary and secondary education by Howard Kalodner; sanitation
by Adam Yarmolinsky and Michael Schwartz; social services by
Bertram Beck; and criminal justice by Richard Danzig. Jeffrey Wood
studied decentralization of housing programs. In addition, Eloise Hirsh
analyzed the City's experience with Model Cities, Community Corporations, and Urban Action Task Forces. An interim report, based on
these special studies and the independent research of this volume's
authors, was distributed to interested members of the association,
City government officials, and others concerned with City affairs.
The association then held a symposium to discuss the interim report.
City officials, municipal union officials, and leading academicians
discussed the political aspects of decentralization, the effect decentralization might have on the quality of key government services, and
fiscal, budgetary, and municipal employment problems. One of the
panels pointed out lessons that could be learned from the City's
education decentralization experience. The symposium panelists
are listed on pages viii, ix and x.

The symposium discussion pointed up the need for further
research and analysis in several areas. The association commissioned
Sol Hoberman and Lewis Kaden to study civil service and municipal
union problems. Dick Netzer, John Forrer, Heather Ruth, and Peter
Goldmark were consulted concerning fiscal affairs, budgeting, and
local taxation. Susanne Farkas helped in analyzing the political problems of decentralization. Finally, Michael Schwartz prepared a
detailed analysis of the effect decentralization might have on the

quality of sanitation services, which is included as an appendix to this study.

The final draft of the study was circulated to the members of the advisory committee in January of 1972. By that time, decentralization had ceased to be a subject of long-term academic interest and had become a major political issue. As a result the draft report has already been circulated among City and state officials and among some community leaders. Hopefully, this study will help public officials, representatives of civic and interest groups, newspaper and broadcast reporters, and concerned citizens to understand better the choices posed by various decentralization proposals and their likely or possible consequences for the quality and cost of the public services the City delivers to its residents.

The study discusses, and ultimately points toward, drastic alterations in the structure of New York City's government. Nonetheless, it is a very conservative document. The authors believe that New York City will not only survive, but triumph—that it will remain America's great city because of its confluence of financial, cultural, and social resources. The nation needs New York and cannot replace it. Moreover, we believe the City's economic and artistic vitality will continue its attractiveness as a place to live for millions of Americans of all income levels. Not that there will be no burdens to living in the City, but compensating advantages and pleasures will outweigh the burdens for vast numbers of old and new New Yorkers.

We are also conservative in envisioning a residential city like today's, with rich residents and poor, but with the vast percentage in between—working people, of all races, who ride the subway, shop, and send their children to public or private schools. Indeed, as we set out at various places in the study, we see the major task of federal, state, and local public policy to be that of bringing to today's poor residents, and especially their children, an opportunity for a way of life similar to that which New York City's middle class enjoys today.

Yet that spirit of endorsing much of the present, expecting it to continue, and, indeed, seeking more of it for more people, leads us to conclude that City government should be altered. Recent events—expansion of public tasks, altered revenue base, new pressures between municipal employees and the consumers of their labor—lead us to conclude that a partially decentralized government might meet the public's demand for municipal services better and at lower cost.

The Special Committee of the Association of the
Bar of the City of New York

Thomas R. Farrell, Co-Chairman
Russell D. Niles, Co-Chairman
Bethuel M. Webster, Vice-Chairman
Fritz W. Alexander II
Herman Badillo
Edward N. Costikyan
Judah Gribetz
Howard N. Mantel
Frederic S. Nathan
Basil A. Paterson
Theodore Pearson
David Ross
Frederick A. O. Schwartz
Elizabeth T. Schack
David Schoenbrod
Jeanne Silver
Robert W. Sweet
Roger W. Wilkins

"CAN NEW YORK CITY BE GOVERNED?"

A Symposium on the Realities of Decentralizing
New York's Government

at the House of the Association of the Bar of
the City of New York

Thursday, December 3, 1970

"Decentralization and the Body Politic"

Chairman: Russell D. Niles, former President of the Association
and former Dean of New York University School of
Law.

Moderator: Walter G. Farr, Jr., Professor of Law, New York University School of Law, former National Director,
Model Cities Program

Panelists: Wallace S. Sayre, Professor of Political Science,
Columbia University. Author (with Herbert Kaufman)
of Governing New York City
Donald H. Elliott, Chairman, City Planning Commission
Alan A. Altschuler, Professor of Political Science,
M. I. T.
Robert Abrams, President of the Borough of The Bronx

"Can Decentralization Deliver?"

Chairman: Edward N. Costikyan, former Democratic Party Leader,
New York County

Moderator: Lance M. Liebman, Professor of Law, Harvard University, former Executive Assistant to Mayor
Lindsay

Panelists: "Personal Services: Health, Welfare, Protection and
                 Justice"
              Jule M. Sugarman, Administrator, Human Resources
                 Administration, New York City
              Gordon Chase, Administrator, Health Service Adminis-
                 tration, New York City
              Henry S. Ruth, Director, Criminal Justice Coordinating
                 Council
              Bertram Beck, Director, Henry Street Settlement House
                 and Committee Consultant for Social Services
              Harvey V. Fineberg, Committee Staff, Health Services
              Richard Danzig, Committee Staff, Criminal Justice
              "Environmental Services: Housing, Zoning and
                 Sanitation"
              Samuel J. Kearing, former Sanitation Commissioner,
                 New York City
              Robert G. Hazen, Commissioner, Department of
                 Development, New York City
              Michael W. Schwartz, Professor of Law, New York
                 University School of Law and Committee Co-Consultant
                 for Sanitation Services
              Adam Yarmolinsky, Professor of Law, Harvard Law
                 School and Committee Co-Consultant for Sanitation
                 Services
              Jeffrey S. Wood, Associate Director of the Special
                 Study and Committee Consultant for Housing Programs

              Address by Mayor John V. Lindsay

Friday, December 4, 1970

                 "The Education Experience"

Chairman: Howard N. Mantel, Study Committee Member

Moderator: Howard I. Kalodner, Professor of Law, New York
                 University School of Law

Panelists: Murry Bergtraum, Chairman, Board of Education,
                 New York City
              Albert Shanker, President, United Federation of Teachers
              James Sullivan, Member of Community School Board
                 No. 13

ix

"Financing Decentralization"

Chairman: Robert W. Sweet, Study Committee Member

Moderator: Norman Redlich, First Assistant Corporation Counsel,
             New York City

Panelists: Dick Netzer, Dean, New York University Graduate
             School of Public Administration
             Edward K. Hamilton, Budget Director, New York City
             Mario Merola, Chairman of the Finance Committee,
             New York City Council
             Horace L. Morancie, Director, Central Brooklyn Model
             Cities Program

"Manpower in a Decentralized City"

Chairman: Walter G. Farr, Jr.

Moderator: Michael I. Sovern, Dean, Columbia University Law School

Panelists: Herbert L. Haber, Director, Office of Collective Bar-
             gaining, New York City
             Victor Gotbaum, President, District Council 37
             Harry H. Wellington, Professor of Labor Law, Yale
             Law School

CONTENTS

List of Tables

STATEMENT OF EDWARD N. COSTIKYAN,
THOMAS R. FARRELL, AND
THEODORE PEARSON

Since the work of this committee commenced and the studies of the staff began the need for decentralization of New York City's government has become increasingly apparent. Two years ago, the notion that New York City's government needed restructuring was relatively new. It was the product of dissatisfaction with the manner in which essentially local services were delivered. It reflected unhappiness with the increasing insulation of the City's governmental mechanism from reaction to legitimate citizen-needs.

In the intervening years, the need for decentralization has become increasingly apparent, and in our view the studies staff has done a careful job in analyzing all the risks implicit in restructuring our City government. It is our view, also, that the risks can and should be taken; that there has been adequate study of the problem; that further delay in implementing the proposals in the staff report can only lead to further deterioration of the City government; and that sooner or later we will have some form of decentralization of New York City government. We believe it is important that it be the right form.

Accordingly, while acknowledging the risks implicit in carrying out the staff's recommendations, we endorse the conclusions. We urge that action be taken by all appropriate governmental authorities forthwith to recast the charter of the City of New York for implementing this.

But action by governmental authorities to create a new structure will not in itself be enough. As the report says, successfully changing to decentralization will need the support of millions of New Yorkers, in the formulation and in the implementation of any new structure. We also urge that a program be instituted to mobilize public support for this action now.

STATEMENT OF ROBERT W. SWEET

"Decentralizing City Government" successfully raises almost all the questions that must be considered before embarking upon the process of decentralization. The study has correctly identified the areas in which some form of decentralized structure already exists. Further analysis and additional study is required concerning these programs, however, particularly relating to the Board of Education and Model Cities, before any final conclusions can be drawn. In addition, realistic models are essential to test the theory of decentralization advanced by the study.

To complete the necessary study, the recently enacted Charter Revision Commission should set itself the task of evaluating the present City Charter and the existing programs of a decentralized nature, determining the boundaries of unified service districts, preparing fiscal legislation incorporating decentralized budgets for such districts, and recommending the services to be decentralized within such districts. Ultimately, the Commission should recommend the extent of any transfer of power, whether administrative or political.

STATEMENT OF DAVID SCHOENBROD,
JOINED BY F. A. O. SCHWARTZ, JR. AND JEAN SILVER.
FRITZ ALEXANDER, II CONCURS
IN THE GENERAL APPROACH OF THIS STATEMENT
BUT TAKES NO POSITION ON THE SPECIFIC ISSUES
OF A DECENTRALIZED CITY'S STRUCTURE.

New Yorkers should begin to decentralize their City now. The greatest need is to bring back to the people a sense of controlling their own destinies.

Those who advocate more experiments tend to forget that New York, as the world's largest city under a single municipal government, is itself a unique experiment in the problems of size.

The process of creating a new structure should adhere to the principles of decentralization; citizens must understand decentralization, participate in the formulation of its ground rules, and assent to its implementation. "Additional study" will not produce more grass roots level understanding. Rather, the public will focus best on the underlying issues when a broadly based commission is charged with the actual drafting of a charter revision, taking into account the recent experience of local programs such as the Community School Boards and the growing block association movement.

State government, which recently redrew legislative boundaries with cynical disregard for neighborhoods, should have a role in the selection and operation of this Commission commensurate with its marginal interest in the City government. City government, which has an interest in the status quo, should not control the process. The drafting group should contain a majority of persons whose primary identification is with neighborhood level institutions or who are elected

as representatives of small areas. Coupling the drafting process
with citywide administrative decentralization, including district-level
budgeting, would heighten public awareness, generate data useful to
the Commission, and prepare the way for political decentralization.
At the end of a year or two, after a discussion of concrete questions—
not on pronouncements handed down by a blue-ribbon commission—
the residents of New York could decide how they wish to govern themselves.

There are ample preliminary studies. The study by this Committee's staff analyzes the issues comprehensively. We agree that
a two-tiered political decentralization has important potential, but
that structure alone cannot cope with many more deeply-seated problems. Our limited disagreements stem from a difference in focus.
We see public participation, access to government, and accountability
as important values in themselves, while the staff report avowedly
treats them only as ways to improve services.

   1. The Districts Should Consist of Existing Communities. The
study ascribes high priority to setting district boundaries for equalizing
wealth, ensuring a population mix, and spreading population evenly
among districts. The result might be roughly 40 districts, each with
a population of 200,000. Such districts would vary from what most
New Yorkers see as communities; many sizable, recognized communities are smaller than 100,000 in population. Equality of wealth
and heterogeneity of population would dictate the splitting of most
poorer or minority neighborhoods.

The study gives two reasons for drawing district lines to produce
cross-sections. First, the staff argues that disparities in district
wealth will lead rich districts to fight for more local taxation and
less city taxation, thus lessening the City's limited role in taxing
according to wealth and providing services according to need. But
there are ways of equalizing access to public services without frac-
turing neighborhoods; the Charter could provide a formula whereby
district level tax revenues would be levied upon or matched according
to the relative wealth of the districts.

Second, the staff argues that majority groups would dominate
the more homogeneous districts and drive out minorities, even if
zoning were handled on a citywide level. Perhaps this failing is
expectable, but heterogeneous districts may not be any better. Block-
level prejudicies and rents probably have much more to do with
determining who lives in a neighborhood than does the political sub-
division in which it falls. So, disregard for community boundaries
may produce more multiracial districts but not necessarily more
multiracial neighborhoods.

There is strong reason to honor existing communities. Only if
the districts follow community lines will minorities have an opportunity to elect their fair share of district officials.

To follow recognized community lines, there should be no fewer than 60 districts, each with an average population of about 125,000, drawn with regard to tradition, public facilities, transportation modes, shopping areas, and natural boundaries. The districting should preserve existing integrated communities, but should not attempt to paper-over racism with a map, because the net result would be to deprive minorities of political representation.

2. <u>Decentralize the Police</u>. To most citizens, decentralization means effective local control over schools, sanitation, and police. Since local government must generate sufficient citizen-interest if it is to succeed, the districts should control all three functions within the foreseeable future. The staff would decentralize sanitation pick-up, but postpone the conforming of community school-board and district-government boundaries, and it would keep the police centralized.

The arguments for decentralization of the police are powerful. Effective police work requires citizen cooperation. What the study describes as the "Leviathan" size of the Police Department makes it difficult for the Department to control its lower levels and communicate with citizen groups. Decentralizing the patrol function would not prevent keeping certain detective and special-service functions at the City level.

The strongest argument to the contrary is that decentralized police would express local prejudices. The danger of prejudice is real, but whose prejudice is most dangerous and how best can it be curbed? The City now fails to deal satisfactorily with the Police Department's own prejudices, particularly in minority areas where the police are seen as an occupying army demanding bribes and obeisance. A centralized police department in a decentralized city offers little hope of curing this problem; it does run the added risk of an even stronger reflection of local prejudice by the police where there is ethnic similarity between the force and the district. As such, this choice may involve the worst combination of alternatives.

3. <u>Give the Districts More Budgetary Autonomy</u>. The power of the purse is the power to control. Thus the districts must have fiscal power concomitant with their operating responsibilities, or budget officers at the City level will run local government.

The study recommends a budgeting system, at least initially, for allocating funds in the form of grants to the districts, to be spent only in broad budget categories. This type of allocation would tie the districts' hands in deciding between, say, more code enforcement and more sanitation service. In theory, it would not hinder them in deciding upon the form of sanitation service, but, in practice, control over district decisions might be greater since city-level officials—with an interest in perpetuating their power—would want to make the grant-categories as narrow as possible.

A better system would allocate funds among the districts, not by program area, but by population and general indicia of need, such as poverty and the number of senior citizens. With this system, the City could continue to administer tax collection and state and federal grant gathering but would allocate the unrestricted proceeds according to overall fiscal needs.

The problems of budgeting merely illustrate the ways in which residual central controls can cripple neighborhood government. Similar problems can arise in central control of capital budgets, collective bargaining, civil service laws, accounting, purchasing, contracting, and bonding requirements. While fiscal integrity and the interests of existing employees require some restraints on districts' choices in such areas, the allocation of authority must leave local government with the ability to govern.

4. Abolish the Offices of Borough President, Comptroller, and President of the City Council as Elected Positions. The accountability of government officials requires that they be visible to their electorate. Even now, visibility is reduced by the large number of officials that voters must elect. Since decentralization would add another level of elected officials, the new structure must dispense with elective positions that are not essential.

The difficulties in perpetuating the ceremonial office of Borough President only begin with the imposition of unnecessary administrative costs and the dilution of the quality of elections. The Borough Presidents, conveniently situated in the middle of jurisdictional disputes between districts and the central City, will undoubtedly attempt to arrange compromises that result in the assumption by them of the disputed powers, in either the formal or the informal chain of command. The result will be a three-tier system of government with the number of jurisdictional disputes cubed.

As in the federal government, the Mayor should appoint the chief fiscal officer, the comptroller; the Council should elect its President.

Decentralization will fail to bring local services to acceptable standards so long as other levels of government and private institutions have the fiscal and other power that the City needs. But if New Yorkers understand this limitation, decentralization is worthwhile. Creating credible local government is an essential step in mounting political support for a fairer distribution of such power.

STATEMENT OF HOWARD N. MANTEL, JUDAH GRIBETZ AND ELIZABETH T. SCHACK

As part of its centennial celebrations, in 1969 the Association of the Bar of the City of New York organized a major study of

decentralization of the New York City government; a Centennial
Committee on the Decentralization Study was created and a study
research team, headed by Walter G. Farr, Jr., of the New York University Law School, was commissioned.

During the course of the work of the study, the Committee met
on numerous occasions and formed a number of working subcommittees.
Its purpose was not to decide the issue of decentralization, which
increasingly became the center of intensive public debate and controversy, but to sift relevant questions and to help frame a basis for an
objective review.

We recognize that neither polemics nor unrealistic conceptual
proposals are likely to aid in the solution of New York's deep-seated
and pervasive problems. Decentralization may offer some assistance
in meeting the quests and service requirements of the City's residents
and businesses. At the same time, it is critical to avoid jumping head-
long into a revamping of the City's governmental fabric without a careful examination of the known and the potential, unknown dangers.

We believe that Professor Farr and his colleagues have contributed
to the probing of many of the searching questions involved. Their
report should aid in the consideration of decentralization, as well as
of other alternatives for upgrading the governmental and participatory
capacities of New York City. Its timeliness is increased with the
advent of a new charter-revision commission.

The committee and the association should take no official view
of decentralization. We respect the right of the authors to reach and
state their own conclusions. Individual members of the Committee
have a wide range of views on the subject as a whole and on particular
aspects. Hence we have intended neither to adopt the study as one
issued by the Committee nor to endorse or reject it. We commend it
for wide public reading and urge continuation and expansion of the
probing process.

In recent years mayors, legislators, newspaper columnists, and the general public have all agreed that the nation is in the midst of an "urban crisis." Congress has declared that "improving the quality of urban life is the most critical domestic problem facing the United States."[1] Crime in the streets, drug addiction, unemployment, welfare dependency, breakdowns in health care and public education, deteriorating housing, dirty streets, and polluted air all are concentrated within our cities, and all seem to be getting worse at once. These tangible problems are matched by a growing dissatisfaction with city government and city services. Urban leaders increasingly employ bitter confrontation tactics; at the same time most members of the new urban minorities and of the ethnic working class seem either apathetic or sullenly hostile. More mobile middle-class residents and businessmen are rapidly moving out of the cities altogether.

New York City, always a city of superlatives, seems to represent the biggest problem of all. In fact, New York is better off in many respects than most other large cities, but its problems always run into the millions, and they are most widely reported in the media. In addition, New York is now, as always, in the forefront in attempting to devise new and better ways to cope with urban problems. New York is then an apt subject for study, both because of the importance of its own problems and because its solutions are frequently copied in other cities.

The mayors and their supporters usually blame their cities' problems on lack of money—especially lack of federal and state support for education, welfare, and all other urban services considered to be necessary by the mayors and their constituents. Money is clearly at the base of much of the urban problem. As the cities increasingly become the principal home of the poor, the minorities, and the aged, and as middle-class residents and businesses flee to the suburbs, cities will become less and less able to pay for the increasing services their residents need and demand. If urban decay, poverty, and racial strife are to be contained, national resource allocation policies must shift radically toward maintenance of a decent environment and toward a more equal sharing of the financial burdens of housing, educating, healing, and maintaining the inner city poor. But no such massive shift seems imminent; in any event more money alone is not a complete answer.

New York City's municipal expenditures have trebled in the past ten years, and the rate of increase in City expenses seems to be accelerating. These increases in expenditures have permitted a 50 percent increase in municipal employment and a smaller but significant increase in actual services. But the changing population, the increasing impatience of minorities for equal opportunity, and such diverse social and economic trends as bulkier packaging of consumer commodities and spreading drug addiction have meant that needs and demands of City residents for municipal services are increasing far more rapidly than is the City's response.

Nor have increases in dollars spent or people employed always meant increased effectiveness of governmental services. New York's public school system was geared to an upwardly mobile clientele in an era of greater individual economic opportunity. It has neither the capability nor the experience to serve the exploding proportion of black and Spanish-speaking students in the school population—from 37 percent in 1960 to 57 percent in 1970. No simple increase in police services can eliminate drug-related thefts and muggings or increase the security and cooperation of those who view the police as an occupying force. Longer vacations, more sick leave, and inefficient utilization of equipment can counteract theoretical gains from introduction of new, more efficient sanitation trucks and sweepers.

Lack of money and poor municipal services account for only part of the resentment and alienation of large numbers of New York residents, who feel that City government does not represent their interests and is not to be trusted. Most New York residents feel they have no access to, or influence over, the decision makers in the great City institutions. The City's general elections of councilmen, borough presidents, the mayor, and other citywide officials rarely involve issues relating to neighborhood services or conditions, which are close to home and important for the average City voter. Low voter turnout at local Community Corporation, Model Cities, and even school board elections reflects in material part the widespread ignorance of the roles of those boards or skepticism that they have real power. In the old days political clubs offered channels of

communication at least to the party faithful. Even this channel is
now closed, partly through the triumph of reform politics. It is widely
assumed that most decisions are fixed by the Manhattan establishment,
by a few powerful union leaders, by party politicians, or by the under-
world.

For all these reasons, it is important to examine the institutional
structure of City government to determine whether institutional change
can help improve the quality of urban life, whatever the level of available funds. We believe that institutional structure is relevant to
government output: the decisions that are made, the quality and quantity
of services that are provided, who is hired and how hard they work,
what tasks they perform, and when they perform them. And purposive
alteration of the machinery of government is not vain: it is possible
to reason about the kind of government product one would like to encourage and about the government structure most likely to achieve
that product, and possible then to contribute to alterations of government structure in the direction one has charted.

During the 73 years since the formation of the five-borough
City of New York, the structure and organization of the City's government has been studied and restudied by the exponents of scientific
management, rational administrative organization, and coordinated,
comprehensive planning. These studies have almost all recommended
greater reliance on professional experts to plan and deliver services
and greater centralization of decision-making authority and administrative control in the central City government and in the office of the
mayor. Almost all of these reforms have been implemented, but the
City's complex network of political party and interest group struggles
has continued to dominate the content and course of public policy.
Although the past decades have witnessed a growing level of competence
and individual capacity at top levels of City government, there has
not been a parallel growth in the ability of the top levels to change
the content of City policy.

The failure of centralized, professional City government led,
in the early 1960's, to a nationwide citizen participation counter-
revolution against notions of policy-neutral administrative expertise
and technical rationality. This movement was based on the view that
laymen, in general, and recipients of services, in particular, could
develop and administer programs more effectively than professionals.*

----

*The terms _effective_, _efficient_, and _satisfactory_ or _responsive_
services will be used throughout this study. While exact definitions
of these terms may not be possible, we will generally be using them
as follows: Effective services are those that are achieving their

Ten years and two federal programs later (Office of Economic Opportunity and Model Cities), the more extreme claims for citizen participation have yet to be proved. But out of the frustrations of efforts to harness citizens and program professionals—particularly poor, minority group citizens and white, middle-class professionals—came arguments for more structured, formal kinds of decentralization. The inquiry shifted to restructuring traditional political and administrative institutions within existing jurisdictions to reduce the scale on which governmental decisions are made and thereby decrease the role of central administrative officials and professional bureaucracies in the process of local policy formulation and service delivery.

This was the background against which the Association of the Bar of the City of New York decided to support a study of the structure of New York City's government as a major project of its 100th anniversary year. Because of widespread concern that the existing centralized government of the City was failing to provide satisfactory service and because of the emerging interest in community control and neighborhood government, the association requested that this inquiry focus on whether or not decentralization of government might improve the quality of New York City's government and increase the satisfaction of City residents.

---

objectives—sanitation services that keep streets and sidewalks clean or schools that train their graduates for existing jobs, prepare graduates for college, or help graduates appreciate books and the arts. Services are efficient when the costs of needed inputs are as low as possible in comparison with the quantity of service—sanitation services are efficient if the costs per trash can emptied are low, even though residents keep the sidewalks littered—and it is efficient for schools to buy first-grade readers in volume and at a discount, though first graders in some areas are not learning to read. Services are satisfactory or responsive when the service recipients feel they are receiving the services they want and need from a service agency they respect and accept—residents who ascribe high priority to the opportunity to obtain well-paying jobs right out of high school and who respect professional educators might find a vocational or commercial high school that is administered tightly through central school headquarters satisfactory and responsive, even though the average life incomes of the school's graduates turn out to be low and the graduates tend not to take advantage of available cultural activities. Others who value college admission highly or minority persons who want their schools to reflect their culture might find those same schools unsatisfactory and unresponsive.

Decentralization means many different things to different people, and it is cited as the solution to many different problems. Some feel that the principal urban problem today is the alienation and powerlessness of its residents, not only poor blacks and Puerto Ricans but also the working class of all ethnic and racial backgrounds. It would follow that participation of the poor and minorities in government should be radically increased, whether or not such increased participation helped or hindered the efficient delivery of traditional government services. At least for now the creation of culturally homogeneous, semiautonomous neighborhoods, to which residents felt they belonged and in which they had some leeway to set their own priorities, would be more important than better preparation for college, improved housing, or more efficient trash collection. Others feel that City government is failing because top elected and appointed officials represent established middle-class and business interests rather than the bulk of New York's white working class or minority poor and that decentralization would assure a more representative government. Other proponents of decentralization feel that the municipal service bureaucracies and their unions have too much power and are serving themselves rather than the City's residents and that decentralization might provide the means to break the stranglehold of the bureaucracy and the unions. Still others are primarily concerned that the atrophying of party politics and of local political clubhouses has left City residents with no access to, or connection with, City government; they believe that decentralization might give new life to the parties or at least provide a substitute means of citizen access and connection.

All of those diagnoses of urban problems have validity, and decentralization might help achieve some or all of those objectives. But the objectives reflect different and somewhat conflicting values of government, social relations, or politics and are inconsistent when applied in specific contexts. This study focuses on the problem of ineffective and unsatisfactory governmental services and considers whether decentralization of some of the City's decision-making authority and service delivery responsibility might make governmental services more effective and more satisfactory to the bulk of New York City residents. From this point of view demands for community control of education, health, or police are seen as reflecting concern that children are not being prepared for college or good jobs, that City youths are failing physical exams on which good jobs depend, that visits to clinics are tedious and impersonal, and that streets and even homes are insecure.

But satisfaction with City services may well depend in material part on whether residents feel that policy makers, administrators, and City employees are responsive to their wishes and are accountable to them. Many New Yorkers also feel that they or their neighbors

deserve a larger share of well-paid, secure City jobs and of government contracts. So the objective of more satisfactory government
service does involve questions of access to government and participation
in governmental decisions.

Residents are much more likely to be satisfied if they feel that
they select their government and that it represents their interests—
in other words, that it is legitimate. The legitimacy of government
may be more important to the ability of teachers to educate than class
size or modern learning equipment and more important to the ability
of police to control crime than the size or frequency of patrols or the
speed of police telecommunications. But for purposes of this study
we treat participation, access, accountability, and legitimacy more
as means to effective services than as ultimate goals of government.
Concrete findings and projections are more feasible with respect to
the relationship of government structure to effectiveness of services
than with respect to the psychological, social, or political benefits of
participation, neighborhood development, or cultural identity. Others
have studied and written about these more abstract, though perhaps
equally important, values and objectives. This study will not attempt
to retrace their steps or argue their conclusions.

Present concern with the idea of decentralization of government
is reflected by the number of current decentralization proposals—
particularly ones relating to New York City. The Committee for
Economic Development, in its recent publication, "Reshaping Government in Metropolitan Areas," endorses the idea that effective government for large metropolitan areas can be found only in a combination
of community and metropolitan units of government. In the spring of
1970 Mayor John V. Lindsay announced a plan for harmonizing City
agency service districts and reducing the number of City-sanctioned
community advisory groups in the City's 62 community districts. In
November 1970 Bronx Borough President Robert Abrams proposed a
return of substantial service delivery responsibilities to the five
boroughs, and the other borough presidents followed with their own
plans. In December 1971 Mayor Lindsay announced a major experiment
in decentralization of the administration of services in five City districts. The Task Force on Jurisdiction and Structure of Governor
Rockefeller's Study Commission for New York City is also focusing
on decentralization. Official and unofficial task forces have been
studying decentralization for Boston, Detroit, and Minneapolis—usually
in the context of new forms of metropolitan government organization.
And numerous civic and community groups in New York and elsewhere
are active in the decentralization debate.

Because decentralization is discussed and espoused or opposed
by individuals and groups with such widely differing interests and
objectives, use of the term itself can lead to great confusion unless it

is carefully defined. Decentralization in the governmental context, as most broadly defined, simply means increasing the number of persons, offices, or institutions that have authority to make or influence governmental decisions or administration. This definition is broad enough to include both the division of authority that occurs when a government of separated executive, legislative, and judicial powers is substituted for a unified government and, also, the division of authority that takes place when a unified territorial political jurisdiction is divided into separate decision-making units. This study is concerned with the latter form of geographic decentralization.

It is customary to distinguish between two forms of geographic decentralization: administrative and political. Administrative decentralization involves the delegation of discretionary decision-making authority to subordinate officials within an administrative hierarchy. It normally also involves the establishment of fiscal or programmatic goals against which the performance of the subordinate official can be measured. Failure to satisfy these goals is sanctioned by withdrawal of the delegated authority. Political decentralization, by contrast, implies a change in the organic structure of government, in which both the authority to make decisions and the power to hold the decision maker accountable are turned over to new political institutions.

Administrative decentralization is more limited and, therefore, safer than political decentralization. Most administrative restructuring poses less threat to City bureaucracies or their unions or to political parties or elected officials than a political restructuring would. However, this study will not devote significant attention to this more limited concept. Administrative decentralization as a means of coping with excessive institutional size and rigidity is nothing new. Private business has long since recognized that bureaucratic structures can become so ponderous and wedded to existing procedures that they cannot adapt to changing conditions. The remedy has normally been to break the business up into separate but subordinate decision-making units, each with a separable task. The central corporation headquarters controls the subunits by holding their managers accountable for achieving agreed upon goals rather than by direct control over operating decisions.

Government officials have been no less aware than their private counterparts of the potentialities for bureaucratic rigidity and stultification through size. Government officials, however, have not been able to restructure administrative bureaucracies as easily as have business corporations. In government the incentives to risk taking by subordinate officials are inadequate, because the rewards for success are not commensurate with the risks of failure. Cities cannot dispense stock options, bonuses, or even vice-presidencies. Senior public officials also lack adequate tools for monitoring and review of subordinates' work, because local government goals and output can rarely be measured in objective terms.

Responsible public officials are therefore unwilling to delegate decisions for which they must shoulder political responsibility; all of the incentives are to take back delegated authority whenever its exercise begins to cause them embarrassment. Thus, administrative decentralization is inherently unstable. The history of unsuccessful attempts to delegate administration of the City's health programs strongly suggests that lasting and effective changes in the location of administrative power are possible only if accompanied by comparable changes in the location of political power.

Moreover administrative decentralization may be less effective than political decentralization in a number of ways. First, it adds little or nothing to the legitimacy of government in the eyes of the governed and is, therefore, unlikely to provide new social or institutional pressures on local residents to cooperate more fully with government in such areas as crime control or sanitation. Second, the advisory board approach to increasing the voice of residents frequently increases frustration because the board is powerless. And local district administrative officials and neighborhood directors or coordinators find it almost impossible to serve two masters: area residents and agency superiors or central City political officials. Third, administrative decentralization would have little effect on coordination of services from different agencies within individual administrative districts, because local service managers would owe allegience to central administrators of their own programs, not to any local official who also controlled the other services with which coordination was needed.

Area-based political decentralization within a large city implies division of the city into a number of subareas or districts, each of which is the basis for a new unit of local government with its own local political institutions. Each such unit would have powers sufficient for the delivery of important municipal services and would be accountable in some way to the residents of that district.

Such decentralization could be total: the City could be fragmented into smaller, separate municipalities. This result would be precisely the reverse of local government consolidation, as in the 1898 unification of New York and Brooklyn. Decentralization could also assume an intermediate form. Some municipal service responsibilities of the existing citywide government would be given up to the new local units of government, while others would be retained by it. The relations between the citywide government and the new local units would then be analogous to those between state government and municipalities within the state.

Complete fragmentation is of only theoretical interest in our large cities. The past two decades of emphasis on the achievement of metropolitan governments and the examples of the suburbs should by now have convinced us of the need for some unified political authority over whole metropolitan areas. Political decentralization in our large cities, if it occurs at all, should be based on a "two-tier" model of government, which places some authority in the hands of new local units of government and leaves other authority in the hands of the pre-existing citywide government.

Decentralization of that kind is closely related to current efforts to create governmental structures capable of coping with problems of metropolitan areas. In earlier attempts to deal with metropolitan problems, the issue was defined, rather too simply, as excessive governmental fragmentation, and governmental consolidation or a new level of unified governmental authority was singled out as the solution. A few city-county consolidations have been accomplished—notably, Jacksonville and Duval County, Florida and Nashville and Davidson County, Tennessee. But such consolidation or supergovernment efforts have more often than not proved unviable; reformers have increasingly turned to intergovernmental structures or systems of intergovernmental cooperation that involve less than complete consolidation and a division or sharing of service responsibilities between areawide organizations and local government units.

Two-tier or federal forms of metropolitan government structure may well provide the best vehicle for solving areawide problems, while still permitting satisfaction of local needs. Federal structures, such as Metropolitan Dade County and Metropolitan Toronto, are similar to the kind of decentralized structure that is the subject of this study.

A fully comprehensive study of New York City would consider the creation of a metropolitan organization covering suburban counties and even parts of New Jersey and Connecticut. Many issues like transportation and development planning certainly do involve the interests of a wider area. But New York City is for many purposes its own metropolitan area. After the great consolidation of 1898, the City was left with dozens of square miles of undeveloped land within its borders. As a result New York was able to plant its first, and much of its second, ring of suburbs within its City limits. Present-day New York City, aside from its greater size, is not unlike Boston plus the suburban communities around it that were built up prior to World War II. While regionalization is important and desirable for New York City, a study of decentralization of the City alone makes practical sense because of the political difficulties of including New York's suburbs in any new governmental structure. And decentralization of the City might facilitate later formation of a metropolitan

formula, since the suburbs could see that, as local districts within
a metropolitan government framework, they could indeed retain
substantial power and independence.

There are two possible patterns that new "lower-tier" units of
political authority might assume within a large city like New York.
In each geographic area, there could be a number of separate local
governing bodies, each responsible for a single service. Or there
could be a unified local government, like a municipality in miniature,
responsible for delivery of a number of services to residents of that
district.

The former approach, which is commonly called "functional
decentralization," is akin to the pattern produced by the overlapping
citizen participation requirements of many federal aid programs—
Model Cities, urban renewal, Community Action agencies, and multi-
service centers. Each program has its own board of citizens, its
own bureaucracy, and its own funding sources. The latter approach
implies that each discrete local district resembles a small municipality,
possessing some, but not all, of the powers of presently existing
cities, such as White Plains, or Yonkers, or any of the thousands of
cities in urbanized America.

The use of separate local political groups for each service or
function is most suitable, however, when those groups are serving
as advisory bodies to locally based arms of central administrative
agencies, and not as autonomous bodies with direct policy-making
and program administration responsibilities. The more separate
governmental units with service delivery responsibilities at the local
level, the harder it is for citizens to know who is responsible for
what services or to exercise their voting power intelligently in local
elections. The creation of local school boards, local health councils,
local social services councils, and local sanitation boards would
probably result in narrowly based groups of persons ending up in
practical control of each of those services.

Functional decentralization also increases the difficulty of
getting qualified people to serve on local policy-setting bodies. It
increases the number of positions to be filled and is likely to discourage
those with broad concerns about the quality and purposes of citizen
government from standing for office. Finally, functional decentralization invites incredible coordination problems. Loyalties, priorities,
and relationships of local district organizations would run to relatively
limited local constituencies and, also, would continue to run along
programmatic and organizational lines to, for example, the state and
federal health and social service establishments.

This study, therefore, does not consider the decentralization
of authority for service delivery to single-purpose local level units
as a wise alternative for New York City. The analysis is based on a

two-tier system of government in the City, involving the creation of new, geographically distinct, multipurpose units of decentralized political authority.

Chapter 2 describes New York City's present structure for decision making and for rendering services to its residents, identifies and discusses a number of specific problems that stem from the City's present structure and practices and which hinder effective service, and suggests some specific problems that any decentralization effort should seek to avoid or at least recognize.

Chapter 3 deals with the issues that must be considered in determining what size and structure of decentralized units of government would best serve the objective of improving services and considers how such new units should relate to the residual central City government.

Chapter 4 considers what government services should be decentralized and analyzes the possible effects of such structural changes on service effectiveness.

Chapter 5 deals with fiscal affairs and budgeting in a decentralized system, including allocation of taxing authority and responsibility, setting and adjusting formulas for distributing centrally raised revenues among local district governments, controlling expenditures to assure municipal solvency, and approving, financing, and building capital projects.

Chapter 6 discusses the role of the civil service system and municipal unions in the City's government, considers possible collective bargaining arrangements in a decentralized system, and discusses the impact decentralization might have on the effectiveness of service management, the productivity of City employees, flexibility in the method of delivery of services, and access of minorities to City jobs.

Chapter 7 sums up the likely advantages and disadvantages of decentralization and suggests some problems and tactics the City would have to consider if a decision to move toward decentralization were made.

2

THE PROBLEMS
OF GOVERNING
NEW YORK CITY

Any estimation of whether and how decentralization of New York City's government might improve its public services must necessarily be based on some understanding of the present structure and operations of the City's government, the character and causes of its present service problems, and the efforts the City has recently been making to deal with the difficulties it perceives. This chapter is therefore intended to provide a basis for the discussion of decentralization. Neither the descriptive nor the analytic material purports to be comprehensive. Others have described New York's government and discussed its substantive programs in great detail.[1] Here, we merely sketch the existing structural framework and highlight those factors that seem to have the most direct bearing on the issues affecting decentralization.

THE STRUCTURE AND OPERATION OF NEW YORK
CITY'S GOVERNMENT

New York City's government performs two sets of functions for the City's residents. First, the City provides public services, performing tasks that economies of scale suggest ought to be undertaken collectively in dense areas. Second, the City government decides public questions for New Yorkers. This means that, within limits set by national and state authority, the City decides what matters are appropriate for municipal decision, selects the processes to use in deciding them, and determines who should participate. These public questions are often closely intertwined with questions of service delivery, and so the two municipal roles often overlap. Among the most important public questions are what services the City should perform, from whom the funds should be obtained for performing them, how services should be allocated among sections of the City, and who should be hired to perform the services. But the City government also decides questions not directly related to service delivery: questions, for instance, of permitted land use, of income redistribution, of whether Fifth Avenue should be closed for a parade on St. Patrick's Day. Generally, the City's decisions are about allocation of limited resources among citizens, but the resources are often intangible and difficult to quantify.

Somewhere in the interstices between delivering services and deciding policy lie most of the difficult questions about the structure of New York City's government. The attention of an individual citizen usually focuses on the services delivered to him: Is his street clean? Is his child admitted to college? Is his aunt protected against muggings? His attention to government as a decision maker may be less personal. He may be in favor of, or against, what are reported to him as increases or decreases in levels of welfare support, or a plan to legalize heroin, or the construction of a park on a pier. Generally, he is in favor of every decision that increases the delivery to him of services he values and opposed to almost all others. One task of local government is to render decisions and organize the delivery of services so that citizens receive more of the services they most want and pay less for them and so that mutually beneficial trade-offs can be achieved. Those who care most about a particular outcome should have their way with respect to that issue and should give up their perferences on matters of less concern to them. Government's other task is to do all of the above by procedures that are fair and just, and that are widely seen as being fair and just. Most of the City's citizens should believe the government represents them and takes their needs and preferences into consideration—and the government should, in fact, do so.

In making decisions, the City of New York functions through both formal and informal structures. Its formal structure can be described relatively simply. The City's principal legislative body, the City Council, has 37 members—27 elected from single-member geographic districts of about 300,000 residents each, plus two elected at large from each borough by a scheme which guarantees that they will be from two different parties. Since most legislation of importance remains within the purview of the state legislature, the council's chief roles are its review of City budgets and its actions on "home rule messages"—the latter required because the state legislature sometimes cannot, and more often will not, adopt legislation solely affecting the City without a message requesting that legislation from the council. Because the council's tasks are not important enough (except annually when the budget must be prepared), mayors and

borough presidents can often ignore its views. The council has recently
tried to strengthen its voice by assuming an investigative role, but so
far without major gain in publicity or power. Most councilmen are in
effect chosen by the Democratic Party apparatus in their district or
borough, and many become judges after they leave the council. Councilmen lack staff resources to maintain significant contact with their
large constituencies. Probably very few New Yorkers even know their
councilman's name, much less his position or role on any issue of
importance to them.

The president of the council, one of three elected citywide
officials, presides over the council, succeeds upon the mayor's retirement or death, and sits on the Board of Estimate. The comptroller,
also elected citywide, keeps the City's accounts and pays its bills.
He has the power to stop, or at least delay, any City payment he deems
improper. He presides over 750 employees and also sits on the Board
of Estimate.

Each borough has a president, elected quadrennially with the
mayor. The borough president once had substantial administrative
duties. Allegations, some of them substantiated, of rampant patronage,
conflict of interest, and inefficient and low-quality service led to
removal of these functions in the 1961 revision of the City Charter.
Now, the borough presidents serve chiefly a ceremonial function,
except for their participation in the Board of Estimate and the Site
Selection Board (which determines the location of public buildings).
A borough president who wishes to do so, however, can command
substantial publicity as spokesman for the concerns of his constituents.
In that way he can become a significant participant in the City's governmental process.

The three citywide elected officials and the borough presidents
sit on the Board of Estimate, a strange outgrowth of the amalgamations
that produced the City's present five-county structure. On the Board
of Estimate, the mayor, City Council president, and comptroller each
has four votes, and each of the five borough presidents has two votes.
Thus, Staten Island gets the same voice as Brooklyn, which is seven
times larger. The mechanics of compiling majorities on such a board
are intricate and confusing. And since a great many issues coming
before the board affect only one borough, the other four borough
presidents are frequently disinterested observers, whose votes can
be won on other bases and with arrangements that combine several
measures.

The Board of Estimate has two chief tasks. It participates in
the budget process, and it must approve all substantial capital projects,
as well as subsidiary decisions, such as street closings, sale of City-
owned land, and leases of real property for City purposes. The
importance and frequency of these tasks make the board a regular,

full-time participant with the mayor in governing the City, a role the
City Council does not have. At some stage nearly everything the
mayor wants to do needs board approval. A lengthy calendar confronts
the board at its twice-monthly meetings, and so most items are rou-
tinely adopted. But anything that has become controversial can be
held up for general scrutiny by an individual member of the board.
This means, for example, that some private person or group that is
concerned about something a mayoral agency is doing can make a
public issue of the matter by gaining access to a single borough
president. However, since the mayor controls most of the City's
patronage and is responsible for most programs of importance to the
borough presidents' constituents, he almost always gets his way with
the board.

The board holds public hearings, open to all, before it acts.
These hearings are an instance of formal citizen participation in City
government. However, they occur only _after_ the board meets in closed
executive session, where agreements are usually reached on how
members will vote. New York's citizens can, and sometimes do,
delay programs by disrupting board hearings, but the agenda is so
complex and the available information so skimpy that they rarely even
realize that issues important to them are to be decided—and even
more rarely do they affect the ultimate outcome of items before the
board.

Especially under the 1961 City Charter, the mayor has the formal
authority to govern the City. His is the principal voice in determining
the level and form of taxation and the way the City's revenues are
spent. He appoints and removes almost all administrators and commissioners, with no provision for legislative consent. And the mayor
is the focus of media attention and public concern. For most citizens
the mayor _is_ the City government.

The mayor exercises his authority through nine superagencies,
each headed by an administrator. All of the superagencies, except
the Finance Administration, contain several departments, each directed
by a commissioner. The superagencies were set up to increase
coordination of related functions, to lessen the administrative burden
on the mayor, and to make it possible for the City to hire able executives. A number of commissioner-headed departments (police, fire,
consumer affairs) are outside the superagency structure, as are a
variety of commissions, boards, and agencies. At least several dozen
officials, with a wide range of duties, report directly to the mayor.

Mayoral supervision takes place through the deputy mayor-
executive and a City Hall staff of several dozen special assistants.
The assignments and relative statuses of these mayoral aides are in
constant flux. Three things about the mayor's palace guard are
important. First, departmental officials are not regularly supervised

by, or even in communication with, the mayor's office. Issues rising
to City Hall concern may be taken up with the responsible commissioner
by a variety of City Hall aides in a variety of ways. Or they may not
be taken up with him at all. More important, matters that are extremely
important in the life of a commissioner, and of the City, may escape
City Hall involvement altogether. Second, persons from outside City
government, if they are important (famous, rich, able to attract media
attention, able to mobilize large demonstrations, though to be influential
in their communities) or lucky, can gain the attention of someone in
City Hall and so sometimes gain action or inaction outside the usual
bureaucratic paths. Third, because time is short and problems many,
the mayor, the deputy mayor-executive, and other City Hall staff
devote most of their attention to the issues that are getting heavy
newspaper or television coverage at that moment. When they concentrate on other subjects, it is usually because they expect them to be
the subject of media headlines in the near future.

Two instrumentalities of mayoral government should be mentioned. In New York City, as in Washington, the complexities of mid-
twentieth-century government and the opportunities to employ new
management techniques led to the development of a strong Bureau of
the Budget. At one time the capital budget branch worked for the
Board of Estimate, but Mayors Wagner and Lindsay, with help from
the 1961 City Charter, established control over the entire bureau. In
New York, indeed, the bureau's control over departmental action
extends to matters of much greater detail than does the control of the
federal Budget Bureau. It is principally the Budget Bureau to whom
a commissioner must answer, and often to some middle-level bureau-
crat, whose concern with long-standing tradition and administrative
tidiness is very great and whose concern with the goals and tasks and
potential innovations of the commissioner's department is much less.
The bureau controls agency expenditures and programmatic decisions,
not only by its power of approval over the original capital and expense
budgets but also by its power to approve, disapprove, or hold up
indefinitely budget modifications (shifts of funds from one specific
purpose to another) and the hiring of new employees. As a result
commissioners never can be sure whether or not they will have the
funds or the staff needed to carry out their programs. The bureau
provides regularity and solvency, but at high cost in innovation and
managerial flexibility.

The second instrumentality is the City Planning Commission.
The chairman of the Planning Commission, like the budget director,
serves at the mayor's pleasure. But, unlike the budget director, the
planning chairman is part of a seven-member body, the other six
members of which are appointed by the mayor for eight-year terms.
The commission, staffed by the Department of City Planning, draws

the federally required master plan, prepares the first draft of the
capital budget, adopts and amends the zoning ordinance, negotiates
with private developers about City approval for their projects, and
passes on sites for City capital projects. The commission has recently
created offices in all five boroughs, staffed by planners who are quite
heavily involved in discussing local problems and needs with local
citizens and groups; it holds public hearings before taking action, and,
generally, its responsiveness to citizens has exceeded that of other
City agencies.

Most New Yorkers' only contact with government is with the
City agencies that collect taxes, deliver services, or regulate business
or personal behavior. In New York more of these agencies officially
report to the mayor than in almost any other city. Mayoral agencies
include fire, police, environmental protection (sanitation, water supply,
water and air pollution), parks and recreation, human resources
(welfare, social services, antipoverty, and narcotics control), public
health services, transportation, housing and development (urban
renewal, housing, and building code enforcement and rent control),
consumer protection, and finance and taxation. Elementary, secondary,
and higher education are all governed by independent boards, though
the City is responsible for most of their funds. The City's subways
and buses are controlled by a commission dominated by gubernatorial
appointees, though again the City must finance most capital costs and
subsidize fares. Until 1970 the City operated a network of large
hospitals. In 1970 it turned them over to a semi-independent Health
and Hospitals Corporation, in order to permit borrowing for buildings
and equipment outside City debt limits and in order to escape the red
tape of City controls over executive salaries, purchasing, construction,
and budgeting.

City agencies, both those responsible to the mayor and those
somewhat independent of him, employ approximately 380,000 persons,
almost all of whom are protected by civil service and represented by
increasingly powerful unions. These municipal unions have become
one of the most powerful forces in City government. They bargain
not only for wages, holidays, and pensions, but also for such program
matters as work load, personnel deployment, and transfer and promotion rules. In most agencies all except the very top supervisors have
risen through the ranks, are union members, and identify more with
the rank and file than with management or the persons served by the
agency.

Theoretically, the agency administrators and commissioners
have substantial power to set agency priorities; to hire, classify,
promote, and assign employees; and to plan and evaluate their programs. In fact, because of a shortage of capable middle managers and
the power of the municipal unions, executives appointed by the mayor

have only limited influence over their widely dispersed employees.
And since the Budget Bureau and other staff agencies regularly review
and modify all agency budgets and personnel requests, few agency
heads have the will or the staff competence to plan, budget, or evaluate
their programs.

Over the years almost all departments have organized service
delivery by geographical districts for their own convenience and to
facilitate some degree of administrative decentralization. Unfortunately, no two departments have drawn the same district lines, so
that the City service map is now a hodgepodge of police precincts and
fire, sanitation, health, mental health, water, sewer, and school districts.
Superimposed on this service district grid are the 62 community
planning districts created in the 1960's to encourage community consideration of development plans, particularly capital project proposals.
The City has also designated 25 poverty areas and set up a Community
Corporation in each one to disburse federal and City Community Action
funds and has created three model neighborhoods for development and
implementation of federal Model Cities programs. None of these
districts coincides with councilmanic, state assembly, state senate,
or congressional districts.

New Yorkers are governed from Washington and Albany, as
well as from City Hall. Federal and state operations within the City
are usually undertaken through instrumentalities of the City government. The federal government makes policies and, by providing
dollars, encourages cities to carry them out.

Similarly, the state government has primarily functioned by
making rules and regulations and leaving the City government to carry
them out. The state has allowed New York City to do very little
legislating and has taken upon itself very little administration. The
result is that City residents think of the mayor and their City government when they think of urban government. Attempts by mayors to
pass the buck—even justified attempts—usually are unsuccessful.

The participation of private persons in New York City's governmental process occurs through a variety of mechanisms. New York's
political parties are highly organized, at least on paper—with party
officials even at the election district level (500 to 750 registered
voters). Their organizational structure has traditionally given county
leaders in the Democratic and Republican parties great power over
their subordinates and, therefore, substantial influence in City affairs.
But over the past few decades, open primaries have become common,
reform clubs have won party elections, and the Liberal and Conservative parties have sometimes been a force. Democratic and Republican
Party leaders have lost much of their control over elected officials
and over the electorate. Their inability to deliver the vote has significantly weakened their influence. Nevertheless, the City's governing

scheme leaves to government officials many discretionary decisions, especially the filling of certain jobs and the selection of firms to receive certain contracts, for which objective criteria are unavailable or easily ignored. Party officials still have a say in those decisions whenever they have been useful to the government official to whose discretion the decision is committed. In that way service to a party can still lead to preferment for a City job or contract. And in that way, as much as through ideology and program, the parties continue to draw their adherents and their contributions.

Other mechanisms of citizen involvement in City government fall into two categories: geographic and subject matter. Many neighborhoods and communities have civic groups or councils of civic groups that are treated by residents and outsiders as being highly representative. These groups are especially strong in Queens, where they are interrelated in areawide confederacies. Many of these councils are quite catholic, embracing religious bodies, homeowner and tenant groups, Boy Scouts, and a variety of other popular organizations. They are frequently looked on in the way the Brooklyn Democratic Party usually is, i.e., as "the" local structure, in which one must play a role and make a name in order to succeed in business as well as politics in that borough.

When a civic council or a political organization is seen as catholic, its power is great, because others assume that it would not take a position on a local issue unless general community sentiment was overwhelmingly behind it. These groups lose their influence when they become, or are seen as being, mere expressions of the few leaders who take the trouble to participate. But since individual City officials have no infallible method for gauging the representativeness of the self-proclaimed community leaders who regularly appeal to them, the leaders' influence is often greater than their actual strength merits.

This is true also of private organizations with a specialized interest in a certain area of City government activity. These bodies can maintain a regular relationship with City bureaucrats and sometimes convince the City workers that they need not look elsewhere for citizen views. More often, however, specialized groups will survive over several years only by becoming the captive of private interests who alone have enough inducement to continue to participate. And when this happens the City officialdom will usually recognize the alteration and discount the organization's views accordingly.

Finally, there are a number of groups whose private power is so great that substantial public influence naturally follows. The City's largest businesses, including Wall Street firms, but also the large retail establishments, the utilities, and the national corporations with a substantial New York presence, play a role. So do the churches, especially the Catholic and Episcopal episcopacies and the less tightly

structured Jewish rabbinate. In these and other cases influence varies
with the issue, the nature and extent of the private party's concern,
and an indecipherable tangle of prior private and public relationships.

The other major private participants in City government are
the news media. Stories in the three daily newspapers are attended
to by most of City officials to a degree far greater than the likely
readership of obscure inside-page City government stories would
suggest. The Long Island Press, with a large Queens and Brooklyn
readership, is also read by City officials, but the Spanish-language
dailies, the Staten Island Advance, and neighborhood weekly papers
are rarely seen by officials with citywide jurisdictions. In the past
decade the 6 p.m. newscasts of the three network television stations
have become a major factor in City government, rivaling even the
influence of the New York Times. Most officials assume that the three
shows together get more attention from City residents and voters than
any other media combination, except perhaps the front-page headline
of the Daily News.

The operating procedures of the media affect the functioning of
City government. Because the significant media are regionwide, a
City government matter must affect an immense number of citizens,
or be extremely poignant or vicious, to command attention. Because
television is visual and the newspapers like illustrable stories matters
that do not photograph well are ignored. Similarly, events must be
capsulable in 60 to 120 seconds, must occur during the day (television
does not like to pay overtime rates for nighttime filming and does not
like to run a 6 p.m. film from the previous evening—unless it is very
colorful, like a riot), and must occur at a predictable time or last long
enough for clumsy equipment to be brought to the scene. It also helps
a great deal if the event occurs in Manhattan, for even newspaper
reporters seem to have difficulty finding their way to an outer borough.
These are necessary rules for the media. As guides to City attention,
which they inevitably become, they are without obvious correlation to
the questions and issues that may be concerning citizens.

PROBLEMS OF CENTRALIZED GOVERNMENT

This brief description of New York City's government and
related public and private institutions suggests a number of general-
izations about the City's problems. The City's tasks seem increasingly
urgent, in part because of the vast expansion in the scope of local
government activity over the past few decades and in part because of
the heightened political consciousness of minority groups following
the civil rights drives and the poverty programs of the 1960's. Some
of the problems reflect the sheer size of the City, the increasing

proportion of disadvantaged residents, and the squeeze of a tax base
that does not increase in proportion to demands for funding. What
follows is a brief catalog of some of the more significant reasons why
the City is having such difficulty rendering effective, satisfactory
service to its residents at a cost they are willing to pay.

Ineffective Program Management

The City's program managers have little opportunity or incentive
to plan and carry out effective programs. Agency heads and their
principal deputies are overwhelmed by the sheer size of their operations. Information systems are sketchy at best; by the time data
reaches an administrator, it has been thoroughly edited to suit the
interests of the echelons through which it has passed. Administrators
do not know the diverse needs of citizens in the various parts of the
City; they do not even know the quantity or the quality of the services
they are delivering to any neighborhood. Without more precise knowledge, administrators tend simply to keep doing what has been done
before and to do the same thing throughout the City. The chains of
command are so long that few subordinate managers in the neighborhoods would receive or act on refinements in program direction anyway.

Despite broad theoretical delegations of authority from the
mayor to his top administrators over program development and personnel management, few agency heads exercise substantial initiative
for very long. They know that the Budget Bureau, and perhaps the
comptroller and other staff agencies, will review and probably modify
every program proposal or alteration, frequently with more of an eye
to short-term savings or citywide standardization than to program
achievement. Since top bureau officials are close to the mayor, and
since even lesser bureau officials can hold up personnel actions or
program modifications almost indefinitely, operating agency officials
rarely oppose the bureau. When they do, they usually lose. If an
agency does find a way to operate more efficiently, it will rarely get
the benefit of any savings. And if an agency head tries to make a
change that displeases an important union leader, he knows the union
leader may have more political influence with the mayor than he does.
As a result agency heads can be certain only of delays if they innovate.
The incentives are to stick to the ways of the past and to standard
programs and procedures; few agencies even develop the staff capacity
for effective program planning or evaluation.

Middle management is even less likely to seek program changes
or cost savings. Almost all agency supervisory personnel are covered
by civil service and are union members. Most of them owe their jobs
to seniority and a written exam that does not test for decisiveness or

devotion to management's viewpoint. Few have had the benefit of in-
service training. Their principal objectives are to get along with
their old friends and to support the union.

An aggressive district supervisor might well find only frustration
if he sought to improve the quality or efficiency of the services of his
unit or to tailor services to some special needs of the residents of
his area. Operating rules in so large a system leave little leeway for
local initiative. In most cases the district supervisor cannot predict
from day to day how many men or how much equipment he will have
at his disposal, as these matters are controlled centrally to assure
citywide flexibility and the capacity to concentrate resources where
most needed. Budgets are not developed locally. Indeed, budgets are
rarely broken down by geographic area. The local unit is not expected
to plan or to evaluate. Under these circumstances local managers
have every right to pass the buck; knowledgeable local residents know
their local service personnel cannot be held accountable for the exercise
of power they do not have.

Low Productivity of Municipal Employees

New York City employees are widely accused of being less
productive than workers in the private sector, and the situation is
thought to be getting worse. The City's expenditures have in fact
tripled in the last 10 years; except for health and welfare benefits,
personnel costs make up most of the budget. The number of employees
has increased only 50 percent; reduced hours, liberal sick leave, and
increased holidays and vacation mean that man-hours on the job have
increased very little. Most City employees probably work just as
hard as those in private industry; yet the stereotype of the lazy civil
servant persists.

For many years the salaries of public employees were significantly lower than those of their counterparts in the private sector.
Civil service protection and widespread private unemployment combined
to attract highly qualified City employees during the 1930's. But those
capable and frequently dedicated civil servants have almost all retired.
For years City employment was not an attractive career, and the
status of the civil servant sank in the eyes of the community and the
public employee alike.

Within the past decade municipal unions have negotiated salaries
up to competitive levels; fringe benefits now exceed those in private
industry.[2] Union leaders and City workers have not been afraid to
strike in violation of state laws. Whether or not the City's health or
welfare has been placed in jeopardy, mayors have felt their political
careers seriously threatened by the piling up of garbage, unprotected

streets, or long school closures. Early retirement with substantial pensions has been relatively easy to negotiate, because pension costs can be deferred and do not force the current mayor to raise taxes right away. And perhaps retirement after 20 years is particularly attractive to men who hold their jobs in low esteem. It is no wonder that many City employees are more loyal to their unions and to the system than to the City or to the residents they serve.

Many of the larger City agencies have attracted employees primarily from particular ethnic or religious groups: policemen and firemen are mostly Irish, teachers have been largely Jewish, sanitationmen traditionally are Italian. In the past overt discrimination reinforced the homogenizing effects of word-of-mouth recruiting and natural preference to work with one's own kind. Today, unnecessarily rigorous employment exams and qualifications may well still screen out qualified blacks and Puerto Ricans. But even with no discrimination the City's newer minority group members are reluctant to join the "Irish" police force or the "Italian" sanitation department. As a result minority neighborhoods are served by white policemen, firemen, sanitationmen, and teachers. These minority residents resent this and not only refuse to cooperate but are sometimes openly hostile. The civil servants frequently reciprocate with equal hostility.

For efficiency reasons and to curb corruption, public employees are regularly shifted from neighborhood to neighborhood. Many unions have bargained for the right of senior employees to transfer to fill any vacancy for which they are qualified—usually into a quieter, more affluent neighborhood. As a result civil servants rarely get to know, or become attached to, the area they serve; individual employees, including supervisors, cannot be held accountable for the state of any particular neighborhood for long. Since more and more City employees live outside the City, few civil servants work among their neighbors.

In addition to obtaining higher wages and fringe benefits, the municipal unions have reinforced traditional civil service security with even broader contract security and uniformity. The firing of a public employee is almost unheard of. If it happens, the dismissed worker can appeal within his agency to the Department of Personnel, to the courts, or to arbitration. Promotion is now almost entirely by written tests plus seniority, the City having recently agreed to do away with performance ratings as a factor in promotion. Lateral entry is almost impossible. While the civil service laws theoretically permit merit increases, management is rarely willing or able to reward individual employee productivity or initiative. The public employee has therefore little or no incentive to work hard, much less to excel, particularly if his job is emptying garbage cans.

Lack of Local Program Coordination

Improved program coordination has become a prime objective of all those who would reform the structure and operations of government. The benefits of coordination are frequently exaggerated, but it is true that unemployment cannot be effectively fought without changes in education, health, and social services; land-use and economic planning; and mass transportation; and the same interrelationships apply to all urban problems and solutions. The federally sponsored poverty and Model Cities programs both were designed in part to coordinate efforts by all levels of government to alleviate the problems of urban slums. Such New York City overhead agencies as personnel, purchasing, real estate, labor relations, city planning, and law are intended to cut down waste by standardizing policies and program inputs, as well as by achieving economies of scale. The Budget Bureau and the Office of Administration are even more directly responsible for preventing overlapping and duplication and for encouraging multi-agency use of more efficient methods and facilities. And Mayor Lindsay's consolidation of more than a score of independent agencies into nine superagencies was aimed specifically at making complementary agencies more effective, by grouping them under a single direction as well as by reducing the number of agencies reporting directly to the overworked mayor.

None of these measures has had much effect in achieving coordination at the local level. In recent soundings taken on behalf of the City's Office of Neighborhood Government, local agency personnel cite their inability to solve problems that cross agency jurisdictional lines as among their greatest frustrations. All program management orders travel vertically; such rewards and punishments as exist are earned by carrying out the tasks of the official's own agency and not from participating in any coordination effort. The creation of service districts by the City's major agencies, each of different size and with different borders, makes local coordination even harder, as each local district supervisor has to deal with a number of different counterparts in other agencies, depending on what part of his district is involved. The existence of semiautonomous authorities, such as the Port of New York Authority and the Metropolitan Transportation Authority, and now the Health and Hospitals Corporation, increases the difficulty of coordination, even at the central City level.

The federal, state, and City governments have all mandated creation of local citizens' advisory or policy committees in every conceivable program area, plus such multipurpose citizens groups as Community Corporation boards, Model Cities committees, and community planning boards. These boards are organized to represent those same overlapping, noncongruent areas. While the objective

was to increase citizen participation in program development and
implementation, a prime result has been to foster bitter rivalries
among the citizen groups, which have consumed most of the participants' energies. Moreover, a whole new set of bureaucracies has
developed, each deeply concerned with the preservation of its own
jobs and status and with the integrity and independence of its own
program area. The net result has generally been less rather than
more coordination.

Welfare funds still pay rent for apartments that violate the
housing code. Vocational high schools still train for jobs that the
City's manpower agencies know do not exist. Two agencies can still
file applications for rat control programs for the same neighborhood,
and neither might know about the other. And it is still impossible to
distinguish between the roles of certain social service agencies and
community mental health agencies, all primarily financed through
the City.

Effective program coordination means more than exchange of
information among different agencies, or use by several agencies of
the same kind of copying machine, or even elimination of obvious
program duplication. Total program resources will be used most
effectively and local urban problems addressed most comprehensively
only if each official responsible for operating decisions has substantial
incentive to allocate resources or make other program decisions in
a way that will maximize the impact of all related services, even if
some decisions mean that the impact of his own program may be less
than it might be. This ideal state of coordination is not likely ever to
be fully achieved, because the problems are so complex that waiting
to coordinate with all related services would mean never getting
started. But any approximation of such coordination requires that the
relevant decision makers all work for the same person or governmental
unit, that they all deal with some area of manageable size, and that
they work in close proximity to each other and to their common
employer. Those conditions could never exist citywide in New York.

Lack of Program Variation To Reflect
Differing Local Needs

New York City's size is matched by its diversity. The problems
and needs of its dozens of neighborhoods are as different as are the
incomes, education levels, jobs, homes, buying habits, and racial,
religious, and ethnic backgrounds of their residents. New York has
been called a melting pot; it has welcomed and nurtured people of all
kinds from all over the world. New York also offers relatively great
employment and recreational and residential mobility to its citizens.

But for reasons of economics, discrimination, and personal preference, people with similar problems, prospects, and needs do tend to cluster in particular geographic areas.

Different parts of New York City need and want different mixes of services and different methods of service delivery. In many neighborhoods expectant mothers do not think of pregancy as a condition requiring medical care. For those areas health education may be the highest priority. The elderly may predominate in other areas, and visiting nursing care may be most needed there. For some places a Monday trash pickup may be more important than more street cleaning. Variations in methods of payment may also make real sense for services such as trash collection or recreation. Sometimes, the differences in demand are not so specific, but, as in the school decentralization fight, those demands may be very strong. Anthony Downs suggests that the intensity of people's desires for goods and services varies directly with their capacity to select among differing styles and qualities.[3] Americans like to be different, he feels, and the standardization of public goods and services is one of the factors that causes them to prefer private consumer goods to public services. Suburban migration probably reflects in part a desire to live where government provides the services the migrant wants, the way he likes them.

A number of factors inhibit government from tailoring services to differing local preferences. Under New York's centralized system of resource allocation and program design, both the central service "line" agencies and the "overhead," or staff, agencies tend to enforce citywide procedures and standardized specifications for supplies and equipment. The teachers union, for example, has bargained a citywide maximum class size. It is also true that most major systems do make a number of important allowances for differing local conditions: each major piece of fire equipment in congested Bedford-Stuyvesant carries more men than the same equipment in middle-class Bayside; some first-grade classes in the slums are smaller than in more affluent neighborhoods; and trash is picked up much more frequently in areas with large apartment houses than in one-family neighborhoods. New York also mounts its share of pilot and experimental projects. But generally, ease of management and the quest for economies of scale result in citywide rules: the same first-grade reader citywide, even though it makes little sense to Harlem children, and standardized window screens delivered a year late, instead of a slightly more expensive special purchase for immediate delivery. It is politically very difficult to treat one neighborhood differently from others; it is bureaucratically much safer for a central office official to insist that local managers go by the book. The central official will be blamed if a local variation fails, and he will get little or no credit if it succeeds.

Lack of Access to, or Influence over, Decision Makers

The effectiveness of government services depends as much on the perceptions of the service recipients as on the efficiency of service deliverers. Residents of New York increasingly seem to feel they are not getting the kind or quality of services they want and deserve in comparison with the taxes they pay. The poor believe the more affluent have all the influence; the working man believes the poor, particularly minorities, are coddled by the City; almost every neighborhood believes it is powerless and that it is being shortchanged.

Frustrated by the feeling of being discriminated against, New Yorkers seem to overreact to service gaps or breakdowns. These overreactions may be due in material part to the widespread feeling of helplessness: there is no place and no person to whom an ordinary person can complain with any hope of redress. The powers and concerns of regular City-elected officials seem remote from day-to-day problems—particularly since the demise of the local political clubs as avenues of access to, and influence over, government. It is almost impossible to find the local agency officials with jurisdiction over the particular problem at issue. Once found, the local official usually turns out to be powerless to act. The only recourse is to protest at City Hall. But such a protest requires a level of organization and commitment that can be generated only rarely and only with respect to matters of high emotional impact. As a result most residents without special connections with City Hall usually complain only to each other and view City government with increasing bitterness and distrust.

Top New York City officials have recognized this growing alienation as a serious problem for several decades and have tried to deal with it. The first response appears to have been the creation of some 60 local planning districts in 1950 and the gradual development of community planning boards. Mayor Lindsay has added neighborhood city halls and Urban Action Task Forces (UATF's). The federal government sponsored local Community Action agencies and local Model Cities boards. And the new community school boards are certainly the City's most ambitious citizen participation effort.

The only citizen participation program with City Charter status is the City's system of 62 community boards, which are empowered to represent their districts with respect to plans for community welfare and orderly development. Each board has up to 50 members, appointed by its respective borough president. No board member is compensated, and staff support is nominal. A board can theoretically consider, hold hearings on, and render advice concerning any social, economic, or physical plan or project affecting its district and can initiate programs. As a practical matter, however, most boards consider only capital projects—and only by reacting to proposals of others. They almost never hold hearings and only occasionally render timely advice on capital projects; rarely is their advice particularly influential.

The community boards are relatively ineffective for a number of reasons. Their role is purely advisory; the most they can force is a short delay in project approval. The boards' principal official connection is the borough president, who has relatively little power. Most boards are not representative of the district population. Residents have no role in selection of board members and, for the most part, do not even know the board exists. Hence, the boards have no significant constituency and frequently speak for no one but themselves. City agencies know this and pay little more attention to advice from a community board than to advice from the numerous other local or citywide interest groups, some of which may be of much greater political significance. With almost no staff support, few boards can keep track of City government proposals, maintain any contact with district residents, plan or conduct hearings, or make use of the media for publicity or persuasion. A few boards, representing particularly sophisticated neighborhoods, such as Manhattan's East Side or Greenwich Village, have had more sustained and affirmative influence; one board in the Inwood-Washington Heights section of Manhattan has acquired funds for permanent staff and is beginning to achieve some standing and influence. But most boards are caught in a vicious circle of lack of legal power, lack of neighborhood constituency, lack of staff, and lack of influence.

Mayor Lindsay's neighborhood city halls and UATF's developed separately—the former as a substitute for ward-level political head-quarters where a resident could get answers to his questions and feel some participation in the processes of City government and the latter as a listening post in riot-prone neighborhoods. But the two were soon merged; now there are local offices responsive to the mayor in about half of the community districts, where local residents can lodge complaints and seek advice in dealing with the bureaucracy and where local leaders can meet periodically with City officials to discuss current neighborhood problems. The mayor assigns a key City official to each local office (usually at the commissioner or deputy commissioner level), orders local agency officials to attend the periodic meetings, and provides staff for each office to get a feel for the neighborhood, to receive complaints, to answer simple procedural questions, and to recruit neighborhood leaders. In addition small amounts of "flexible" money are provided for emergencies or special projects and for modest summer youth programs.

The thousands of complaints and requests for advice each month attest to concentration of neighborhood concern on visible issues, such as police patrol, sanitation collections and street cleaning, over-crowded schools, subway breakdowns, and park maintenance. They also show the extent of the need for some local means of access to government. In those districts where the mayor's representative has been particularly zealous and the staff person particularly resourceful, the local meetings have generated significant interest—especially if the mayor's representative is able to deliver on requests for a special cleanup of a local park or an extra patrolman for a busy intersection and if the flexible funds are judiciously parceled out among participating civic organizations. Also, some useful, but short-lived, self-help efforts have evolved. But local leaders have not been encouraged to confront local priorities or to press for important changes. The task force system could not respond to any such requests, because it has no power to reorder City priorities, much less generate additional resources. For example, the task force could not even get Monday trash service in place of Thursday or Wednesday service for a neighborhood whose citizens named that as the top priority at every meeting over a two-year period.

In general, the characteristics of the UATF's are a mirror image of those of community boards: they are essentially informal instead of statutorily authorized; have direct lines to the mayor instead of to the borough presidents; have changing, self-selecting membership instead of a limited, appointed body; and are regularly concerned with daily service delivery instead of with capital questions. The result, however, is about the same: another organization seeking to speak for the community, giving a different group of local residents a structured voice in City government, but a voice which—partly because of limitations of structure and partly because it has not been exploited imaginatively—is rarely raised coherently and even more rarely heard.

The federally sponsored Community Action and Model Cities programs were also intended in part to help residents of poor neighborhoods obtain greater access to governmental decision makers and greater influence over their decisions. These federal programs differ from the City-sponsored citizen participation efforts in that both channel substantial amounts of program money through City systems that involve locally elected neighborhood boards with power or influence over program design and implementation. While the Community Action Program was initially intended to perform a coordinating role, in New York and in most other cities, the Community Action programs came to be entirely separate from other City services or activities. In effect 25 locally elected Community Corporation boards in New York City's poverty areas have been given several million dollars apiece to spend as they see fit, usually for recreation, job referral, tenant organizing, or similar high-personnel, high operating cost programs in which success or failure is hard to measure.

The federal guidelines for the Model Cities Program envisioned
a partnership of City government and poverty neighborhood boards
and use of Model Cities funds to induce constructive changes in regular
City programs in the model neighborhoods. But in New York the
tradition of virtually autonomous Community Corporations originally
made overt City government control seem politically infeasible. The
City solved its dilemma by leaving the power of the local Model Cities
boards deliberately ambiguous. The net result has been a great deal
of confusion and distrust, a few useful programs, but, in general,
extremely slow program development and very little actual expenditure
or impact. In early 1970 the City took control of the program away
from the local boards, but the promise of quick program implementation
and visible neighborhood improvement remains unfulfilled.

Despite the lack of substantive program impact, both of these
poverty area efforts have had significant influence on the tone and
processes of government. A whole new group of leaders has emerged,
learned the ways of the bureaucracy, and entrenched themselves as
middle-class officials—just as interested and as capable of preserving
their status as are their longer-term counterparts elsewhere in government. These leaders tend to be better educated, better organized,
more middle class than the average slum resident, but nevertheless
to be more representative of their neighbors and better spokesmen
for their interests than other elected or appointed officials. The rest
of City government has become more aware of poverty neighborhood
views and more deferential to those views. There has been a small
shift of power to the poor and to their slum districts.

The poverty and Model Cities programs also suggest several
general lessons. First, widespread, sustained community participation
is probably impossible in poor neighborhoods. Turnouts will be small
for any election, but they will be infinitesimal if the electors feel that
the boards to be chosen will have little or no effect on neighborhood
conditions, either because the resources available are small or the
board's power is insubstantial or unclear. Second, changing the ways
of City agencies is extremely difficult—impossible for outsiders, even
with substantial leverage money. If the powers of the central overhead
agencies (particularly the Budget Bureau), of the major operating
agencies, and of the bureaucracies and their unions are not changed,
their essential conservatism will overcome any peripheral effort,
even if supported by the mayor and other senior officials.

New York City has "decentralized" one giant service. After a
half-dozen major reports and three famous experiments, the state
legislature in 1969 mandated transfer of important authority over
elementary and intermediate schools from the central Board of
Education to 30 elected local boards. The educational decentralization experiments, especially Ocean Hill-Brownsville, have been

adequately chronicled.[4] As befits the subject, the published accounts reach widely varying conclusions about the facts, the causes of strife, and the educational and political outcomes. The new districts have had power for less than three years and an adequate appraisal is not yet possible. The school story, however, does suggest or reinforce certain conclusions relevant to the general subject of decentralization.

First, even in local elections for positions widely regarded as important, those with money and education can achieve dominance out of proportion to their numbers. This dominance may have been increased in the school elections by the complicated proportional representation system, which few voters could understand.

Second, political decentralization with no administrative delegation is unlikely to be productive. Important segments of political control over education policy have gone out from central headquarters to the district boards. But the system remains administratively centralized: professionals are in a rigid hierarchy, the important parts of which are managed citywide. Thus, conflict between the reward system of the teachers and the desires of the elected local boards is inevitable, and the local boards face much frustration as they seek to achieve their goals.

Third, taking over a complicated and well-established machine is slow and difficult. This is always true, but it is especially the case for part-time citizens whose statutory mandates are ambiguous, who face a strong union, and who must function in an age of superheated ethnic and other disputes.

Finally, the school boards have had to spend a great deal of effort establishing themselves locally. Their odd districts, not coterminous with any of the City's dozen other boundary schemes, confuse constituents. Since school programs overlap with other City efforts (for example, with recreation, antipoverty, drug abuse, and land-use decisions), school boards must get along with other local representatives, all of whom have a variety of public and private axes to grind. Such fragmentation of local participation discourages accountability to residents and effective handling of the matters committed to the neighborhood level.

Lack of Bargaining Power for Neighborhood Needs

The government of New York City, like that of most other cities, is essentially a bargaining process. While the mayor is the central figure, he does not always have the strongest bargaining position. The other major players are lesser elected City officials, the bureaucracy and its unions, the political parties, functional interest groups ranging from the National Welfare Rights Organization to the

Downtown Lower Manhattan Association, the state and federal governments, major foundations, the media, and local civic associations.
All of these groups have citywide or Manhattan-based interests, except
the local civic associations and, to a limited extent, borough presidents,
councilmen, and political parties. During the 1960's the bureaucracy
and the municipal unions have probably had the most influence. They
have known or cared little about local problems. The daily newspapers
and TV stations probably command more of City Hall's time than any
other interest, and they rarely report local concerns. There is no
powerful voice for local interests to force the City to adapt its services
to local needs. With so little power residents of the outer boroughs
have little positive interest in City government or in helping to improve
City services. They have learned how to veto action they dislike but
not how to initiate or follow through on programs they want.

Lack of Local Understanding of Costs and Trade-Offs
in Government Services

City statistics have always been developed and reported along
functional lines. It is almost impossible to assemble comprehensive
statistics with respect to any subarea within the City. Only in the last
few years, with the City Charter requirement for drawing community
district lines, has any attempt been made to break information down
geographically. Capital projects are now listed by community districts;
it is just becoming possible to collect some taxation statistics by
district. Since the local districts for other services are all different
from the community districts, comprehensive information may be
years away. This means that no one even tries to develop comprehensive neighborhood plans or to evaluate the total impact of programs
on the total quality of life in any area.

This lack of data about conditions in any neighborhood or about
the costs or accomplishments of government services contributes to
the almost total lack of understanding by City residents about what
the City does for them and for others, what services cost, or what
additional services might be provided at what costs. There seems to
be no comprehension as to what the trade-offs might be between increases in preferred services and decreases in other services or
increases in taxes. The ordinary citizen rarely seems to connect
increases in civil service wages, pensions, or other fringe benefits
with possible reductions in service to him or increases in his taxes.
Overall City expenditure figures are so large that they are almost
meaningless; everyone assumes that cost increases can be made up
by reductions in services to someone else or in some other part of the
City. This lack of understanding of costs and trade-offs reduces the

City's bargaining power with unions, because the effects of a strike, by contrast, are clear and present. The average citizen's uninformed attitude also fans dissatisfaction with high taxes and with the supposed gap between the services the City provides and the services New Yorkers believe they need and deserve. And everyone seems to believe that he and his neighborhood pay more than their proper share of taxes and receive back less than their just share of service.

Government by Crisis

The absence of local decision makers with authority, the lack of powerful representatives of local interests in the governmental bargaining process, and the lack of information and understanding about the quantity or costs of government services to the individual and his neighborhood all contribute to two other significant problems in governing New York City: government by crisis and failure or refusal of most citizens to cooperate with government in improving their own environment.

Citizens of all social and economic backgrounds now realize that they can hope for a positive response only from a top level agency administrator or the mayor himself—both of whom already are called upon to make too many decisions with too little information. A visit to City Hall means that some citizens are angry or frustrated about some issue and that they have organized a protest. It does not necessarily mean the issue is more important than thousands of others. A TV report on a problem means that the problem is interesting and conveniently photographable, not necessarily that it is of special importance. But City Hall seems to feel it must react. Not only do such demands on City Hall result in government by crisis, they also block the ability of central City officials to concentrate on the issues that affect the maintenance of the City as a viable, employment-providing economic and social entity. There is no way of discriminating between a dispute that has reached the mayor's desk because he is the political court of last resort and a dispute that has intrinsic significance for the whole City.

Lack of Citizen Cooperation with Government Services

Clean streets and sidewalks, enjoyable parks and playgrounds, efficient fire prevention or fire-fighting services, and neighborhood security all depend as much on the behavior and attitudes of neighborhood residents as on the efficiency of governmental services. There

are many explanations for the low level of citizen cooperation or of
sustained self-help efforts in most of the City's neighborhoods, but
lack of understanding or identification with government must be a
substantial contributing factor.

Special Minority Problems

Blacks and Puerto Ricans have special problems under New
York's centralized governmental system. Only a small percentage of
elegible blacks and Puerto Ricans vote in elections of any kind, and
they are not as successful as other interest groups in organizing for
proportional representation or block voting or in putting together
voting coalitions. As a result blacks and Puerto Ricans are significantly underrepresented among the City's elected officials. Under
present conditions neither blacks nor Puerto Ricans are likely to win
elections, except in districts in which a large majority of the eligible
voters are black or Puerto Rican and unless the stakes are high and
the election system is simple and well publicized.

Minorities also occupy far less than their proportionate share
of City jobs, particularly highly paid or supervisory jobs. And
minority firms get almost none of the City's construction or consulting
business or of the City's contracts for purchase of equipment, supplies,
or services, which could launch new minority-owned businesses.
City employees and procurement officers can justifiably claim that
there are few competitive minority applicants for the better jobs and
few qualified minority-owned suppliers. But blacks and Puerto Ricans
can point to the traditional system under which good jobs and lucrative
contracts always go to friends or associates of the employer or buyer
or at least to persons of similar backgrounds whom the employer or
buyer understands and trusts. This traditional system is sometimes
called "institutional racism"; it saps the initiative of blacks and
Puerto Ricans, who assume there is no use trying to qualify oneself
for the good jobs or the big contracts.

Minority neighborhoods are served by predominantly white
policemen, firemen, teachers, doctors, and social workers. Many
blacks and Puerto Ricans feel that the police arrest innocent youths
who congregate on street corners but avoid drug pushers, that white
teachers believe minority children are incapable of learning and
therefore emphasize discipline rather than instruction, and that social
workers preach good housekeeping or look for welfare cheaters rather
than advise poor people of their rights. Indeed, many minority persons
believe that white civil servants, in general, are insensitive to minority
needs, are primarily interested in their own security and job benefits
instead of the welfare of the minority residents, and are holding jobs

that should go to minority group persons. Whether or not these feelings
are justified, they cut down on the effectiveness of services, because
the minority residents refuse to cooperate and frequently interfere
with police, firemen, or sanitationmen. The prophecy of white insen-
sitivity then becomes self-fulfilling.

Special White Working-Class Problems

White working-class families that have only recently escaped
slum life also feel especially neglected and threatened. They believe
they are being taxed to pay for welfare and services to blacks and
Puerto Ricans who do not work, and they resent it. They also resent
the City's efforts to locate public housing in their single- and two-
family house neighborhoods, both because it means they will become
neighbors with the poor minority persons they have just escaped and
because they fear crime will increase and their schools will deteriorate.
As residents of areas in outer boroughs far removed from downtown
Manhattan, they feel they are being governed by the liberal upper-
middle class, which is almost as alien to them as it is to blacks and
Puerto Ricans. Many see little benefit to them in being part of New
York City and little opportunity to exercise the same self-interest
rights that their suburban neighbors enjoy.

POSSIBLE DISADVANTAGES OF
DECENTRALIZATION

Demonstrating that New York City's centralized structure poses
serious problems for effective and satisfactory governmental service
and that the City's citizen participation experiments have thus far
been ineffectual is not the same as demonstrating that multipurpose,
political decentralization will solve all those problems or will actually
improve services. Indeed, decentralization, like any radical change,
can be expected to introduce new problems that could well vitiate its
beneficial effects. Before analyzing how the City's government might
be decentralized therefore, it seems appropriate to suggest some of
the possible disadvantages of decentralization that also need to be
reflected in the analysis of how decentralization might work.

Greater political responsiveness would mean less professional
independence. It could lead to corruption and incompetence, with an
increase in patronage politics, particularly since the watchdog job
performed by the citywide media and civic associations might be less
effectively performed under decentralization. Some way must be
found to make sure that local governments are watched and that
dishonesty, favoritism, and inefficiency are promptly exposed.

The metropolitan government movement seeks economies of scale; decentralization must not sacrifice these economies where they are substantial. Volume purchasing can save money. Some problems, like pollution or mass transportation, require solution on a scale larger than the City. Some services, for example, waste disposal, can benefit greatly from large-scale technology. In other functional areas, such as zoning, costs of local decision making could spill over to neighboring districts or to the City as a whole. Some regulation of private behavior, such as the building code, could raise costs of doing business, if decentralized. And the City's capacity to experiment and innovate must be preserved.

New York's economy is complex and, perhaps, fragile. If the City lost its appeal for corporate headquarters and for the financial, legal, and advertising community, the whole metropolitan region would suffer, and the City would be unable to find employment for its citizens. Such a loss could follow substantial deterioration in services, a serious escalation of political or racial conflict, or a fragmentation of commercial or development authority. Equally damaging would be further erosion of the attractiveness of the City as a place for the middle class to live.

Decentralization should bring a substantial shift of power from citywide or Manhattan interests to local district interests. Within those districts, however, tyranny by a district majority could develop, or even tyranny by an aggressive minority. The kind of shifting coalitions that characterize today's City politics and provide some protection for minorities would be less likely to occur in smaller districts, where a particular interest group might be able to take and keep control. Furthermore, the addition of some 40 new power centers could mean 40 new and stronger vetoes against change. It is already far too difficult to launch new projects; additional bottlenecks could mean virtual paralysis.

One of the principal benefits of decentralization could be better information about program costs and accomplishments, organized on the basis of moderate-sized districts, so that interested citizens could understand and evaluate government services and the available options for change. But more widespread understanding will not necessarily produce only enlightened decisions. Political decentralization, accompanied by clearer understanding of how City taxes are spent, could make it much harder for the City to tax those who can afford to pay in order to help those in the greatest need, especially if that means redistributing substantial funds from residents of relatively affluent districts to residents of poorer districts.

The decentralization solution applied to the special problems of blacks and Puerto Ricans and of the white working-class residents of the outer boroughs is pregnant with serious problems of its own.

Leaders of both groups seek greater homogeneity in new districts and greater local power over program design and over government employment. But a federation of homogeneous, autonomous districts could well mean reduced mobility in housing, education, social and recreational activities, and employment. The advantages of self-determination and the opportunity for blacks and Puerto Ricans to run their own governments must then be weighed against the dangers of jeopardizing progress toward integration.

Many of the City programs that might be decentralized are financed in substantial part by federal or state grants and are, therefore, subject to federal or state oversight and regulation. But because of the vast size of New York's citywide programs, state and federal agencies tend to interfere less in New York City program management than in the management of smaller cities' programs. Fragmentation of the City's programs among a number of smaller districts might mean an increase in the role of state or federal program officials and a lessening of local control.

The fiscal future of the City depends to a large extent on the capacity of the mayor to bargain for support in Albany and in Washington. Election of local district officials would diffuse power, and the mayor might no longer be able to speak as effectively for the City as a whole. If decentralization materially lessened the mayor's bargaining power, the City might obtain less financial support than would otherwise be the case.

Finally, any major change is disruptive, as school decentralization has so recently demonstrated. And in a multifaceted bargaining system like the government of New York City, approval of, or acquiescence to, change must usually be purchased. If the disruption is too great or the purchase price too high, the change might well not be worth it.

CONCLUSION

New York City's problems in rendering effective services provide ample basis for demands for change in the structure and operations of the City's government. But change and even improvement can seem deceptively easy as long as analysis is kept theoretical and general. The hard questions are how structural change would affect the behavior and output of the City's political structure, its service delivery agencies, its fiscal and budgeting system, and its employment system. Only by analysis in some detail of the impact of decentralization on those institutions can one predict whether decentralization would solve existing City problems and avoid creating serious new ones.

3

**LOCAL
DISTRICT
GOVERNMENTS**

A two-tier system of government for New York City would
require the creation of new local government districts and new political
institutions to govern those districts. The success of any such decentralization effort would depend in material part on how the new
local governments interact with the continuing central City government.
The quality of this interaction would in turn depend upon the internal
political structure new local units chose or were required to adopt,
what service responsibilities they assumed, how these services were
financed, and how their employees were chosen and directed. Our
analysis of these closely intertwined matters begins by considering
the issues involved in determining local size and boundaries, the
internal political structure of local district governments, the effects
of decentralization on the structure and functions of the continuing
central City government, and the extent to which the continuing central
City government should intervene in internal local district political
matters.

DISTRICT SIZE

Choosing the size for new decentralized government units is
difficult for the same reason that confronts all the structural choices
in this chapter: the relatively narrow goal of improving the delivery
of public services must compete with other ends that people use local
government to achieve. For example, questions about direct individual
participation in the making of political decisions, racial integration,
organization and staffing of new units of local government, and the
distribution of population and taxable resources are all relevant to
the size of new districts, but they suggest conflicting answers.

On one issue all considerations point in the same direction. If
local districts are to develop viable local political institutions and a

sense of political identity, they must constitute sociogeographic entities This means that boundaries should follow major natural and man-made barriers—rivers, railroads, expressways, industrial areas—and should not create enclaves or pockets separated by such features from the body of the local unit. This principal probably deserves adherence, even if it causes units to be larger or smaller than might seem desirable from an abstract service-delivery viewpoint.

New local districts should observe, as well, existing patterns of neighborhood organization. This might mean recognition of existing service area boundaries, such as community school districts or other City-defined boundaries within which political organization has occured. It might mean observance of existing, spontaneous patterns or organization in areas like Greenwich Village or Bay Ridge. Or it might mean no more than recognition of the informal organization of local public transportation routes and the shopping, walking, and recreational patterns that define the urban neighborhood of the sociologist.

Great disparities in wealth, population, or formal powers among local districts would probably make much more difficult the task of developing effective new local political institutions. Size and power disparities would tend to encourage claims for ever-greater autonomy by the larger local units. Power and status differentials would affect the trade-offs among districts in the central City political institutions, as well as diminish the ability of less-powerful districts to attract and hold highly qualified officials and administrators. Substantial wealth differentials would also increase the likelihood that more wealthy local units would seek greater autonomy in order to escape the burden of contributing funds to less-wealthy units. Accordingly, large deviations from the "average" local district, in size, powers, or accessibility to taxable resources should be permitted to exist only when other factors make them unavoidable.

But boundary and uniformity criteria do not come to grips with the question of how large the typical local units should be. Should local units be the urban equivalent of the village, encompassing an area of 20,000 or 30,000 people? Or should the present boroughs, or units approaching them in size, be the recipients of decentralized powers?

If one believes that there should remain a significant central City government after decentralization, then borough-size units (with the exception of Staten Island) are probably too large to serve as second-tier units. If each borough had major service delivery responsibilities, some fiscal autonomy, and full-fledged borough legislative and executive bodies, the boroughs might eclipse the central City. Moreover, such upgrading of the boroughs would probably not yield many of the gains hoped for from decentralization. The four major boroughs are so large that most of the problems of size outlined in

Chapter 2 would apply to them as well. As a result, the only gain
might be freedom of the outer boroughs from the real or imagined
dominance of Manhattan—a retrograde step if it meant loss of ultimate
citywide authority over environmental protection, zoning, or transportation planning and development.

There are a number of reasons for prefering units much smaller
than the present boroughs—units as small as 50,000 or 60,000 people.
Decentralization that yielded relative homogeneity of population within
individual districts (in comparison to the diversity of the City as a
whole or of whole boroughs) might help reduce both the frequency and
intensity of intergroup conflict within the City. When all important
decisions for the City are made at City Hall, the decision of one group
to press its demands upon the mayor or his department heads encourages other groups to mobilize, even if their interests are only
symbolically at stake. Because every decision tends to serve as a
precedent for subsequent similar decisions, groups cannot afford to
ignore decisions with possible adverse implications. Lessening the
scale of decision making would both decrease the precedential value
of any given local decision and also decrease the number of groups
likely to come into conflict over a single decision.

Such small units, coupled with existing City residential patterns,
would enable minority groups to control many local units. The precedential value of the recent elections of the 31 new community school
boards is somewhat obscured by the special form of proportional
representation used for those elections. But the school board election
experience does indicate the possibility that, in large units, organized,
middle-class white groups can control local elections, even though
they represent only a minority of potential voters. By fostering the
creation of autonomous minority-controlled political institutions,
decentralization to relatively small units might also help minority
economic development and might also help minority groups develop
the group confidence and individual skills needed to deal on equal
terms with the dominant institutions of the society.[1]

Our largest cities seem to be those in which there is the least
resident understanding of the interplay among services, municipal
wage levels, and tax rates and, also, the least resident concern about
the costs that individual behavior can impose on environmental
amenity and public safety. Although undoubtedly this situation results
in part from urban population densities and the incredible intricacy
of urban economic interactions, smaller units would at least provide
a focus for emphasizing the relationship between individual behavior
and the cost of providing public services and, perhaps, would also
strengthen the resolve of citizens and public officials to take a tougher
stance in public employee collective bargaining.

One of the tangible gains that could flow from multiplicity of local governments is the opportunity for choice among alternative possible combinations of government services and among styles of government operations. The suburbs are attractive in part because they permit some interarea variation in the level and mix of government services. They also provide a basis for interunit competition in the quality of services, which is lacking in large cities. In New York, where it is virtually impossible to relate tax increases to improved services for a given neighborhood, no one is willing to consent to a tax increase to finance improved services. Relatively smaller units might stimulate this kind of competition and willingness to spend money for public purposes.

Finally, for those to whom direct, day-by-day resident contact with the making of decisions about local government services is important, very small units would be a necessity. True "citizen participation" in policy making is impossible when a political unit has a population so large that frequent direct consultation and representation through block-level units becomes logistically impractical. A unit of 50,000 persons surely would be at the upper limit of the size at which such representation and consultation would be practicable.

There are, nevertheless, a number of reasons why units of 50,000 population or less would be unrealistically small for primary service delivery units in a city with the population and complexity of New York. "Thinking small" has a number of disadvantages, particularly in relation to values of equity, equality, and racial integration. The flexibility and variety offered by multiple suburban jurisdictions often is available only to those of above-average incomes. The opportunities for choice among alternative service packages in various individual jurisdictions more often than not boil down to dividing people according to incomes—so that those who make the greatest demands upon public resources are carefully segregated from those with the greatest capacity to pay. To some extent this could be avoided in a two-tier City government by restricting the fiscal and zoning autonomy of the local units. But the smaller the individual unit, the greater the incentive and the opportunity for the dominant group within the unit to attempt, consciously or unconsciously, to become the sole group.

A related concern with very small units would be their impact on mobility and employment diversity within the City. At present, however segregated by race or income parts of the City may be, most people still travel throughout most of the City for social, educational, employment, recreational, or other purposes, without thinking much about what they are doing. The substitution of a large number of local units would decrease this mobility, and the impact would increase as individual districts became more homogeneous. Upwardly mobile minority group members might find it increasingly difficult to move into areas in which their middle-class incomes could be reflected in middle-class life styles. Although local district governments controlled by blacks or Puerto Ricans might benefit from their ability to deal with white units as equals, the net results for blacks and Puerto Ricans in the City as a whole might not be positive. There is no way that reasonable boundaries could be drawn to ensure that some minority group members were not in white-dominated areas, and many areas in a two-tier City would probably be relatively unreceptive to the goals and aspirations of minority residents or potential minority immigrants.

Such tendencies toward individual district conservatism would be an inevitable part of any move to a two-tier system. The federal government has been more sensitive to the needs of the poor and of minority group members than most state and local governments. There is no reason to expect that smaller units within New York City would not show the same tendency, on the average, to increased conservatism. This tendency could be minimized by ensuring that individual second-tier units are large enough so that most such units would face common problems. If districts perceived no such common problems, they would be less interested in working together among themselves or within the legislative councils of the City. Each would prefer expenditures that met its peculiar needs and would oppose taxation and expenditure to meet other needs. The net result would more probably be inadequate public expenditure, rather than a complicated horse trade involving something for everybody.

Beyond the possible adverse impact of small units on the levels of equality, opportunity, and integration possible in the City, there are practical reasons for suspecting that in a city the size of New York, second-tier units as small as 50,000 people might not prove to be viable. First, as suggested in Chapter 1, it is not clear that many New Yorkers are interested in participating actively or consistently in the relatively unglamorous tasks of local government. When trash is not collected, people are interested in registering a loud complaint but not in devoting much of their time to improving service. Second, in higher-density areas of the City, units of 50,000 persons would be small enough to relate only with difficulty to an existing commercial center, public facilities, or natural boundaries. Such districts would frequently cover so little territory that many decisions affecting local residents would be made by adjacent districts over which local residents would have no control. In turn, such a district's exercise of its own powers would be likely to impose "spillover" costs on neighboring districts.

The natural tendency with quite small districts would therefore be to grant them only noncontroversial responsibilities and to draw back power once granted. But as demonstrated by the experience with the present City boroughs, too little power would cause local residents to lose interest in the local unit of government, except as

a safety valve. Local officials might have the power to receive and
pass on complaints, with little responsibility. This would not be the
road either to improved service delivery or increased resident satisfaction with City services.

In addition, if most residents of a given district were employed
outside of that district, sought their recreation opportunities outside
of it, and perhaps even did most of their shopping elsewhere, they
would pay little attention to the conduct of local district political and
administrative affairs. And the larger the number of local units, the
more difficult it would be for the various news media to cover internal
district politics and the greater would be the economic difficulties of
establishing local newspapers or cable television service. Nor would
word of mouth and local acquaintances always suffice, because a large
proportion of the acquaintances of many residents would be from
different districts. Accordingly, participation, or at least knowledgeable participation, might not be improved by smaller districts.

Choice of unit size probably would also have an impact on the
administration and service delivery capacity of second-tier units of
government Unfortunately, even though public services are delivered
in the United States and abroad by governmental units of virtually
every size, there is no reliable information about the presence or
absence of economies or diseconomies of scale, at least so long as
the unit has a population of more than 50,000.[2] But one implication
of unit size for service effectiveness can be drawn. New second-tier
units would need to develop new cadres of managerial and senior
administrative personnel. New York's present, highly centralized
agency structure has produced few middle-management officials
capable of assuming senior administrative responsibilities in new
local units. Thus, the greater the number of new units, the more
difficult would be the task of recruiting competent local administrators
and the more likely it would be that service quality would decline in
the early years of a two-tier system. Any such decline significant
enough to annoy large numbers of New Yorkers could lead to elimination of a two-tier system before it was fairly tested.

The size and flexibility of local district budgets would also
have impact on local effectiveness and on local ability to innovate.
Competent, qualified persons are attracted by the magnitude of the
challenge and of the resources that may be commanded. Officials in
very small districts might find little incentive to hold office, except
for their own salaries and the few local jobs that might be dispensed.
Local districts could hardly be innovative if their budgets were so
small that there were no flexible funds for experimental activities or
programs. It would always be easier to stick with the status quo if
experimenting would require cutting back on traditional services.

Lastly, central City officials would probably be more likely to ignore or override local preferences of small districts. With local districts large enough to have some political significance at the city-wide level, this possibility would become more remote. Moreover, the smaller the local units, the more difficult it would be to transfer partial or exclusive control over any of the City's present tax base to new second-tier units.

The authors of this study ascribe higher priority to political viability and capacity to provide effective service than to widespread citizen participation or maximization of choice among local districts. Accordingly, they conclude that local government districts in New York City should serve populations of not less than 125,000 or more than 300,000. This choice of range is somewhat corroborated by the fact that the City's existing planning and service districts fall within it. For example, the 31 community school districts average 270,000 residents, the 62 community districts average about 125,000 and go up over 250,000, and the 58 sanitation districts average 135,000 residents. Within that range there are no compelling social or economic reasons for any particular size. But both the transition and continuing central-local relations would be easier with fewer districts. And there is much to be said for keeping districts about the same size and making them as equal in wealth as possible. With necessary adjustments for rational boundaries and wealth equalization, therefore, some 40 districts, each with about 200,000 population, would seem as good a compromise as any among the conflicting pressures and values.

DISTRICT STRUCTURE

The primary consideration in defining the structure of the new district governments should be their capacity to make decisions and assure that they would be carried out. But the satisfaction and co-operation of district residents would depend not only on the vigor and efficiency of the local governments but also on whether residents perceive those governments to be their legitimate representatives. Local government must therefore be accessible, and participation of local residents in local elections must be made as easy and effective as possible.

Any design of a new governmental structure in New York City must take into account the enormous complexity of the City's public and private institutions and recognize the difficulties and dangers of any radical change. The new local district governments would be assuming extensive and controversial responsibilities. They would need to recruit top management personnel almost immediately and

to build relationships with thousands of municipal employees and their
union leaders, whose enthusiasm for decentralization might be lukewarm
at best. The residual central operating agencies, the Budget Bureau,
and other central staff agencies might well cling to their former powers
and cooperate only to the extent absolutely necessary. Resident expectations would be high, and the new governments would soon discover
that they did not have the resources to meet those expectations.

Ideally, the residents of each district should be permitted to
choose their own form of government, but that freedom of choice might
not be feasible, at least at first. Regardless of how enthusiastic some
district residents might be for decentralization, the local districts
would probably not start out as effective political units. There is no
evidence to suggest that local political parties would be well organized
or that there would be news media capable of effective collection or
distribution of local news. No matter how carefully the transition were
made, fiscal, budgetary, personnel, and program arrangements would
be full of uncertainties and unresolved problems. If decentralization
is to survive its shakedown years, the districts should not be allowed
to become bogged down in organizational struggles.

There should be one person in each local district who could be
held responsible for the quality of local district services. Therefore,
each local district should have a chief elected official—comparable
to a strong local mayor or to the elected county executive in Westchester or Nassau counties. Collective district council responsibility
for the administration of local government services would be too
likely to diffuse accountability for decisions. Or if individual councilmen
assumed responsibility for specific programs, coordination would
suffer as each councilman would focus on his own program and would
tend not to inquire closely about what other councilmen were doing
within the limits of their program areas.

With districts of about 200,000 people, district residents could
neither legislate nor monitor program performances directly. Representative legislative bodies would be necessary. The issues become
their size and the way in which representatives would be chosen. A
small local unit council would be more desirable than a relatively
large one for several reasons. With a large council, it would be
difficult to pay the stipends necessary to encourage the participation,
even on a part-time basis, of mothers, wage earners, or small
businessmen. The larger the council, the more costly it would be to
provide council members with some kind of staff assistance, so that
they could respond to constituent requests and obtain the information
necessary for responsible council participation. Without such assistance, however, the price of a large council might be permanent
amateur standing for its members.

In addition, most Americans, other than those who have spent all their lives in our five or ten largest cities, are accustomed to relatively small city councils or similar bodies. The relatively large size of councils in cities like New York or Chicago is more a response to the problems of obtaining reasonable patterns of representation in a large city than it is a testimony to the efficacy of large councils. The experience in the United Kingdom with relatively large urban councils is not necessarily a satisfactory precedent for the United States. Such large councils appear likely to function most effectively in relatively homogeneous cities, where there are undoubtedly sterner standards of public service and official rectitude.

A small council might be anywhere from five to perhaps as many as eleven persons. For example, with districts of about 200,000 population, a seven-man council would mean about 30,000 residents per councilman, and a nine-man council would mean around 23,000 residents per councilman.

District councilmen should be elected. A system of appointment of some or all of the members might assure that a larger proportion of councilmen would have government experience and would be able to deal effectively with bureaucrats in and out of their districts. But appointive techniques that make sense for advisory boards would be less attractive when applied to a general purpose legislative body with formal budgeting, priority-setting, and policy-determining powers. Appointive politics would soon become interest group politics, as each organized constituency sought representation. If the appointing power were independent of the majority of voters in the district, the council would not be a local autonomous legislative institution but a collegiate administrative arm of some higher level of political authority. Finally, group representation patterns assume that people with some common characteristic, such as background, would indeed have common interests—an assumption that grows more unreasonable the wider the range of discretion given to the representative.

In view of the history of low participation in local elections, every effort should be made to stimulate voting in district elections. For purposes of determining the local district franchise, the statutory requirements for eligibility in citywide elections should apply. In view of the high rates of intracity mobility, however, there should be no district residency requirement other than the time lag between the close of registration and the holding of elections. This time lag should be as short as possible. Property owners in local districts should not receive a special franchise by virtue of that fact, just as property owners living outside of New York City are not entitled to vote in New York City elections.

New York's school decentralization experience does not yet support the use of proportional representation techniques for local district elections. Although theoretically desirable as a way of giving all interests a chance for representation, those methods that produce statistically fair results appear to be too complicated for the comprehension of the average voter. Accountability and voter participation might better be fostered if the local district were divided into local council election districts of equal population. And, since residential patterns in the City produce ethnic and economic interest group neighborhoods, council election districts of about 20,000 people should help ensure that substantial minority groups within each district have a chance of representation. After the first two or three years of decentralization, however, local districts might be given the option to adopt proportional representation elections.

The parties could play an important role in assisting voters to identify candidates and to have some idea of their political positions. The out-of-office party would have a vested interest in organized scrutiny of the behavior and decisions of those in office, thus helping to overcome the concern that decentralized politics would be unpublicized politics. Elections for local office in areas that were heavily composed of unregistered but otherwise eligible voters would provide local party groups with an incentive to increase registrations, whether or not an increased number of black and Puerto Rican voters seemed likely to upset the stability of existing county-level party organizations. In any event the City's political parties are still powerful enough to block any major governmental damage that would exclude them from participation. But with local council election districts of about 20,000 people, the task of winning a seat on the council would mean the ability to attract no more than about 5,000 votes. Therefore, the parties would not be able to obtain a stranglehold on candidacies for the local council simply because of the financing and campaign apparatus required.

The local council would have the same kinds of authority that a council would have in strong mayor cities. For example, if the authority to establish regulations for local sanitation services or local parks were vested in local districts, the local council would have that authority. The actual preparation of detailed rules and regulations would of course be delegated to local agency administrators. If local districts were given powers to regulate parking, to define minor misdemeanors, or to modify the terms of the housing code, the council should be required to act. The council should also pass on any decision for or against the local assumption of additional government responsibilities.

Fiscal matters are discussed in Chapter 5, but, in general, the local council would have the same kinds of powers with respect to the local budget that the present Board of Estimate and City Council have over the City's budget, including approval of the local budget document, control over budget modifications during the year, and approval of the annual requests for capital projects. If local districts were given the right to impose taxes or user charges, this authority should also rest with the council.

In the initial stages of any move toward political decentralization, the administrative structure of the new local district government would be determined for some time to come by the pattern of organization at the time of transfer. The initial structure of the operating agencies would presumably be the traditional one of a series of program administrators, who would become the equivalent of department heads and would constitute a "cabinet" under the local district executive.

Districts that wished to appoint a chief administrative officer or city manager should be free to do so, but this should not be required. The city manager system is difficult to combine with a chief elected official and historically has worked best in homogeneous communities—an unlikely situation in districts of 125,000 to 300,000 people in New York City.

DISTRICT RELATIONS TO
CENTRAL CITY GOVERNMENT

While the failure of New York City's centralized government to respond effectively to local interests supports serious consideration of decentralization, no reorganization should be adopted that would undermine the values of the City as a whole or leave citywide interests unrepresented. Federations of existing municipalities into a metropolitan structure seek to retain the advantages of both local and metropolitan governments; decentralization should have the same objective.

A proper balance between local and central or citywide interests could be maintained if the state or some other neutral body acted as a continuing arbitrator or referee. Or balance could result from the natural interplay of political forces operating within the new governmental structure. There is no reason to believe that the state government, the courts, or any other independent body could satisfactorily accommodate the many local and citywide interests that would be at stake. The state legislature now has almost complete power over New York City's affairs.[3] In the absence of radical state constitutional change, which is unlikely, that power will continue. But the less it is used to affect relationships within City government, the better. We would prefer to rely primarily on the City's voters and on the bargaining process that constitutes City government. Such reliance on forces within the City does, however, increase the importance of proper structuring of the relations between the central and local governments.

Since the central government would still be needed to make taxing, land-use, and other decisions that will not be popular in any district, local district governments should not have too much power over the central executive or legislative branches. The slowness with which the Metropolitan Council of Toronto embarked on controversial projects during its early years has been attributed in part to the fact that the members of the Metropolitan Council were elected primarily as officials of the constituent municipalities rather than as officials of a metropolitanwide government.[4] Since New York City's reorganization need not be passed upon by existing local governments, this problem of the Toronto system need not be repeated.

But local district interests must also be protected from unbridled central government power. The central New York City government would be allocating City funds between central and local functions and, under at least one of the possible fiscal systems, even among the several local functions. The central executive and legislature would presumably also have some power to change the structure of the decentralized government itself. Since such powerful interests as the existing central agency managers and unionized bureaucracy would probably try to preserve or recapture centralized authority, the new governmental structure should assure a powerful voice to representatives of the local districts, both as to ongoing governmental decisions and as to any reallocation of governmental powers.

The mayor should continue to be elected directly by a citywide electorate. He would be responsible to all New Yorkers for delivery of central City services and for decisions with respect to taxation, budget allocations, planning, economic development, and other important matters. And he would continue to speak for the City in Albany and in Washington. A mayor chosen by local district chief executives, local district councils, or the central City Council would be compelled to exercise his programmatic and budgetary powers with a view to their effect on the political coalition that placed him in office. This would leave the City as a whole without an effective leader or advocate.

The central City legislative body should be structured to assure a strong voice for local district interests. But the composition of the central council should not foster defensive parochialism. If the central legislative body were composed of local district officials sitting ex officio, the central City government might become the captive of local district politics in ways that prevented its achieving the important but controversial purposes for which the central government would still be responsible. A log-rolling system, under which each legislator sought primarily to achieve the goals of his own district, would also be encouraged to some extent by selecting City legislators from districts coterminous with the decentralized boundaries. On the other hand a certain amount of "trade-off" politics

is inevitable and might even facilitate the making of acceptable citywide
policy. Since at-large elections for the City legislature seem impractical, the realistic choice is among a legislature composed of local
district agents, one made up of delegates elected from districts
coterminous with the local units and one consisting of members elected
from different districts.

The choice among these options involves four considerations:
(a) the peculiar historical division of legislative powers in New York
City between the Board of Estimate and the City Council; (b) the
likelihood that all or a substantial portion of local district fiscal
resources will be determined by political decisions made in the citywide legislative body; (c) the one-man/one-vote rule, as applied to
local governments by the Supreme Court; and (d) the importance of
conforming district boundaries to existing conditions of social geography.

Any changes in the central City legislature must either provide
a continuing role for the borough presidents, whose principal activity
is Board of Estimate membership, or be able to garner sufficient
political support to ignore them and the county political party organizations to which they belong. The other three considerations are at
least partially inconsistent with each other. Centralized control over
allocation of funds to local districts supports an argument for units
of legislative representation that would be coterminous with local
district boundaries. The one-man/one-vote rule probably requires
that newly created units of legislative representation be of substantially
equal population. Adherence to boundaries that respect physical
barriers and existing patterns of community organization, shopping,
and transportation could not occur in many cases unless districts were
of unequal size. Since the Supreme Court is unlikely to reverse its
one-man/one-vote rule, either local government district boundaries
will have to do a certain amount of violence to conditions of physical
and social geography or the election districts for the central City
legislature could not be coterminous with local government districts.

With each central legislator representing a local government
district, it would be easier for a district government to obtain the
attention of central City agencies in the event of disagreement with
the way those agencies were delivering services to its residents. If
legislative districts were not identical with the local districts, then
residents of a piece of one local unit would be likely to find that
they were in a legislative district primarily composed of an adjoining
local unit and might be able to make little claim on their legislator's
time or assistance. But even if local districts and councilmanic
boundaries were the same, a legislator might feel he owed none of
his votes to a particular area within the district from which he was
elected, and a similar risk of ignoring that area's interests would
be created.

Another reason for making central City councilmanic districts coterminous with local government districts would be to simplify the ballot and focus the voters' attention on his district as a jurisdiction of social and political significance to him. Voter recognition of the structure and boundaries of the local government system would both encourage informed voting and assist resident efforts to influence government behavior other than through the ballot box.

On the other hand the many natural and man-made geographic barriers to communications might well create substantial service delivery problems if district populations were not permitted to deviate by more than 10 or 15 percent. Moreover, the need to redraw legislative district boundaries periodically in order to reflect population change would entail the redrawing of local governmental unit boundaries as well. Potential future population growth in Staten Island and the outer Bronx and Queens and population declines in the older areas of Brooklyn, Manhattan, and the Bronx could mean substantial boundary changes. Such changes would adversely affect the development of internal political cohesiveness and working political institutions. They would also cause administrative and programmatic upheavals, as they would involve shifting personnel and adjusting local district budgets. In some cases boundary shifts might even change the kind of services provided to the affected residents because the new district might be providing a different service mix than the old one.

While it would be important that the viewpoint of local districts be strongly represented in the City Council's considerations of budget allocations between central and local functions, it would not be as necessary that the point of view of each district be represented. If either of the fiscal and budgetary systems recommended in Chapter 5 were adopted, allocations of funds among the districts would be determined by formulas based on district population and appropriate factors that measure relative need. There should be no political maneuvering to favor one district over another. Indeed, the greater the identification of central legislators with individual districts, the greater the danger that budget sessions would veer away from considerations of total needs and division of funds among the various functions of government, central and local, and toward acrimonious debates as to whether individual districts gain or lose by decisions that should have broader objectives.

The key factor then might be whether central City legislators who are elected from districts with boundaries substantially different from those of the local district governments would represent the local district governments' point of view strongly enough to counteract the other powerful centralizing forces in the City. It is hazardous to predict how such legislators would behave, but there is real danger that they would consider themselves primarily citywide officials and

that the necessary balance of central and local interests would not
be achieved. We would prefer, therefore, that central legislators'
districts be the local government districts and would hope that the
flexibility demonstrated by the U.S. Supreme Court in the recent
Rockland County case would be extended to permit the drawing of
plausible district boundaries.

If, however, considerations of equal apportionment should bar
councilmanic districts identical to local districts, we would favor
permitting the local district councils each to select a central City
councilman. This device seems permissible under the U.S. Supreme
Court's Sailors decision and would prevent the fragmentation of local
district cohesion, responsibility, and recognition, which could seriously
undercut the decentralization effort.

What role does this leave for New York City's Board of Estimate?
The board how has no authority over regular legislative matters, but
does have substantial influence on the budget, on capital projects, and
on a series of administrative matters. It resembles, but is not
equivalent to, an upper house in the traditional bicameral legislative
structure at the state and federal level. The board is one of a kind,
a unique product of New York City's consolidation; it continues to
exist primarily because it has been politically impractical to eliminate
it.

In considering the future of the Board of Estimate in a decentralized New York City, there are three distinct issues: (a) the impact
of one-man/one-vote on the Board of Estimate, (b) the political role
of borough representation at the central City level, and (c) the politics
of accountability in a quasilegislative body that includes officials
elected on a citywide basis other than the mayor. The one-man/one-
vote rule probably means that the Board of Estimate would be in
violation of the Constitution if the board gained any share in the
general legislative powers now possessed by the City Council. Broadening of the board's powers thus would require that it give up borough
representation.

The notion of at-large representation on a central City legislative body was rejected above because such elections would automatically produce rivals for citywide leadership. The same concern
exists with the comptroller and the president of the council. In a
two-tier City it would be preferable for there to be only one focus
for the central City government—the mayor. The tendencies for
local districts to try to pull away from central control from time to
time will be strong without the existence of other citywide elected
officials with substantial budgetary powers who can try to use.this
dissatisfaction to build their own separate constituencies.

The temptation for the comptroller and the council president
to try to establish their own citywide constituencies is increased

by the present structure and role of the Board of Estimate. The board resembles a parliamentary legislative body, in which the prime minister (the mayor) has no party behind him. The mayor has the formal responsibility for governing the City—supervising the work of its agencies, preparing and presenting a budget, and obtaining necessary programmatic and fiscal support from state and federal governments. He is expected to do all this through the vehicle of the Board of Estimate, on which he controls four out of 22 votes. Unlike a parliamentary system, however, the remaining members of the Board of Estimate bear no responsibility for opposition, because the voters cannot determine the extent to which action or inaction of the board is responsible for the mayor's failure to achieve his proclaimed goals.[5]

However, there are several practical reasons for retaining an institution like the board. It would not hurt the preservation of the City as a unified whole if some City officials other than the mayor had a political base that compelled them to think in terms much broader than individual districts. Furthermore, the existing boroughs are very large themselves. The borough presidents would be the logical persons around whom to build organizations of district executives comparable to "councils of local governments" to facilitate cooperation among local districts within the boroughs. If there is a role that the borough presidents can usefully play, it makes no sense to propose eliminating them in order to simplify the organization charts for a two-tier structure of local government. A great deal of political and emotional capital is tied up with the existing boroughs and with the system of elected borough representatives. If the rest of the gains from decentralization are felt to be worthwhile, the battle to achieve the somewhat nominal gains from a pure unicameral legislative structure at the central City level might well not be worth fighting— because it is not at all clear that the borough presidents would lose.

On balance, therefore, the most desirable alternative would be a Board of Estimate limited to borough presidents and the mayor, in which the voting structure was set up so that the mayor, plus two borough presidents, would constitute a majority. Such a revised Board of Estimate would have a single point of citywide leadership—the mayor—and would be likely to enhance, rather than downgrade, the role of the borough presidents as regional representatives.

SPECIAL CENTRAL CITY DISTRICT

Downtown and midtown Manhattan should probably be constituted as a special central city district, financed and governed by the central City government. These are the areas where most of the City's office buildings, hotels, and theaters are located and where most federal, state, and City officials work. Less than 100,000 people live in these areas, which yield a large fraction of the City's tax revenues and account for a large part of the City's employment base. They need excellent public safety and environmental services if New York is to remain the corporate, financial, and cultural capital of the world, but there is relatively little need for public education, health, or social services. Almost every governmental decision involving these areas would have a substantial citywide effect.

The boundaries of the central district should be drawn to include as many of the City's existing and proposed business and government buildings as possible, while excluding areas that are now residential and likely to remain so for the next decade. These areas would be governed out of the mayor's office and served by central City agencies. Such personal services as elementary education and social services might be provided by contracts with adjoining government districts. Some services, such as trash collection, might be provided by contract with private enterprise. There should probably be some kind of citizens' council, perhaps even an elected one, but it should be advisory only; residents of these areas would have to recognize that citywide interests would probably be determinative in most matters.

SUMMARY

The primacy of the objective of improving the quality of government services would significantly affect most decisions with respect to size and boundaries of local districts in a two-tier system of City government, as well as the structure of local district governments and their relationship with the continuing central government. But factors such as physical and social geography, the attitudes and behavior of the City's voters, and the incentives and pressures likely to influence legislators would probably be more important to the success of decentralization than concepts of scale efficiency or scientific principles of organization and management. The most important factor would be existing social and political interests, which could not be ignored to achieve theoretical benefits. The framing of local district government must therefore involve a balancing among social and political values, and the ultimate structure would result more from the relative bargaining strength of interest groups than from the logic of public administrators.

Some 40 local districts should emerge from such a bargaining process, each with a population of about 200,000. Local district boundaries should reflect natural and man-made barriers to communication, existing patterns of neighborhood identification, and the distribution of commercial, recreational, and public facilities. Substantial differences in size or wealth should be avoided. Each district should have a strong elected chief executive. District legislative councils should be elected from subdistricts of about 20,000 in population each and should have powers parallel to those of the central City Council. Local districts should be permitted to establish their own administrative structures. The mayor should continue to be selected in direct citywide elections. The central City Council should, if possible, be elected from districts coterminous with local government districts. The Board of Estimate should be continued but should include only the mayor and the borough presidents. The comptroller and president of the City Council should still be elected citywide, but should not sit on the Board of Estimate.

4

ALLOCATION
OF RESPONSIBILITY
FOR SERVICES

The success of decentralization will depend primarily on whether
New Yorkers are satisfied with the quality of decentralized services.
New local district governments should therefore assume responsibility
only for those services and activities that they could administer more
effectively than could the central City government. The governmental
structure described in Chapter 3 was designed to provide a framework for improved services. Few program specialists would select
that exact structure as the best possible base for their programs.
But the proposed district governments should be capable of managing
a broad spectrum of personal and local environmental services, and
the central City should then be able to concentrate on improving those
remaining services and activities that demand citywide attention.

While the decision as to whether to decentralize responsibility
for delivery of each governmental service should be based largely on
factors peculiar to that service, there are several considerations of
general applicability that should influence all allocation decisions.[1]
First, the new units of local government must have responsibilities
that are of continuing, daily importance to a majority of their residents.
A governmental unit responsible for only one or two services could
all too easily become responsive only to those who specialized in
activities related to those services. Residents who do not represent
any special interest would vote in local elections in substantial numbers only if the new local governments had a "critical mass" of responsibilities and powers. And between elections, civic groups, opposition party leaders, and the media would actively monitor the local
governments only if their activities excited widespread interest.

Second, where the effectiveness of a service depends upon
the active cooperation of local residents or even on the general conduct and attitudes of local residents, smaller unit size should be an
asset. The larger the unit, the greater the tendency for the individual

to view his own conduct as irrelevant and to center his expectations solely upon the level of efforts of municipal employees. With a smaller unit, relationships between the quantity and quality of public services and tax levels could be more readily established, and greater pressures could be exerted on individuals and groups to adapt their own behavior to facilitate the efforts of local services, such as street cleaning, solid waste collection, or law enforcement. The individual's self-interest in such cooperation should become more apparent. More significantly, the chances of effective social sanctions would be increased.

Third, a series of relatively small units of government could, at least in theory, be more flexible than one large government, with long traditions and a comprehensive system of checks and balances. The smaller units should therefore be made responsible for services that might benefit from experimentation and from local variations in output, techniques, or style.

Fourth, there are some services, such as zoning and waste disposal, which, when performed by small units, involve a high likelihood of the imposition of costs on adjacent units. At a minimum, substantial interunit cooperation would be necessary to reduce the likelihood of such external, or "spillover," costs. But when individual local units would be likely to measure the benefits and costs of their actions in emotional terms, rather than in monetary equivalents, interdistrict cooperation would become difficult to achieve. Separate units of government could agree on joint purchasing plans more easily than they could agree on joint zoning schemes. When a service would have both a high potential for external costs and high emotional content, responsibility should be left with a larger, more inclusive unit of government.

Finally, many activities of municipal governments are intended to serve related goals or depend for their success upon the effective performance of one or more other services. Such overlapping or mutually reinforcing services or activities should, to the extent feasible, be assigned to the same unit of local government.

Most of New York's governmental services can be classified under three broad headings, with a fourth residual category. The first group covers personal services that are directed at satisfying individual needs by acting directly on individuals or on their immediate families. Some of the more important of these services are old age and childrens' services, personal health services, social services (including day care, family-planning, and homemaker's services), and manpower training and retraining. In view of the impact of housing and education on individual and family problems of urban residents, this group should also include elementary and secondary education and major aspects of public housing management.

The second group covers activities of government directed at the quality of the local physical environment, such as trash and garbage collection, street sweeping, parks and open space maintenance, street maintenance, parking controls, and enforcement of housing codes and pollution controls. These services are somewhat more diverse than those in the first group, but they are substantially interdependent. Effective trash and garbage collection and control depend upon enforcement of housing code rules governing placement and storage of waste prior to collection. Clean streets are possible only with enforcement of parking regulations. And parks maintenance cannot be separated from care of streets and sidewalks.

The third group covers regulatory and service functions, the geographic scope of which is defined in terms of economic market areas or natural geographic areas, such as air and water pollution control, transportation planning and mass transportation operations, economic development, land-use planning and control, formulation of building and housing code standards, consumer protection, and rent control.

The fourth group of less easily classifiable services includes police, fire, and large-scale renewal or housing projects. These services are clearly related to services included in all three of the other groups. But each has unique characteristics that argue for special consideration.

PERSONAL SERVICES

The personal services all involve attempts to better the lives of families and individuals by direct delivery to them of various forms of information and assistance, such as social counseling, health services, service to tenants of public housing, and education. Their emphasis is on helping individuals, rather than on changing external conditions and forces, although the community organization aspects of social work and the environmental aspects of public health services do attempt to deal with some of the external causes of individual dissatisfaction or discomfort.

There is little certainty about the relative effectiveness of different approaches to delivery of these personal services in improving individual and family well-being. Within broad limits one technique of intervention may help people as much as another; recipients may be more receptive to the notion that somebody cares than to program details or philosophy.

Even if it were clear that some methods of supplying personal services are better than others, it is most unlikely that any set of service methods would be equally successful for all people, regardless of differing cultural or economic backgrounds. Personal services almost surely need to vary in response to the perceived needs of different clientele groups. Even for all clientele groups with the same socioeconomic characteristics, there is still generally no one professionally certifiable approach.

The transfer of responsibility for personal services to local district governments would make possible the creation of more unified personal service programs than exist today. Coordination of personal services programs seems to be impossible under the present super-agency structure. Coordination and cooperation within the Health Services Administration and the Human Resources Administration (HRA) have been difficult to achieve. The several commissioners and program directors sometimes reach sufficient agreement to issue policy statements about the interrelation of social work and health services, for example, but translating those statements into action might require the kind of shake-up in existing ways of professional and agency thinking and doing business that could be achieved only through major changes in the structure of political accountability for service delivery.

Social Services

In addition to distributing welfare payments to the needy, government today provides or finances a wide range of social services: (a) counseling and advice to welfare recipients; (b) child welfare services, including day care; (c) adoption services; (d) foster care and institutions for children requiring placement outside of their own homes; (e) counseling of present and potential drug addicts; (f) services for the aged; (g) employment and vocational training services; and (h) settlement house and community organization activities. To this list probably should be added probation services, which are usually categorized as part of the criminal justice system and are delivered by officials who tend to be even more overburdened and underfinanced than their social work counterparts in other fields of service.

Publicly funded social services are presently delivered through a complex mixture of public and private agencies and organizations. Although the formation of the HRA in Mayor Lindsay's first term ostensibly brought most public social services under a single umbrella agency, the unification was more in form than in substance. The agency was reorganized in late 1971, but it is too early to tell whether this latest effort will increase internal coordination. Many services were and are provided by private voluntary agencies, operating under contract with the City and funded partly with local, partly with state, and occasionally with federal funds. These private, often sectarian agencies are required to meet service standards set by public officials, but they do not always concentrate their efforts where the need is greatest. Many other services are provided by privately funded agencies, operating alongside of, and often relieving the demand upon, publicly funded social services.

Other services are provided by public agencies only nominally subject to City control. Community Action agency "special emphasis" programs, operating under federal standards and constituting virtually required uses of federal funds, are "local" programs only insofar as the HRA is expected to assume responsibility for ensuring against misuse of the federal funds. Day care centers are the responsibility of the HRA, but must be administered in accordance with elaborate federal and state requirements. Some local manpower-training programs operate with direct federal funding and exclusively federal guidelines.

The City's social services thus are already decentralized, both organizationally and financially. But this present decentralized structure has not developed with any consideration for the kind of pattern most likely to meet the needs of potential clientele. New agencies wax and wane within the HRA, as social service styles and funding patterns change. Many private agencies seem to relate to social service needs of earlier generations. The connections of social service agencies with each other and with related educational and health activities are often tenuous, if in existence at all. With so many independent units of power and authority, only the expert can find his way around the system.

Moreover, the decentralization that does exist is, as suggested above, along functional or programmatic lines and not in terms of geographic areas. Yet, there are no compelling reasons for the delivery of social services of a given type on a uniform citywide basis. Virtually no economies of scale would be lost if authority were transferred to social service delivery units serving as few as 50,000 people, with appropriate size variations for very poor or very wealthy areas. Spillover costs are likely to be low as long as the level of welfare payments is not varied from district to district. Few persons would migrate in search of better services without any fiscal incentive. Any effects of local ineptitude would therefore remain relatively localized.

If responsibility for social services were decentralized, the citywide government would merely stipulate that certain basic kinds of services should be provided. Most local district social service programs would continue to be financed largely out of earmarked state and federal funds, subject to state and federal standards. No additional requirements should be set at the central City level, unless it became apparent that some districts were failing to fill important service needs.

With the present lack of certainty about the ways in which the social services can best accomplish their goals of improving the ability of individuals to function in a complex society, fixed rules and professional control should give way to more flexible lay direction. For social services, customer accountability makes real sense. And for such accountability to be effective, social services should operate through units that are small enough to make it relatively easy for consumer complaints to reach the level at which authoritative administrative decisions can be made. Such local control should increase the likelihood that program decisions would be reflected in changes at the level of client contact.

While New York City has pioneered new social service concepts, it has not been as able to translate those concepts into ongoing patterns of social service delivery. The City's capacity to experiment could be preserved by maintaining a small, central social services operation for technical assistance, by the funding of special demonstration programs developed by the central City or by local units, and by informational monitoring of local activities. But social service departments within the local district governments should be responsible for delivery of all services and for professional as well as administrative supervision of social workers.

Most importantly, decentralization of social services could counter the present tendency to organize services to suit the convenience of existing patterns of professional specialization or current social therapy theories. While unified social services departments are not a cure-all, acceptance of the primacy of consumer convenience would seem to be a more promising basis for improving social service effectiveness than competition among specialized public and private agencies. Decentralization might well provide the kind of shake-up in existing patterns of official behavior that would be necessary to achieve this change in approach.

The HRA is indeed now faced with the possibility that the federal government will assume administrative responsibility for administering the federally assisted welfare transfer payment system. Such a move would free up to several thousand professional and paraprofessional social workers from their present responsibilities of policing welfare eligibility rules. While many City officials might well be sympathetic to assigning those social workers to local organizations, so that they could become responsive to local needs and desires, no local existing organizations, including the Community Corporations, have the stature or competence to assume that responsibility. Many of the Community Corporations can exert effective pressure for government action, and all of them provide employment and leadership training for persons who might not otherwise have those opportunities. But none has the professional stature of a competent settlement house or the political stature of a local district government.

Even assuming the existence of local district governments, de-centralization of responsibility for manpower training and placement could result in wasted effort if not carefully controlled. There can be economies of scale in training, particularly training for specialized, skilled jobs. Furthermore, selection of training subjects should be based on areawide labor market conditions, and placement services need to be coordinated on a citywide or even a metropolitan area basis. It might be possible to decentralize basic manpower training, while maintaining central specialized skill centers. And, since local districts would not deliberately train for vanishing job categories, a central information system about employment trends should provide adequate guidance for local training content.

Placement presents harder problems. A citywide placement service should theoretically be more efficient, but such large, im-personal systems can be ineffective when dealing with disadvantaged, minority group unemployed and underemployed persons. Local dis-trict training centers would have greater incentive to place their trainees and to provide follow-up guidance to help them retain their jobs. A centralized job information system could work as well with local placement agencies as with one central agency. The resultant competition among local agencies for the available jobs might mean more pressure on private employers and more placements.

Manpower programs have had a poor record of performance, however structured—given declining job opportunities for the unskilled, unrealistic expectations of job seekers, the competition of welfare, "hustling," and the life style of the street—and, above all, given per-vasive institutional racism. Under these circumstances aggressive local manpower projects might be as likely to have impact as any citywide system, despite loss of theoretical scale economies.

Because publicly provided social services are significant only to a minority of the City's residents, the central City would have to watch local performance closely to see that the poor were not being neglected. Some districts would have few residents who need or desire publicly assisted social services. Other districts might accept such traditional social services as old-age assistance or child care but be more hostile to services aimed at persons of employable age. If left to themselves such districts might choose to slight social services and spend more money on nonsocial service programs or reduce local taxes. To the extent that financing for local districts came in the form of transfers from the central City government that were ear-marked for specific program areas, this reluctance to spend on social services could not have much effect. A local district government would have discretion only within the broad area of social services, and that discretion would be further limited by the requirements that attach to the federal or state funds that would be included in the transfer package. But if local districts were financed by a single revenue-sharing grant from the central City, the only external protection for poor people would derive from state and federal legislation.

If federal and state protections proved inadequate, it might make sense for the central City to reserve the power to take back the responsibility for providing some or all social services directly to residents of districts that fall below minimum standards. The central City would then deduct the cost of those services from the revenue-sharing grants to the delinquent districts. But any such reserved power to step in should a district fall below standards would be inconsistent with many of the basic goals of decentralization. Creation of new local district social service administrators and policy makers, while leaving the central City with reserve administrative and policy-making powers, could well add to bureaucratic confusion and delays. Objective performance standards simply do not exist for personal services; so the central City evaluators could be quite permissive or very strict, depending on their values and aggressiveness. While the central City would rarely, if ever, exercise its power of reversion, the existence of such power would enable aggressive central officials to maintain a continuing, close overview, to make suggestions, large and small, and ultimately to assume effective responsibility for local performance.

On balance, then, it might be best to rely on the political process to regulate local performance. If local district indifference or discrimination became a serious problem, the state or the City could adopt corrective legislation. Any other course might undercut decentralization before it had a chance to prove itself.

The role of voluntary social agencies would almost surely be controversial in any program for decentralization of responsibility for the social services. Those agencies that operate on a local basis in the City would need to deal with new sources of public funding—the local district governments rather than the existing central City government. Those agencies that operate on a citywide basis might find themselves in greater difficulties. There is no reason in principle, however, why a voluntary agency should be exempt from the principle that personal services ought to be delivered, or at least supervised, on a unified basis by more controllable, accountable units of government than the present citywide HRA. Voluntary agencies financed from private sources or from direct state of federal grants could theoretically continue to operate as they do now, but hopefully the new public social service structure would force private agencies to reorganize also and to respond better to local needs. Those agencies that rely on City-controlled funds would receive financing from local district governments only if they provided services the local district wanted and were competitive in price and quality with other alternative sources of service.

Any proposal for making new second-tier units of government responsible for social services delivery must be capable of coping with the challenge presented by the present welfare transfer payments system. The City's Department of Social Services, under the HRA, is responsible for the administration of the welfare payments system. Funds for the welfare payments system are derived about 70 percent from state and federal transfers and about 30 percent from the City's own taxation. Standards for welfare payments are determined in part by the federal government, in part by the state, and in part by the City itself.

Local districts could probably become eligible for handling welfare payments. With such an approach, the central City government would give up responsibility for both the social service system and the welfare payment system. But the poorer local districts could not possibly raise the approximately 30 percent local share of welfare payments from their own resources. If the central City continued to be responsible for funding the local share of welfare payments, it probably should also be responsible for administering the distribution of such payments, because local district administrators would feel little or no responsibility for the efficient use of funds, all of which represent transfers from the tax receipts of other, more inclusive units of government. Local district voters in poor neighborhoods would not become deeply concerned over misapplication of such 100 percent transfer grants. The pressures on the local districts would be to maximize the flow of money to local residents, not to enforce the administrative rules and eligibility requirements set up by higher levels of government. The welfare payment system should, therefore, remain with the central City, and perhaps in the near future become the exclusive responsibility of the federal government.

Education

Since the responsibility for primary and secondary education in New York City has already been partially decentralized, the principal issue for this study involves the relationship of the existing community school districts to decentralized responsibility for other personal services of local government. This is a serious problem because the tradition of educational autonomy from other local political institutions makes it all too likely that responsibility for social and health services would be transferred to units with boundaries and political institutions quite separate from those of the school boards. Such an outcome would tend to lessen, not increase, local resident control over priorities and coordination among personal services.

At present, the mayor and the City's legislative bodies are authorized to decide on the allocation of City funds among social services, health service, and educational functions. Even though this power is limited by inflexible City budgeting processes, collective bargaining agreements, and the requirements of state and federal categorical assistance programs, the mayor can respond somewhat to changing citywide priorities and to different local priorities. But if education were decentralized to one group of local officials and social and health services to another group of local officials, the result would be the kind of functional decentralization rejected in Chapter 1. It would be impossible for district residents and civic groups to express their priorities among these sets of services through the election process or otherwise. Indeed, the proliferation of local policy boards would keep down voter participation and increase the likelihood that each local board would be dominated by the professionals in its functional area. If different boundaries also existed, so that each board had a different constitutency, lay control would be further diluted, for there would be no single forum in which choices could be made. And if decentralization involved giving each local board some independent fiscal capacity, local priorities would be measured by the relative fund-raising effectiveness of the several boards. If the school board had access to the more elastic tax base, more teachers than social workers would be hired or a duplicate set of school-based social workers and social service centers would be created. The net effect would be a decrease in citywide unified authority over these services, without the creation of a new local source of unified authority with the power and authority to husband scarce resources and commit them to the areas of highest community priority.

Integration of public schools into a local district governmental structure would involve certain practical difficulties. The present population catchment areas of high schools, and even of some junior high or intermediate schools, may bear little relation to boundaries that make sense for the creation of local government districts. At the junior high school level, it might be possible to give jurisdiction over a school to the district from which the bulk of its pupils were drawn, even if it were located within the boundaries of an adjacent local district government. With judicious redrawing of school attendance areas, an overwhelming majority of the students at each school would come from the district that controlled it. Residents of the district in which such a school were located might be given the choice of sending their children to the closer school or to a more distant school controlled by the local district in which they lived. Parents would then need to decide between control or convenience. If they opted for convenience, the district of residence would be expected to pay tuition to the district that operated the extraterritorial school.

This option would probably not be available for high schools, however, even though in theory it would make sense ultimately to decentralize them as well. Their catchment areas are too large, and their locations reflect long-changed patterns of population and even transportation. In the early years of decentralization, high schools should remain a central responsibility. Over time each local district would have to buy a high school from the central City. In effect, each local district would bargain for a high school in the capital fund allocation process.

But there are more basic arguments for keeping the school system separate from the new local district governments. Education would be the largest, most complex, and most controversial decentralized service. The existence of separate, and usually autonomous, school boards in most cities with populations of 125,000 to 250,000 suggests that most Americans believe their schools are complex and important enough to be separately managed. In New York the new community school boards are just beginning to take hold, and the educational bureaucracy and their unions are just beginning to adjust to the change. Another redistricting and restructuring would be disruptive and would certainly be resisted by the new community school boards, as well as by teachers and supervisors and their unions.

As a compromise, at least for an interim transition period, the borders of the school districts could be realigned to match the new local government districts, but separate school boards could be retained. Local district governments could be given substantial control over allocation of City funds between schools and other local functions—in much the same way as the central City now sets program priorities. (See Chapter 5 for discussion of local district budget and fiscal powers.) But such a compromise would not reduce disruption or bureaucratic and union opposition if it also involved greatly increased decentralization of school personnel decisions, as well as new school district lines. And if local district governments were not to control schools, they would command substantially less resident and media attention, in terms both of cooperation and monitoring. In the long run the residents of each local district should be permitted to decide how autonomous their school system should be.

Health Services*

Health services in New York City have become a massive enterprise. Over 20 percent of the City's 1970/71 expense budget was

---

*Much of this analysis of City health services is based on the research of Harvey Fineberg, a Harvard Medical School student, who

allocated to health services. Of total employment in New York City,
5 percent is health service related.

Health services in the City can be broken down into four major
classifications: (a) direct patient treatment for physiological health,
including inpatient hospital services for transient and chronic patients
and outpatient services, both for preventive and remedial care; (b)
direct patient treatment for mental health, including both inpatient and
outpatient care, but under contemporary health service standards and
largely limited to remedial programs; (c) related social service support functions, such as home care programs, nutrition education programs, ambulance transportation services, and general patient counseling; and (d) public and environmental health programs for control
of communicable diseases, public information and education, setting
standards for food handling, regulating public accommodations, and
sanitary inspections.

The City itself has a monopoly only over public and environmental
health programs. The others are provided by a complex maze of private practitioners and public and private clinics, hospitals, and other
institutions. The list does not include the City's vast teaching and
medical research facilities, most of which are closely tied to major
voluntary hospitals, or the City's Medical Examiner. This section
does not deal specifically with either of those operations.

Analysis of the possible scope of health services decentralization
in New York City is complicated by the vast gap between theories of
comprehensive health services delivery and actual practice. Accordingly, the discussion is broken up into two parts: the first part sets
forth one possible pattern for decentralized health services delivery
and the second describes practical limits to the implementation of
such a model in New York City today.

A Model Form for Health Services Decentralization

A plausible health services delivery system for a two-tier city
can be derived from the 1967 Piel Report[2] on health services organization in New York City. The model contemplates a concentric system of medical facilities. A teaching hospital complex was to be
situated at the center of each area of 1.5 million population, with facilities for the treatment of particularly severe or unusual medical
conditions requiring the use of highly capital-intensive treatment
processes. Community hospitals, with facilities for most common
medical problems, were to service areas with populations of 200,000

---

also worked for the City's Health Services Administration.

to 300,000 persons surrounding the teaching hospitals. Paired with these hospitals were to be chronic care facilities, which could be built and operated more cheaply than hospitals and, therefore, should not share hospital facilities. At the lowest level were to be ambulatory health service facilities, providing both preventive and remedial health services to population units of 30,000 to 50,000 people.

Since decentralization of responsibility for public education and for social services would involve districts with approximately the same size populations as would be served by community hospitals in the Piel model, ideally health service decentralization should take place at the community hospital level. Under such an ideal system the feasibility of transferring community hospitals and ambulatory health service facilities to local district governments would appear to depend upon whether rules and procedures could be defined to govern access to central hospital facilities from local units and, also, upon whether arrangements could be made to ensure adequate staffing of the community hospitals. These two issues arise continuously in other parts of the country not so well endowed with medical schools as New York City and are handled, if not perfectly, at least in a manner that permits smaller hospitals to attract personnel and to gain access to the facilities of more comprehensive hospitals. It therefore seems reasonable to assume that in a two-tier system of government for New York City, local units of government could be made responsible for individual community hospitals and for the ambulatory care centers subordinate to those hospitals.

Such decentralization of health service responsibilities could bring substantial benefits. The fragmentation of health services into competing specializations, such as psychiatry, heart, ear/nose/throat, and obstetrics, makes the exercise of lay political control particularly appropriate, as long as public funds that can be spent on health care are limited. The medical profession has no inherent qualification for deciding that funds ought to be spent on cancer treatment instead of on prenatal care or narcotics treatment. The profession may be qualified to say that a given amount spent on narcotics treatment is likely to save fewer lives or result in fewer cures or cost more per patient than the same amount spent on cancer programs. But the decision on which expenditure pattern is preferable for the community as a whole is not a medical decision, because it depends upon which problem is deemed more important to combat or solve. Residents of an area with high levels of infant mortality could well conclude that cancer is unfortunate but less important than saving the lives of children.

Decisions about the manner or style in which health services are delivered should also be subject to lay influence. Health care, like social services, is provided because people both need and want it.

There is a voluntary producer-consumer relationship in health services, except for certain aspects of mental health care. When health services are publicly financed, therefore, representatives of the public ought to be able to define the basic terms and conditions on which it is provided, such as hours of service and kinds of facilities.

Public health decisions by local district governments would not for the most part be likely to impose severe burdens on neighboring districts or on the City as a whole. The central City should probably retain the power to set environmental health standards and, perhaps, even to enforce those standards, because of the density and mobility of the City's population. The central City would also retain some controls over investment in expensive facilities through the capital budget process. And uniform records should be prescribed, because of the frequency with which New Yorkers change residence.

Of greater concern in any decentralization of political responsibility for health services delivery would be whether local units should be required to perform various services and whether the quality of local services should be subject to any review by citywide agencies. Special City quality control should not be necessary in view of broad standards of accreditation of hospitals and state or federal grant-in-aid requirements, though state monitoring and enforcement should be stepped up. But the City would not want a local district to be able to refuse to provide certain important services, particularly those used primarily by low-income residents. While a person who wanted services unavailable in his district could always move to another district, such freedom to select the kinds of health services to be offered would invite districts to make service decisions that would tend to exclude classes of residents.

If significant nationwide health insurance coverage came into existence, this issue would largely disappear, because insured persons, who were not offered the care they needed by publicly financed sources in their communities, would have the means to seek private health care. In any event this issue of possible local district indifference or discrimination in health care matters is essentially the same as the one discussed under social services. Our conclusion as to the desirability of reserved central City powers is also the same: if local abuse became too great, new City or state legislation could be adopted. In the meantime give decentralization the benefit of the doubt.

Practical Barriers to Health Services Decentralization

Unfortunately, the Piel Report model is far removed from the actual organization of health services in New York City. A central city government can only decentralize authority or capacity it presently has: New York City, as a practical matter, does not itself have either

the authority or the capacity to provide or effectively regulate the
delivery of comprehensive health services.

Health services today are a hodgepodge of public and private,
institutional, and individual endeavors. In New York City there are
over 140 public, private nonprofit (voluntary), and private profit-
making (propriety) hospitals, some 300 mental health facilities, over
150 nursing homes, and more than 36 community health care centers.
The Directory of Social and Health Agencies of New York City lists
over 1,200 voluntary and public organizations concerned with health
and welfare. The only major services the City itself fully controls
are the 18 municipal hospitals now operated by the Health and Hospitals Corporation, plus a few broad-range outpatient clinics, some
22 diagnostic clinics, and almost 100 maternity and infant clinics,
all scattered unevenly throughout the City.

Funding patterns are as complex as the administrative organization. As of late 1970 no fewer than twenty-five separate agencies
of government—six federal, five state, and fourteen municipal—participated in the distribution of money for various health care activities
in New York City. One health agency alone, the Department of Mental
Health and Mental Retardation Services, distributed 45 percent of its
funds in 1969 and 1970 to 13 voluntary hospitals for inpatient psychia-
tric care, and roughly 100 additional voluntary agency contracts for
outpatient, rehabilitation, retardation, consultation, and other services.
Although most of its remaining funds flowed through the Health and
Hospitals Corporation, mental health funds also went to the Board of
Education, the Department of Correction, the Family Court, and the
Department of Parks.

The overlapping of public and private responsibility is at its
greatest in the provision of traditional hospital services. The political
compromises required to steer Medicare and Medicaid through Congress resulted in a program designed to encourage the utilization of
private practitioners and voluntary hospitals rather than municipal
or group practice facilities. The cost-plus reimbursement provisions
of these programs permit utilization of private facilities without regard to cost differentials. Since the voluntary hospitals reputedly,
and probably in fact, have provided higher-quality health care, federally insured patients have chosen to use the voluntary hospitals and
private practitioners. Before 1966, when Medicaid and Medicare
began in New York, more outpatient and emergency visits were made
to municipal hospitals than to the voluntaries. By 1968 the roles were
reversed. A similar shift in utilization of hospital inpatient services
occurred. By 1970/71, New York City was budgeting over $200 million
for payments to voluntary hospitals for inpatient services, and an
additional $300 million for payments to individual doctors and other
private and voluntary organizations.

New York City's unique system of affiliation contracts also com-
plicates the situation. Under those contracts professional medical
services in all but two of the City's eighteen municipal hospitals are
provided by affiliated voluntary hospitals or teaching hospitals. The
system had its origin in the late 1950's, when obsolete facilities, patient overcrowding, and staff shortages appeared to threaten some
municipal hospitals with loss of accreditation. In 1963/64 the contractual value of the affiliation services was only $16 million; by
1970/71, after expansion of services and the Medicaid/Medicare-fueled
inflation in medical care costs, the voluntaries received about $160
million.

Despite the affiliation contracts and large City subsidies, the
municipal hospitals are still considered to be inferior as facilities
and in terms of medical care. It is not yet clear whether the new
Health and Hospitals Corporation can erase the stigma of "second-
class" health care attached to the municipal hospital system. The
corporation took over the City's municipals on July 1, 1970. Based
on recommendations of the Piel Commission, the corporation is relatively free of the controls and restraints imposed on City operating
agencies by the Budget Bureau, the Personnel Department, the comptroller, and other overhead agencies. In particular, the corporation
can buy and sell property, let contracts, borrow money and float bonds,
and set its own terms and conditions of employment—except for a
grandfather clause for employees as of July 1, 1970, subject to negotiation with the young and vigorous Hospital Workers' Union, Local
1199. The corporation does, however, continue to depend upon the
City for operating funds and is subject to the policy direction of the
Health Services Administration. The primary job of the corporation
is to make it possible for City hospitals to deliver quality care at
costs that are at least no greater than the costs of private hospitals.

Given this background a realistic starting point for decentralization might be the existing outpatient clinics of various types (the
lowest tier in the Piel model). These could with reasonable ease be
brought under the jurisdiction of local district governments. As funds
become available additional clinics could be developed by them at
much less expense than developing inpatient hospital facilities. The
local districts could, and hopefully would, tie such new health facilities
in with outreach social service centers; in many cases the two operations serve similar social needs.

These outpatient facilities would draw patients from relatively
small areas within each local district and could properly be financed
by formula grants from the central City to the districts. This financing could then be supplemented by small user fees and local district
taxes or such reimbursement as could be obtained under applicable
state and federal health assistance programs. Local lay participation

in decision making for such operations should result in a mix of services, within any City or state minimum-service requirement restraints, to match the needs of district residents; moreover, these
decisions on service mix would not be likely to have a significant impact outside of each district. The local district governments, as the
responsible administrators of these facilities, would also have the
power to make arrangements for backup service from nearby municipal
or voluntary hospitals.

The future local district role with respect to larger-scale municipal health facilities, however, is less clear. Transfer of responsibility for existing City-owned hospitals to local district governments
would be difficult to accomplish. As already noted hospitals are not
distributed in accordance with health service needs or with the probable boundaries of any future local districts. Many of the existing
hospitals, therefore, would draw patients from the residents of a
number of local districts, so that identification of a single appropriate
controlling district would be politically sensitive.

Further, it seems quite unlikely that the City would ever have
the funds to develop a citywide comprehensive health system along
the lines of the Piel model. Certainly, City taxes will never generate
the large sums needed. No foreseeable federal program for financing
health care would be likely to channel funds through City governments.
In all probability federal funds will finance health expenditures made
by individuals for care at public or private hospitals or clinics and
for treatment by individual or group practitioners. No preference to
municipally owned or controlled facilities can be expected. If insured
payments continue to be made on a cost reimbursement basis, there
is every reason to expect that most insured persons would prefer
voluntary hospitals and private practitioners, unless the Health and
Hospitals Corporation is extraordinarily successful in upgrading the
hospitals it controls.

In that case it may be argued that the City and the Health and
Hospitals Corporation should sell off all facilities that are not essential to the City's public and environmental health obligations. Municipal government has not in recent years been particularly effective
as an owner and manager of health facilities that compete with private
facilities, and it might make sense simply to get out of that business.

But there are a number of reasons for continuing a local government role beyond public and environmental health programs. Even
under a national health insurance program, doctors will be slow to locate in the poorest areas of the City. Professional reluctance to serve
minority groups and the poor is not just a matter of economics; these
groups tend to have more health and health-related problems and less
capacity to cope with them, so that they are more difficult to serve
well. Therefore, even after federal assistance becomes available,

local government might have to continue a leadership role in supplying health services to such areas, although it might tend to withdraw from direct service delivery in more affluent areas.

Furthermore, in any insurance-based federal financing pattern, continued governmental involvement is likely to be necessary to monitor the quality of health care provided by private sources and to ensure against overdevelopment of specialized facilities or overconcentration in particular areas. Both of these responsibilities could be left with the federal government, as adjuncts to its health care fiscal responsibilities. But the responsiveness of federal reviewing and monitoring officials to local needs and conditions is bound to be less than that of officials of a local government with an active interest and experience in health care delivery. The federal government might well delegate these responsibilities to local government, retaining authority for federal intervention if local monitoring did not meet federal standards. In New York, the facilities-control function could be left as a citywide responsibility, paralleling the present Health and Hospital Advisory Council. Responsibility for monitoring quality and coverage could become the responsibility of local district governments, but the City would also have to have a role, as location of facilities would depend on quality and coverage.

Finally, even if there were no broad system for a publicly owned or controlled health care system, local district governments could still be authorized to acquire or even build community hospitals or set up clinics or group practice units. Any such facilities would probably have to be self-supporting, i.e., to support themselves out of federal insurance funds or on the basis of private fees; they therefore would be able to compete only to the extent that they could do a better job than privately organized services. But they could provide a yardstick against which the quality of private care could be measured.

If, however, federal financing and program arrangements were available for comprehensive public health systems, like those envisioned in the Piel Report, the Health and Hospitals Corporation should have the authority and the capacity, with the advice and consent of the local districts concerned, to develop a system of community hospitals and subordinate ambulatory care facilities for the City as a whole or for those parts of the City most in need of public facilities. These facilities could then be transferred to subsidiary corporations (which the Health and Hospitals Corporation is already empowered to create), serving areas coterminous with local government districts. A local district government could appoint a majority of the board of directors of the corporation in its area and thereby, for daily administrative purposes, operate it as the focal point of its health services program.

But development of such a system would be slow and difficult. The Health and Hospitals Corporation would still have to cope with

the present uneven distribution of health services facilities around the
City and with the desire of most districts to have their own subsidiary
hospital corporation if one district obtained such a corporation. Because of the location pattern of existing facilities, boundary problems
would be rife. It might be necessary to require the facilities in one
local district to treat residents from another local district, with billing
back of costs to the latter district's government. Some districts would
have populations likely to continue relying on voluntary hospitals and
private physicians; other districts might be amply served by voluntary
hospitals, yet for political reasons seek their own hospitals. This
kind of overbuilding would have to be discouraged. It would make more
sense for the district governments to contract with smaller voluntary
or proprietary hospitals or to convert them into true public institutions.

Housing Management

Local governments own and manage public housing through
relatively independent local housing authorities. But experience with
public housing since World War II has made it clear that adequate
housing alone is no cure-all for the whole cycle of troubles that can
beset inadequately educated parents, broken families, rural families
in urban environments, members of minority groups subject to widespread discrimination, or people with severe physical and mental
health problems. Moreover, with the advantage of hindsight, it is
easy to see that lumping large numbers of such people together can
quickly lead to the deterioration of physically sound housing units.

The management burden on local housing authorities has been
increased in recent years by federal administrative and judicial restraints on housing authority discretion in selecting and evicting tenants. Many housing authorities, including the New York City Housing
Authority, had long sought to control pressures on housing project
stability by denying admission to families showing high propensities
for social disturbance, as evidenced by criminal convictions, narcotics
arrests, prostitution arrests, and alcohol problems. They also used
their broad eviction powers to cull tenant ranks of persons thought
to threaten project stability. Persistent abuse of these powers, especially the eviction power, coupled with litigation and widespread
publicity by tenant groups, has changed this picture over the last five
years. Housing authorities now have much less control over who will
become or continue as public housing tenants. This lessening of control is almost sure to increase the proportion of "problem" tenants
in public housing and make more urgent the task of meeting the nonhousing needs of public housing residents.

The task of meeting these nonhousing needs is going to be made more difficult the greater the separation between the responsibility for housing project management and the responsibility for personnel services. If the local districts provided social services and outpatient health care to low- and moderate-income persons, then maintaining housing project management responsibility as the separate province of central government would increase the difficulty of providing those services to project residents. With such separation there would be no mechanism for making the kinds of trade-offs required in deciding, for example, how much space in a project should go to day care operations, evening health clinics, or similar services.

In addition, once a family has been placed in a public housing project, the future of that family, its integration into the project, and its interactions with surrounding public facilities are all matters more of local, rather than central, concern. A centralized housing authority, with no responsibility for other functions of local government, would have neither the capacity nor the incentive to create links between public housing facilities and existing community services. In the interests of public housing tenants and the areas in which they are located, decentralization of responsibility for health and social services should therefore be followed by significant decentralization of public housing management responsibilities.

Local district governments could become public housing agencies for all purposes under federal public housing legislation. But that would mean that the local district governments would be in control of public housing construction, a step backwards if one believes that the poor should not be concentrated in existing slums and, perhaps, even illegal under new federal site selection guidelines. But for public housing construction powers to remain with the central City, the federal public housing officials would have to be willing to permit the central City to engage in housing construction and, then, turn over management to local districts. Although the definition of "public housing agency" in the federal housing laws does not indicate that the functions of project development and project administration are inseparable, neither does it encourage such severed responsibility.[3] However, there would appear to be no reason why a local district, either directly or through the vehicle of a government corporation, could not be formally delegated the management authority for public housing within its boundaries.

Such a delegation of authority would not result in the full integration of public housing management decisions with other local personal service decisions. Without major change in federal law, public housing financial accounts would still have to be kept separately from the general revenues and expenditures of a local district government. Therefore, there still would not be full encouragement of trade-offs between direct housing maintenance and management costs and other, alternative forms of provision of service to public housing tenants. But the pressures and opportunities for cooperation between public housing services, narrowly defined, and the other personal services delivered by local district governments should be substantially enhanced.

On the other hand it would make no sense in a city like New York to eliminate all central authority over the public housing supply. Although the central City should not have to be concerned with daily management details, it should still be able to ensure that those displaced by central City actions have access to public housing, that those persons placed in projects by the central City are treated on a parity with those placed by the local districts themselves, and that all public housing tenants receive the treatment to which they were entitled by law and federal regulation.

Thus, under a system of delegated housing management, responsibility, minimum standards governing tenant selection, tenant evictions, tenant participation in management decisions, and rental schedules might well be set in the first instance by applicable federal rules and regulations. The central City's power would be in the nature of a residual power, to ensure access of persons to housing and to ensure that tenants placed by the central City are not subject to post-placement discrimination.

The central City should retain the power to construct new public housing units. There is no reason to expect that formal decentralized local units of government would be much more receptive to new housing for the poor than are informal neighborhood organizations today. (The central City role in housing construction and renewal programs in a two-tier City is discussed in a subsequent subsection of this chapter.) Nevertheless, there is no reason why a local district government actively supporting public housing construction should be prohibited from developing its own projects. In the light of New York City's shortage of standard housing, districts that actively seek more housing should be discouraged from doing so only if concentrations of public housing or minority group tenants make particular sites unacceptable. Also, if both the central City and the local districts are able to carry out public housing development activities, more housing funds may flow into New York City, since sometimes two claimants for federal largess may together obtain more assistance than would a single claimant serving the same population and geographic area.

LOCAL ENVIRONMENTAL SERVICES

To the residents of many New York City neighborhoods, a decent home and a suitable living environment may seem further away than they did in 1949, when the Congress set forth these two parallel goals as the objective of American housing policy. Such persons may, with considerable justification, look upon the promises of the Housing Act of 1949 as better evidence of Congressional rhetoric than of national conviction. But the deterioration of urban neighborhoods is not simply a matter of government housing programs that provide either too little too late or which have destroyed neighborhoods rather than preserved them.

Much of the deterioration of the urban housing supply has resulted from social and economic pressures largely unrelated either to the housing programs aimed at innercity deterioration or to the structure of city government. Changes in mortgage finance patterns, federal subsidization of suburban housing (available largely to whites) through the Federal Housing Administration (FHA) postwar programs, shifting patterns of industrial location and demand for low-wage labor, and increasing reliance upon transportation by automobile all have played a role in the decline of urban neighborhoods.

In spite of all these factors, achievement of the goals of a decent home and a suitable living environment does have some relation to the structure of local government. First, neither owners nor landlords are likely to be interested in maintaining housing unless the surrounding dwellings and public areas are also reasonably well maintained. Governmental programs, such as housing code enforcement, must be closely related to the other local housekeeping activities of City government directed at maintaining the physical quality of a neighborhood. Housing code enforcement, local sanitation programs, park and recreational facilities, and street lighting and parking control efforts are all highly interdependent. For any one to achieve its stated goals, all must be administered with high regard for maximizing interdepartmental communication and coordination, and the sanctions for departmental stubbornness must be high.

At present, as suggested in Chapter 2, the administrators and commissioners of the sprawling central environmental protection, public works, and housing development agencies have difficulty pulling together the programs for which they are responsible, much less coordinating their services with those of other agencies. The local supervisors who work for these agencies in the field have almost no contact with each other, not only because all lines of communication and authority are vertical but also because their offices are in different places and the districts for which they are responsible are not congruent. Even if local supervisors could get together, they lack the authority or the incentive to change their own programs to reinforce the programs of other departments.

Under decentralization the officials responsible for street cleaning and trash collection, housing code and pollution enforcement,

local parks and recreational facilities, local street and sidewalk maintenance, street lighting, and local parking would all be appointed by
the elected district executive. With more restricted geographic responsibilities these officials should be more readily able to exchange
information and agree upon local district actions and priorities. They
should have the knowledge of actual operating details within the district
and the access to the employees at the operating level necessary to
ensure that decisions reflect local realities and have some chance of
being translated into direct action. If, at the same time, decentralization is politically successful, local residents, block clubs, civic organizations, opposition politicians and political clubs, and the media
will hold these elected officials accountable for the cumulative impact
of local services on neighborhood conditions. Under those circumstances there would be ample incentive, as well as authority, for a
coordinated effort.

Secondly, the quality of a neighborhood's environment depends
more than anything else on how the residents maintain their own
dwellings, yards, and sidewalks, how well they obey traffic and parking
regulations, and how they treat parks and other public facilities. City
officials have been unable to persuade most New Yorkers to face up to
their own responsibilities. The City usually responds to loud complaints
by temporarily borrowing men or equipment from another neighborhood, rather than by improving services to which the complaining
neighborhood is entitled or by encouraging residents to change their
own behavior. This lack of resident understanding and cooperation
is compounded in black and Puerto Rican neighborhoods, where tensions are high between City employees and local residents.

Creation of new districts with populations of perhaps 200,000
would not assure substantially greater resident understanding and
cooperation. But officials would be closer to residents, and there
would be less opportunity to shuttle in men or equipment from another
area of the City or to pass the buck to central headquarters. Local
elected officials would have to stimulate local self-help, just as they
would have to stimulate more aggressive managerial efforts by the
service supervisors they appoint.

Even in the newer, more affluent of the City's neighborhoods,
these local environmental services are extremely important to local
residents. The presidents of the outer boroughs report that most of
the complaints they receive relate to these housekeeping services.
And the needs and desires for these services vary substantially among
neighborhoods. With responsibility decentralized, residents could
more readily express their views to officials with authority to adapt
services to local preferences.

Local environmental services could be decentralized with little
danger of spillover costs. The impact of these services is felt

primarily by the residents of the geographic area in which they are
delivered. Substandard conditions might deter visitors, but aside
from this, the potential spillover costs associated with these services
would be relatively low.

The following paragraphs discuss how some of these local environmental services could be adapted to a decentralized system.

Sanitation

The operations of the present centralized sanitation department
are described in some detail in the appendix to this study, written
by Michael Schwartz. Schwartz also projects the impact decentralization might have on sanitation services. The discussion here, therefore, will be brief.

The sanitation department today is highly centralized, with
deployment of men and machines controlled in part at central headquarters and in part at eleven borough command offices. The 68 district supervisors have little or no opportunity to plan ahead, to exercise managerial discretion, or to vary services in response to local
needs. But centralized control does permit citywide flexibility in
allocation of scarce resources. Although many of the sanitation trucks
are quite new, over one-third of them are down for repairs on the
average working day, which makes for inefficient deployment of personnel and more night work.

The recently won eligibility for retirement and pension after
twenty years' service has meant an almost complete turnover in middle management. Most field supervisors have been recently promoted
from the ranks, without special training or much concern for their administrative capabilities. They lack managerial experience and tend
to identify with line sanitationmen and the union rather than with the
City or management. Indeed, sanitation union officials largely determine personnel matters, including qualifications for initial hire
and promotion, transfer rights, discipline, and work rules. The sanitationmen themselves are better paid than their counterparts who
work for private cartmen or for other cities, but the younger men
seem to derive little satisfaction from their jobs and feel little loyalty
to the City or rapport with the residents they serve. There are very
few black or Puerto Rican sanitationmen, and the department was
relatively unsuccessful in attracting minority persons to apply the
last time examinations were given. Minority neighborhoods are therefore served by white sanitationmen; hostility runs high between them
and local residents.

Dirty streets and sidewalks, uncollected trash, and slow snow
removal have become major political issues in recent years. During

1971 the City increased department strength by 1,400 men, despite a
general personnel freeze, and brought in a new aggressive commissioner, who has tried to schedule work more efficiently. Sanitation
service seems to have improved. At the same time the department
has been making some attempt to communicate with neighborhood
residents, but mostly to explain the department's problems rather
than to find out how services could be improved. The department also
plans to test substantial administrative decentralization in several
districts. But departmental hopes for improved service depend largely
on more men, particularly on Mondays, better equipment maintenance,
and more efficient scheduling, not on decentralization.

Street cleaning and trash collection are, nevertheless, readily
adaptable to decentralization, with little danger of unacceptable spillover effects, as long as minimum public health levels can be maintained.
District variations in regulations affecting trash containers, commercial waste handling, sidewalk placement of materials to be collected,
empty lot maintenance, and handling and storage of waste within buildings should not have adverse effects on adjacent neighborhoods. Since
minimum health standards are probably significantly below public tolerance levels today, the central government would normally not have
to worry about the quality of local district performance. But since
the central City would remain responsible for waste disposal, it would
have to bind local districts to certain technical standards, to ensure,
for example, local district equipment compatability with disposal or
transfer point unloading equipment. At the same time economies of
scale in waste collection are fairly low, and the level of services could
be varied widely over the relatively small areas.

The combination of easily achievable geographic service variations
and user charges would make it relatively easy to tailor services to
meet the expressed needs of neighborhoods. Waste pickup service
could readily be billed to individuals, so local units would also be
able to experiment with user charges. Local block or civic associations could, for example, contract with the local district for the performance of extra services. This kind of ability to tailor services
to local neighborhood needs could have other benefits as well. For
example, if the cost of storage of trash within buildings for 48 hours
and the cost of antilitter law enforcement were balanced against the
cost of daily trash pickups, many neighborhoods might prefer less
frequent pickups and more effective regulatory enforcement. Neighborhood willingness to make this kind of trade-off would be heightened
by the fact that any net savings could be applied to other neighborhood
uses. Today, in the centralized City, private effort to realize public
savings offers little corresponding private gain. If local districts
could adjust sanitation services to permit local neighborhoods' within
each district to make such trade-offs and devote savings to local parks

maintenance or to street lighting, the chances of enlisting private
action for public benefit would be substantially enhanced.

The major areas in which scale economies could theoretically
be realized are in equipment purchases and maintenance capacity.
But the experience of Boston, which contracts out waste collection
to a number of private companies, and of private haulers in New York
City does not indicate that extremely large size is necessary to realize
such economies. Moreover, most of the costs of sanitation services
are labor costs. Government should therefore concentrate on keeping
equipment in service and on efficient utilization of labor, rather than
on minimizing capital costs. The existing fixed location of sanitation
garages would be a major short-run headache in any shift to decentralized local district responsibility for waste collection, but such facilities
could be operated jointly and need not be within the boundaries of the
district that they serve. Unlike other public buildings, such as police
or fire stations, existing garages have some usefulness to private
business: they could be sold or rented, and replacement structures
could be obtained relatively easily.

Under decentralization each local supervisor could have full
managerial authority over the men and machines in his district. Local
supervisors would be close enough to the "firing line" to have some
hope of translating policies into operating realities and should have
a strong incentive to increase service effectiveness and adjust service
mix to local desires. This relationship between residents and sanitation officials should flow the other way as well. Local government
officials should be better able to explain that public efforts to keep
the district clean depend as much on the actions of home owners,
landlords and tenants, and businessmen as they do on the hard-pressed
sanitationmen. They might be better able to enforce sanctions for
failure of property owners and tenants to carry their share of the
sanitation burden. Although small town cohesiveness could not be
achieved in an area of some 200,000 people, there should be a somewhat clearer sense of the relation between individual behavior and
community quality than there is under the present citywide system.

Black- or Puerto Rican-controlled district governments should
be more successful in recruiting black or Puerto Rican sanitationmen.
Local management and local employees should reduce hostility in those
areas and increase social pressures within the community for greater
cooperation and self-help.

Improvement of sanitation services would then depend largely
on greater citizen understanding and cooperation, on more vigorous
district level management, and on improved employee productivity.
Decentralization would mean no increase in resources. It might mean
less, as local district sanitation directors might well consider it
necessary, or at least prudent, to keep some men and trucks in a

central reserve for the inevitable crises; this would mean fewer men and machines for regular service.

Local Parks and Recreational Facilities, Parking Regulations, and Street Maintenance

Decentralization of responsibility for development and maintenance of small, locally patronized parks and recreational facilities would permit local districts to decide for themselves what kinds of facilities and equipment should be provided and how parks and open space utilization patterns should fit in, for example, with the needs of local schools and housing developments. Any losses in scale economies could be overcome by arrangements for joint maintenance services.

Control of local parking would be closely related to the ability of local governments to carry out street sweeping and, more broadly, to the quality of a neighborhood and the safety of its residents. But the City as a whole would still have a major interest in parking on major transportation arteries and in particularly congested areas. Accordingly, local districts should have the power to regulate parking, with an override authority in a central City transportation department for major thoroughfares and for designated major business of commercial areas.

Street maintenance was the province of the borough presidents until 1961, when it was transferred to the central City because of widespread inefficiencies, excessive patronage, and some evidence of graft. But the size of the borough as the unit for street maintenance probably had little or nothing to do with the shortcomings of pre-1961 street maintenance performance. The borough presidents' combined job of chief executive, borough legislator, and county party spokesman was not, and is not, conducive to efficient management of services.

A local district government should be as capable of maintaining streets as is the present City government. Major projects could be contracted out, just as the City today contracts out major street resurfacing projects. The difficulties with local street maintenance responsibilities would rather be of a different kind. Such local responsibilities could interfere with central City responsibilities for major traffic management patterns and decisions. Moreover, much of the excavation that causes damage to the streets is done by agencies like Consolidated Edison, the Transit Authority, and the Water Department, over which a local district government would have no control. Many of the street "maintenance" controversies in the more recently developed areas of the City are really street-building controversies, since decent streets have never been built, either because

of plans for sewers that have not been carried out or because of more
urgent priorities for capital funds. Any transfer of street maintenance
responsibilities to local units would have to recognize in some way
the differences in present comparative need caused by prior neglect.

If the last issue can be satisfactorily resolved, district governments could be responsible for local residential street maintenance.
This would have the advantage of making the trade-off between local
taxes or even block assessments and street quality much clearer than
it is today. Citywide agreements with independent bodies, such as
Consolidated Edison and the Transit Authority, would still be necessary
to set guidelines for responsibility for strict maintenance, but local
districts would be better able to exert specific pressure on those
bodies than are today's unorganized neighborhoods.

Housing Code Enforcement
and Housing Maintenance

The primary mechanism for direct government intervention in
the quality of existing housing is the housing code. Housing codes
designed to regulate the quality of rental housing developed out of the
public health and tenement house movements of the nineteenth century.
Today, housing codes also regulate room size and structural matters
and even include provisions for tenant safety and security, such as
peepholes in the outer door of apartments, mirrors in elevators, and
front door buzzer systems.

Housing codes are enforced through inspection systems. In
theory, most jurisdictions, including New York City, try to establish
cyclical inspection patterns, so that every unit is inspected with a
certain minimum frequency. In practice, in most large cities cyclical
inspections are difficult to maintain. Repeated reports of violations
begin to pile up in more deteriorated areas of the City. Efforts to
inspect are hampered because complaining tenants are not always
home, and landlords in marginal buildings are often difficult to find.
On top of this the enforcement process can be extremely slow in cities
such as New York, where violations still must be proceeded against
in court rather than in less formal administrative proceedings. All
too often the result is a backlog of missed scheduled inspections,
uninvestigated complaints, and unprosecuted violations.

Code enforcement by itself is of doubtful utility as a tool for
maintaining the quality of much of the City's rental housing stock.
Whatever the level of governmental sanctions for failure to maintain
his building, a landlord must somehow receive enough money to cover
maintenance and operating costs, pay taxes, amortize his capital investment, cover interest payments, and provide a minimally attractive

rate of return on invested equity. Maintenance costs are thus only one element of the landlord's costs. At a given level of actual maintenance, moreover, a landlord's total cash flow requirements rise with any increase in wage levels, price of supplies and equipment, and taxes or interest rates. In addition, as a housing unit ages, the level of real maintenance required to ensure a given level of housing quality will tend to increase.[4]

The landlord's rational response, if his net cash flow decreases, will be to seek ways of decreasing costs or increasing revenues. Rent control has prevented revenue increases in housing for the middle class. In slum areas welfare policies and poverty set the effective rent ceiling. In either case an increase in cash flow requirements must be offset by some change on the expense side of the landlord's budget, since revenues are relatively fixed. He may cut costs by decreasing the level of real maintenance (either through cutting back absolutely on services and repairs or by substituting inferior goods and services). Or he may try to utilize other expedients, such as delaying payment of interest, amortization, or taxes that come due. But taxing authorities and mortgage lenders can legally seize the premises for nonpayment of debt, interest, or taxes. Tenants and code enforcers have no such powerful sanctions. Hence, the landlord's first preference will tend to be cutbacks in maintenance or equipment replacement.

If housing is in short supply, the market will not exert pressure on landlords to conform to housing codes; the threat of the City to close dwelling units simply will not be credible as long as minimal public health requirements are met. If housing within the range of low-income persons is in short supply, strict code enforcement may make the poor worse off by excluding them from housing that otherwise might have been available to them. Code enforcement in the latter situation can too easily become a program for removal of the poor to other communities.

Given this gloomy assessment of the possibilities of housing code enforcement, of what relevance is the notion of its decentralization? The answer lies in the concept of comprehensive decentralization of the various environmental services of municipal government that affect the physical quality of life of discrete areas of the City, as described at the beginning of this section. Without some power to enforce housing maintenance requirements or to choose where requirements will be more strictly or less strictly enforced, local district governments would lack leverage over a major aspect of local environmental quality.

Moreover, housing code enforcement can be most helpful in just those neighborhoods that a single, central City government is most likely to overlook. It would be politically difficult for any unitary

City government to avoid concentrating its code enforcement efforts in the areas with the greatest number of violations. But the housing and public facilities in such areas are usually too deteriorated for housing code enforcement to have much effect. The tenants cannot afford rent increases and usually lack the incentive or the capacity for self-help maintenance efforts. The areas most likely to be helped by vigorous housing code enforcement efforts are older, marginal areas, which seem likely to decline toward slums through combinations of overcrowding and increasing absentee ownership, and those areas attempting to struggle upward through programs of home ownership and rehabilitation. Decentralized district governments should be more able than the central City to concentrate their enforcement activities on such neighborhoods.

On the other hand decentralization of housing code enforcement responsibilities would involve greater long-run risks than decentralization of responsibilities for direct service delivery programs, such as sanitation or even the City's emergency repairs program. Unlike the latter activities housing codes attempt to regulate private behavior and expenditure decisions in a systematic manner. Because the City's housing market will not conveniently break up into separate markets to conform to the boundaries of local districts, variations in local district code enforcement policies could impose significant costs on the rest of the City in a number of ways. Local policies that discourage investment in tax-paying structures or encourage their abandonment could adversely affect the City's tax base. Local districts might attempt, deliberately or unconsciously, to utilize their power to expel from the district economic, racial, or ethnic groups that did not "fit."[5] If housing code standards in one district were much below the levels of adjacent districts, those adjacent districts would find it difficult to enforce their higher standards in areas close to the more lenient district. And local policies that lead to deterioration of sound areas would have the longer-term impact of increasing the demand for renewal and redevelopment capital funds.

Central retention of the power to establish and interpret housing code standards would reduce the danger that local districts would impose external costs without grossly interfering with local housing preservation programs. Central definition of housing standards would make it difficult for local districts to use code enforcement as a substitute for restrictive zoning or other techniques of maintaining economic or cultural homogeneity. But centrally defined standards should not inhibit local district efforts to improve tenant conduct and reduce maintenance costs or to develop new techniques for code enforcement, for emergency repairs, or for receivership or tenant management of abandoned buildings.

Local districts should also be required to exercise the same financial responsibility for relocation of persons displaced by housing maintenance programs as is the present central City government. If further caution were required, districts could be given the duty of creating or accepting as many new low-income or moderate-income housing units as they eliminate through local activities or programs. This would prevent a district from arming its displacees with relocation payments and sending them out into the rest of the City to look for housing. In a tight market this would only force doubling-up of households. If rent control did not exist, it would drive up rents for low-income housing in general.

Finally, to capitalize on scale economies, some elements of the code enforcement process should continue to be a central responsibility. For example, complaint processing can work efficiently only if it is supported by a comprehensive, rapid response information system. This part of the process should therefore continue to be centralized, to take advantage of modern computer-based information technology. Local districts could bear the cost on a minimum-fee-plus-usage basis.

If an administrative housing court for the handling of housing code violations as civil cases has not already passed the state legislature, it should be part of any decentralization package. But a housing court should not be established for each district. If the housing court were broken down on a district basis, some districts would generate almost no cases—yet institutional mechanisms for resolving them would still need to exist. More significantly, if uniform interpretation of the centrally established housing code were to be maintained, there would have to be a "second tier," or appellate division, of the housing court. This would reduce the speed with which final administrative decisions could be made and would also increase the administrative costs.

Much of the benefit of better local understanding of district conditions could be obtained, even with a central housing court, if the prosecutorial function were handled by local district representatives. If local districts were responsible for working out arrangements for housing improvement with local owners and landlords (including decisions to waive sanctions pending repairs or to combine modified sanctions with compliance programs), local districts should also be responsible for initiating housing court actions.

AREAWIDE SERVICES

Responsibility for many public services should be kept citywide or even consolidated at a regional or metropolitan level in order to achieve economies of scale, to reflect relevant geographic or market area boundaries, or to avoid increasing the costs of private activities. For capital facilities such as water treatment or sewage treatment plants, cost per gallon of water supplied or sewage treated falls as the size of the facility increases, over a very wide range. Other capital facilities require high initial investment—whether few or many people are served. Subway systems, airports, and specialized medical equipment can only be supported by governments serving large populations.

A number of services—including land-use planning, transportation, and traffic control—need to respond to circumstances or forces that do not heed political boundaries. Automobile journey patterns and urban land markets are defined by residence patterns, geography, and technological limitations. Geographical fragmentation of governmental responsibility over these matters would be costly and disruptive.

Unified governmental control is also important in regulation of private behavior. In this case the service activity, such as inspection or enforcement, is not the desired end product. Instead, output is measured in terms of the extent to which the desired private conduct is achieved, and the costs of achieving that output include not only the salaries of inspectors but also the burden that compliance with the regulatory policy places on society as a whole. A builder, a restaurant chain, or a union can comply with government policy at much less expense if the regulations are uniform throughout the area of its activity.

Many of the services that fall into this classification do not need discussion. Their scale or technical complexity leaves no serious question as to the need for centralized control. For example, decentralization of responsibilities for water supply would make no sense, since the City depends on water sources reaching miles away into the headwaters of the Delaware River. Local responsibility for installation and maintenance of water delivery services might be possible without increasing costs, but in the absence of compelling technical reasons or public dissatisfaction with present performance, such a change does not seem worthwhile. Decentralization of responsibility for basic mass transit services would also not be a feasible option, although one might well authorize new local district governments to operate supplemental internal transportation services or to contract with the transportation agency for additional services of primary benefit to their residents or merchants.

This section will focus on three areas of governmental activity often suggested as candidates for partial or complete administration by smaller units of government—regulation of private business activities, land-use planning and zoning, and environmental protection

and waste disposal. Although smaller units might play some supplementary role, we believe the City as a whole should have the final
authority in each of these areas.

Regulation of Private Business

Governmental responsibilities for regulating businesses are
divided among a number of different City, state, and federal agencies.
Professionals, such as lawyers and doctors, some banking institutions,
and insurance companies are regulated largely at the state level.
Nongovernmental labor unions, transportation companies, financial
markets, and other banking institutions are subject primarily to federal regulation. Major City responsibilities include the following:
(a) regulation of construction trades and the manner of building construction by the Department of Buildings of the Housing Development
Administration (HDA); (b) regulation of weights and measures and
control of deceptive practices by the Department of Consumer Affairs;
(c) regulation of food handling and the operations of privately operated
medical facilities by the Health Services Administration; (d) regulation
of building uses and means of access and exit for fire protection purposes by the Fire Department; and (e) regulation of emission of wastes
and noise by the Environmental Protection Administration (EPA).
Because it is difficult to predict the magnitude of the costs that
might result from regulatory fragmentation, it would be wise to exercise restraint in turning over responsibility for business and consumer
protection matters to new local units of government. While City officials are often criticized for being too lenient with regulatory violations by business and commercial interests, local district administrators might be under even greater pressure for accommodation and
might have less media backing for strict controls. Individual firms
could threaten to relocate outside the districts, and competition for
employment-generating activities could force down local standards.
And a fragmented regulatory system would probably impose higher
costs upon residents of the City as a whole. Businesses operating
in a number of districts would have to bear the burden of compliance
with multiple regulatory schemes. Furthermore, mobility of consumers might simply mean that the residents of areas with tough consumer protection regulations would make their credit purchases in
less stringent neighboring districts.
Decentralization would clearly be a step backward in the case
of building construction codes. The tendency throughout the country
in recent years has been to widen the geographic area within which
individual building codes apply and to increase the flexibility with
which such codes are applied. Without areawide, uniform codes, both

large-scale conventional builders and builders using new technologies
find it difficult to compete effectively with small local builders. Restrictive local codes make it difficult for the large-scale or indus-
trialized builder to bring its organizational and cost advantages to
bear. Nor are there any obvious compensating gains from decentralizing the responsibility for building construction codes, other than
increasing the political power of local district governments. Building
codes and building code administration do not impede employment of
minority-owned construction firms. Instead, the chief concern with
building code administration in most communities is the temptation
for graft and dishonesty inherent in the building code inspection and
enforcement process, where decisions by individual field inspectors
can mean thousands of dollars to a contractor or an owner. Decentralization and increased fragmentation of inspection responsibilities
would not make the control of such dishonesty any easier.

Decentralization would also make no economic sense for such
regulatory responsibilities as restaurant health standards, commercial property rent control, or licensing for trades such as those of
taxi driver, locksmith, or electrician. Significant local variation in
standards or enforcement patterns could skew business location choices
and generate compliance costs that would materially increase costs
to consumers. Such local fragmentation might even accelerate the
flight of businesses from the City.

Local districts should therefore not be given responsibilities
in the area of administrative regulation of private conduct, at least
at the start of any decentralization program. Enforcement of housing,
health, and sanitary codes is likely to be difficult enough for local
districts, even though they involve matters in which a majority of
local residents should be deeply interested. Decentralizing direct
business regulatory responsibilities, when there is no commitment
to such regulation at the local level, might simply be an invitation to
the trades and businesses involved to dominate the local regulatory
and enforcement process.

Planning, Zoning, and Development

Many persons equate City decentralization with the granting of
power, or at least veto power, over land-use and development decisions to local units of government within the City. But such delegation
of ultimate zoning power to local district governments could cause
more social, economic, and political problems than any other aspect
of decentralization.

The major problem with localized land-use decisions in any
large urban area is the danger that such local decisions frequently

will be made in ways that, deliberately or inadvertently, impose external, or "spillover," costs upon the rest of the City. Narrowing the geographic area within which individual planning decisions are made increases the likelihood that local decisions take into account only local benefits and exclude the more broadly distributed costs flowing from those decisions. This tendency is inherent in all public land-use decisions. The responsible agency will always tend to overestimate the costs or benefits felt by its immediate constituents and underestimate the benefits or costs placed upon those to whom the agency is not required to be responsive.

Thus, when the residents of a relatively small area are permitted to control future land use in that area, they will normally seek to cause unpleasant land uses to go somewhere else. A small local unit would always tend to rationalize its exclusionary attitude with the thought that there must be land available in another location and would fail to see any need for it to make the hard choice between, for example, a new transit yard within its jurisdiction or no transit service.

In New York City, whatever the future structure of the City's government, the economic interdependence of the various areas and neighborhoods of the City seems certain to remain high enough so that major development and planning decisions in one area will have inevitable repercussions across wide areas of the City. For many purposes, therefore, including overall transport and economic development planning, as well as land-use controls, the City, and ultimately the region, must be considered a single planning and development area. Full local-zoning autonomy would seriously undercut any comprehensive citywide efforts to guide the City's physical development. Creation of separate local authorities could also lead to disparate patterns of land-use classification, varying bulk and setback provisions, and diverging standards for special permit uses or variances. The only people likely to profit in the long run from substantial local variations of this nature are real estate speculators and lawyers—hardly the intended beneficiaries of decentralization.

Before considering what decentralization might mean for the City's planning and zoning institutions, it might be helpful briefly to set forth the major official players in New York City's "zoning game." A seven-member City Planning Commission oversees and recommends changes in the zoning resolution and is responsible for preparing a master plan for the development of the City. The other players include the mayor, who appoints the commission; the Board of Estimate, whose approval is required for changes in the zoning resolution; the Board of Standards and Appeals, which is empowered to grant certain "hardship" variances and special permit uses; and the community boards. The latter, appointed by the borough presidents, have the right to be consulted on all land-use and City capital budget decisions

affecting their areas. As yet, however, they have no power to compel
acceptance of their views. Each community board is limited to the
influence its members have as individuals or to their skill, as a board,
in making an issue so visible that it captures the fancy of the media
and other persons with power or influence.

This land-use planning structure is often criticized as insensitive
to local interests. Although the criticism may be justified, land-use
controls are not nearly so centralized as the mayor must sometimes
desire. His control over Planning Commission membership is offset
by the critical position of the Board of Estimate, in which he has only
four of twenty-two votes. Because of their position on the Board of
Estimate, their power to appoint the local community boards, and
their membership on the City's capital project Site Selection Board,
the borough presidents control multiple levers of power at least the
collective equal of the mayor's power. Thus, formal decentralization
of land-use planning authority in New York City today consists primarily of fragmentation of authority at the central City level, rather
than the explicit delegation or devolution of authority to smaller geographic units. Although the borough presidents do individually represent areas smaller than the City as a whole, four of them represent
such large areas that they are highly unlikely, at any point in time,
to be able to take positions that do not require substantial compromise
of, and balancing among, various local positions within their boroughs.

It seems clear that there are real costs associated with the
making of all land-use and zoning decisions through a central planning
institution (or central planning institutions) in a city the size of New
York. It is all too easy to concentrate planning and development efforts
on the heart of Manhattan, where major private investment and employment-generating decisions are made. The cost of such concentration of effort is often inadequate attention to the needs of lesser
commercial and residential development areas of the City. The City's
Planning Department has, over the past decade, moved to counter this
tendency, by establishing separate planning offices in each of the City's
five boroughs. But such offices alone are likely to have little effect.
Implementation of borough planning office recommendations will still
depend on affirmative action by the mayor and the Planning Commission. When their attention is diverted from the most interesting problems of the midtown and downtown Manhattan business districts, it
will normally turn to those neighborhoods that make the most noise—
which are not always those with the greatest needs.

Centralized planning institutions are also more likely to lack,
or be less sensitive to, the information necessary to measure the
costs to individual neighborhoods from proposed land-use changes.
The tough, controversial land-use decisions in any large city today
are those that involve the making of substantial changes in existing

land-use patterns in a small area. The cost-benefit analysis ideally
applied to land-use decisions is difficult to use when the benefits of
change are diffused across the City as a whole (or, indeed, the metropolitan area) and when the costs are heavily concentrated upon those
in the immediate vicinity of the proposed change.

But in spite of the lack of universal satisfaction with many recent New York City zoning and land-use decisions, it is wrong to conclude that the City's officials do not respond to the concerns of specific
neighborhoods, if that opposition is vocal and at all organized. It has
proven impossible to ignore highly localized opposition. The last two
or three years have seen, for example, the defeat of proposals to re-
zone lower Third Avenue, to construct the Lower Manhattan Express-
way, to take 60 homes in the Corona area of Queens for a playing field
for a new high school, and to use a cut-and-cover method of taking
the new Sixty-Third Street subway through the southeast corner of
Central Park. In fact, some critics maintain that the unity and growth
of the City is already impaired—and imperiled—by the strength of
localized interests in the making of planning and development decisions.[6]

Moreover, if land-use decisions had to be bargained out among
individual units—each of which could hold out for the maximum "market" price in making decisions desired by other districts in the City—
a far more insular pattern of decisions would undoubtedly exist. A
locality with underdeveloped or undeveloped land within its borders
could claim for itself the full benefits of that land, regardless of the
effect of its decisions on neighboring districts or of the distorting
effects on the distribution of income among local district residents,
which would be likely to result from such a bargaining system. Poor
areas of the City would be condemned to the status of a Bayonne or a
Jersey City—isolated and without resources.

Such a "bargaining" system exists in Greater London; there,
significant weaknesses have already been identified. Formal planning and development control responsibilities are divided between
the thirty-two London boroughs and the Greater London Council (GLC).
Primary responsibility is in the boroughs, and the GLC has little authority to direct or supersede the planning decisions of the individual
boroughs. In particular, the GLC has no specific power to plan in
any detail for the vital central area of the City or even to supervise
most borough planning decisions affecting that area.[7] With this kind
of autonomous local planning authority, the danger is that

>   the shape of the London of the future will be determined
>   more by what the thirty-two boroughs . . . individually
>   plan with their eyes on their own areas than by the GLC's
>   view of what is needed for London as a whole . . . It may

be that from this dialogue between the GLC and the boroughs there will emerge a coherent plan for London, but
it is probably more likely that we shall see a compromise
between conflicting interests which in the end will satisfy
hardly anyone.[8]

Moreover, there is more cause to worry about parochial exercise of decentralized planning and development authority in New
York City. The extremes of wealth and poverty, of racial antagonism,
and of population density and land values are greater here than in
London. As of 1968, two nonresort cities in England, Oxford and
Luton, have higher rateable values per capital (roughly equivalent
to the American property tax base per capita) than does the poorest
greater London borough.[9]

Nor is it possible to divide authority by identifying some kinds
of decisions that are appropriate for local resolution and other kinds
that are appropriate for central resolution. There is no way of fore-
casting those matters in which local autonomy will necessarily lead
to unsatisfactory results citywide. Urban needs and conditions change,
and the aggregate of individual small decisions can be of significance
to citywide housing, transportation, and employment patterns. Therefore, efforts to divide authority formally are likely to be more productive of litigation than clarity.

The compromise between local anarchy and complete centralization is not found in artificial efforts to divide authority, but rather
in decision-making systems that permit a citywide planning body to
intervene effectively in those cases in which local decisions will impair achievement of citywide goals or impose costs on other local
areas in unacceptable ways. Certain land-use decision-making authority can be delegated to local districts. The local district, for
example, could be authorized to make formal land-use decisions, subject to administrative review and reversal at the central City level
under defined standards. In the absence of any central review, the
local decision would be final, much as the unreviewed decision of the
lower court becomes final.

Local district governments in such a two-tier system would be
able to initiate zoning changes within their areas, insofar as such
changes were needed to facilitate the carrying out of local unit responsibilities—for example, selecting a site for a new school, were
that a local district responsibility. They would also be the point of
initial hearing of private requests for changes in the permitted uses
for specific sites, as well as for variances from centrally established
bulk, setback, or similar restrictions.

As a general principle, local district decisions against local
district residents and landowners should be final, assuming that

applicable procedural requirements and standards of honesty were
observed at the local level. But another local district, a central City
operating agency, or the staff of the central planning agency could request central review because of the impact of the local decision on
citywide or neighboring district interests. In such a system the central City would retain overall responsibility for establishing general
development goals and for definition of the following: (a) basic land-
use classifications; (b) bulk, setback, and light and air rules; and (c)
standards applicable to the granting of variances and special-use permits. It might also establish additional parameters for local decisions
by defining average population density targets or minimum allocations
of land for industrial, residential, commercial, and recreational purposes.[10] Certain decisions of initial widespread concern—major redevelopment projects or major condemnations proposed by central
City agencies—would probably best be handled from the beginning at
the central level, with the planning staff of the local district for which
the project is proposed representing the district before the central
planning and zoning agency.

Retention of central authority over all land-use decisions through
the possibility of central reversal could mean that all decisions, no
matter how local in nature, would in fact come before the central City
planning body. But the tendency to recentralize decision-making authority that has been decentralized would be greatly reduced if power
were delegated to autonomous units of local government rather than
to a regional branch office of a central administrative agency. Although delegated authority would technically be made subject to discretionary, and even arbitrary, withdrawal by the central City, the
political power of the local units would make such withdrawal of authority less practicable than would be the case within a single government agency. With two tiers of municipal government, the central
City would be subject to the same political constraints as a state
governor dealing with county and municipal officials.

A more valid concern is the impact of such local authority on
the level of racial and economic integration in the City. A strong local
voice in land-use decisions would undoubtedly make integration of
some areas of the City more difficult to achieve. But this is likely to
be true as soon as any kind of political autonomy is given to local
areas of the City, whether or not they actually receive formal land-
use decision-making powers. More pragmatically, decentralization
may not make things much worse. Given the present tendency for
racial residential integration to occur only where older and poorer
whites have not moved out or where younger and richer whites are
moving in once again, it is not clear that the giving of autonomy to
local areas of the City would result in substantial lessening of integration, except insofar as local control might lead to the tipping of
transitional neighborhoods toward domination by a single racial group.

Furthermore, the retained power of the central City over land-use decisions for central City activities, coupled with the power of the central City to engage in housing and redevelopment programs (as described in the following section of this chapter), would mean that local districts would not be able to erect complete barriers to members of groups other than the dominant local group. If, in addition, the responsibility for enforcing fair housing laws (the present City Human Rights Commission) is left with the central City government, decentralization at least would not have a dramatically worsening impact on the level of integration. To the extent that district residents felt they had greater control over the future of their own neighborhoods, they might even come to separate questions of racial integration from those of economic integration: the arrival of a few middle-class minority group families might not be seen as the thin entering wedge of the problems of slum life styles.

If local units of government were given delegated land-use planning and zoning powers, they ought also to receive the right to expend funds generally for economic development purposes. The responsibility to engage in the rational development of the local district would be difficult to carry out unless local districts had some carrots, as well as some sticks, with which to encourage private investment decisions. Given the kinds of demands likely to be made on local districts for basic local environmental and personal services, local district governments would not feel free to spend massive amounts of money for development purposes. But there is no need or obvious justification for concentration of all power in a single citywide agency to assist businesses and aid in the creation of new sources of employment. Local power to act in this area could complement local manpower-training efforts or locally sponsored apprenticeship programs.

Moreover, the tendency would always be for the single, citywide agency to concentrate on the area or issue currently occupying the attention of the public, the media, or the economic development experts. Conditions in Staten Island are not the same as those in Brownsville, and neither has much relation to the needs of small businesses in areas facing major private and public redevelopment in the next decade—such as those along Ninth and Tenth Avenues in Manhattan.

Decisions to preserve or encourage small employment-generating centers or to make use of existing plots of underutilized commercial or manufacturing land ought to be within the power of local units of government within the City. The extent of such power, of course, would need to be linked to the financial capacity of any new local government units. If these units were not responsible for determining property tax levels, it would be inappropriate to give them unbridled discretion in determining the extent to which local economic

development activities would receive tax relief benefits. But to the
extent local units were to have command over resources, they should
be able to use them in economic development efforts for the local
area, provided they conformed to local and central land-use decisions
and were not counterproductive in relation to central City development efforts. Undoubtedly, there would be occasions in which local
governments would tend to abuse this power—most likely, by giving
preferential treatment to particular businesses or landowners. But
as long as local governments were required to observe basic procedural standards of fairness, the remainder of the worrying about
preferential local decisions should be left to the citizens of the local
district, for they would be most concerned about the application of
funds that might otherwise have been used for local services, such
as education, or parks maintenance, or schools.

Environmental Protection
and Waste Disposal

To be effective regulation of waste emissions requires substantial uniformity of standards and enforcement patterns over the entire
airshed or watershed. A local standard-setting enforcement authority
would be tempted to set or enforce ineffective standards whenever it
could export its waste emissions or could afford to ignore them, as
in the case of municipalities that are primarily industrial enclaves.
For the New York City area, where both air and water pollution are
bistate problems, involving both New York and New Jersey, increased
fragmentation of responsibility for environmental protection standards
would make little sense. The primary need within the metropolitan
area is for effective standard setting and enforcement across the area
as a whole. Accordingly, the responsibility for setting environmental
protection standards for the City itself should be left where it is today—in the City's EPA. Any fragmentation within the City of the power
to set basic emission control and waterborne or solid waste disposal
standards would only make it more difficult to achieve a rational system of protecting the air, land, and water of the metropolitan area as
a whole.

If waste disposal controls were not enforced over an area large
enough to internalize both costs and benefits flowing from the choice
of technology and facility site, producers of waste within the area
would not get the proper market signals about the costs of waste disposal. The community with a poor incinerator or an inadequate sewage
disposal plant, discharging wastes on downwind or downstream neighbors, would not be charging its residents the true social costs of
handling waste, thus providing them with an incentive to overproduce

it. Were the community required to reduce solid particle emissions, it might concentrate its effort on ways of increasing resident incentives to reduce the volume or change the composition of waste delivered for disposal. Similarly, if solid waste disposal remained the responsibility of the City as a whole but collection responsibilities were decentralized, the charges made by the central City to local units for such disposal should be based on the amount and the quality of waste delivered for central disposal. Flat per capita charges for local use of central disposal facilities would not give the local unit any incentives to transmit to its resident waste producers to sort waste for recycling or otherwise change the composition or reduce the amount of waste delivered for disposal.

Some districts might want to establish higher-than-minimum environmental protection standards, but a community with the power to raise standards, involving water pollution, air pollution, and noise pollution, or aesthetic regulations, such as junkyard controls, would have almost as much control over local land uses as a local area with its own zoning powers. The use of such controls to exclude commercial or industrial operations or public facilities intended to serve a wider area of the City could easily result in a situation in which non-residents of restrictive districts bear the costs of the exclusion, while the benefits are enjoyed by the local community. Local authority over environmental protection standards should therefore be limited in the same way as local zoning authority. Local power to impose stricter pollution control standards should be limited to residential or retail commercial land uses and, even there, should be subject to central City override.

Economies of scale and the unsavory nature of waste disposal facilities also argue against giving significant authority over waste disposal facilities to smaller units of government within the City. Engineering economies of scale in both liquid and solid waste treatment operations are normally substantial up to very large plant sizes. But perhaps even more important in a densely developed area like New York City is the lack of suitable sites for disposal operations in many parts of the City. Sewage disposal requires water courses for disposal of processed waste, land fill dumps must be large and isolated, and even incineration facilities require space to dispose of incombustible materials and ash.

Some system of interdistrict contracting might theoretically permit both joint use of facilities of economic scale and a market-based selection of sites for waste treatment and disposal. But, in practice, market forces would be unlikely to result in a rational and equitable allocation of such facilities, because poorer districts would have little or no bargaining power and relatively wealthy districts would probably exclude such facilities, regardless of ecological factors. For these reasons site selection authority should remain the responsibility of the central City or, better still, a regional governmental unit.

UNCLASSIFIED SERVICES

A number of municipal government responsibilities combine elements of significant areawide concern with either highly localized impact or frequent and widespread day-to-day public contact. This section focuses on housing and renewal programs and the criminal justice system as two of the most important and controversial examples of these less easily classified services. Fire Department decentralization is not discussed. Dissatisfaction with the Fire Department today seems to be based on the low number of minority group employees in the department rather than on the quality of Fire Department services. Compelling evidence that decentralization is the best way to solve this problem is absent; thus, Fire Department decentralization would be premature, at least at the outset of any decentralization program.

Housing and Renewal Programs

Housing and renewal efforts do not constitute a single, coherent activity of municipal government. There are many different federal, state, and municipal programs, each of which was created for slightly different reasons and each of which can be used to achieve varying goals. Beyond this, control over project construction, ownership, management, and occupancy frequently becomes a goal in itself, because of the political and economic power such control confers on its possessors. Many contemporary debates over community control of housing decisions are not about the merits of housing project design or site choice. Instead, they are actually conflicts over which community group will be able to choose or influence the choice of site, architect, contractor, tenants, and management.

The New York City Housing Authority, the Housing and Development Agency (HDA), and the City Planning Commission share primary responsibility for the City's housing and renewal programs. Roughly speaking, the Planning Commission's role ceases once site selection and the basic project scope decisions have been made, and the Housing Authority or the HDA takes over responsibility from that point. But the controversy inevitably encountered in housing and renewal projects means that decisions are seldom limited to these formal participants. Site selection inevitably brings in the Board of Estimate, with its formal powers in relation to amendments of the zoning resolution, and normally the mayor and the City Council as well. The impact of major housing or renewal projects on other services—sanitation, recreation, schools, police, traffic, and fire—means that the appropriate City agencies and the interest groups associated with them will all tend to seek to influence housing and renewal decisions.

Nevertheless, the administrative responsibility for carrying out housing and renewal projects remains with the Housing Authority and the HDA. The Housing Authority has been the major volume producer of low-income rental housing in the City. Between 1935 and 1970 it produced close to 150,000 units. Construction of most of these units was financed by capital grants from the federal Department of Housing and Urban Development (HUD) and its predecessors. Some, however, were financed through smaller but similar state and City public housing programs. Once public housing sites have been approved by the Planning Commission and the Board of Estimate, the Housing Authority has a relatively free hand (as far as City government is concerned) in construction, tenant selection, and project management. The primary curbs on its discretion arise out of state enabling legislation (such as the requirement of certain forms of competitive bidding for project construction) and the various rules and regulations set by HUD.

Other housing for persons of low and moderate income is produced through a mixed bag of federal, state, and City programs, designed to reduce housing costs by reducing permanent mortgage interest costs. Although most of the funding for such housing comes from the FHA or the state-funded Mitchell-Lama program and technically goes directly to the project owner or cooperators, the City has a substantial formal and informal voice in these projects. The state and federal funding agencies frequently will not consider requests for assistance unless the requests first have City clearance. More importantly, most new low- and moderate-income multifamily housing in the City, as well as most new public housing, is dependent upon the low-cost land provided through the write-downs under the federal urban renewal program. The City, through its control over the content of renewal and redevelopment plans, thus has de facto control over most mortgage assistance projects in the City.

In addition to the major housing construction assistance programs and federally funded urban renewal, the City also stimulates the production of standard housing units through various other programs. The FHA provides some funds for rehabilitation. The City has its own rehabilitation loan program and also uses property tax abatements to encourage new construction, as well as rehabilitation. More recently, the Planning Commission has begun to experiment with the implicit land cost subsidy possible through granting high-density

zoning for land that has been purchased at prices based on less intensive permitted uses.

There are two commonly expressed dissatisfactions with present
City renewal and housing development efforts. First, it is alleged that
the City is not an efficient builder or redeveloper. Project lead times
are enormously long, in part because the procedure for obtaining
project approval is so complex. Project costs, therefore, invariably
come to be much greater than originally anticipated. Some observers
also feel that the City's bureaucracy is too cumbersome. Scandals,
such as those in the City's rehabilitation program, are virtually inevitable.

Second, there is dissatisfaction with the substantive results of
housing and renewal programs. Much of the pressure for community
control and citizen participation in urban government has grown out
of opposition to the results of the federally funded housing and redevelopment efforts. Public housing and FHA-assisted housing have
often added to the concentration of poor and minority group residents
in particular areas of the City. Renewal was often a euphemism for
removal of low-income residents from land deemed suitable for commercial use, civic facilities, or higher-income dwelling units. Concentration on physical measurements of dwelling unit age and relative
deterioration have consigned more than one reasonably stable, low-
income neighborhood to the bulldozers.

As a result of this experience, federal and local housing and
redevelopment programs have placed increasing emphasis on letting
local project area residents participate in decisions. But participation
and consultation have proven unsatisfactory consolation prizes for
those who perceive the very prospect of redevelopment to be against
their best interests. As a result project area residents increasingly
argue that any redevelopment and land-use changes must benefit existing neighborhood residents and must meet with their prior approval.

Once enunciated, this essentially conservative philosophy cannot be confined to the residents of poor, powerless neighborhoods.
It has been adopted, all over the country, by more fortunate neighborhoods, anxious to keep out low-income or minority group residents
or simply fearful of change. To further complicate the politics of
housing and redevelopment decisions, individuals and groups searching
for ways to increase nascent power or to bolster existing political
power often look on housing and redevelopment projects as convenient
sources of power, without regard to the values sought to be advanced
by the projects' proponents. Housing and redevelopment proposals
thus become the focal point, both for the fear of change felt by established City residents and for the efforts of new groups in the City and
its neighborhoods to achieve positions of political power.

Decentralization of political power and authority to units of 125,000 to 250,000 people would not eliminate conflict and dispute over housing and renewal site and planning decisions. Such a local district would be substantially larger than even a major redevelopment project. No such district could realistically be expected to be homogeneous enough to avoid conflict between the interests of those in the immediate area of the site and the interests of the district as a whole. (The notion of renewal, indeed, is antithetical to the notion of deference to the wishes of existing site residents. The whole program is based on the premise of changing and, in theory, improving land uses at the project site.) Moreover, efforts to use control over housing and redevelopment projects as stepping stones to political power cannot be expected to decrease simply because the relevant governmental unit is smaller.

Also, substantial involvement of local districts in housing development decisions beyond the purely advisory level could lead to the same kind of local imposition of intolerable costs on the rest of the City as would local control of zoning. For example, those committed to achieving and maintaining some racial and economic residential integration must seek to keep some housing and renewal authority in the central City government. Even the existing citywide political structure finds it difficult to arrive at any consensus on such questions. But if the central government were not to retain such authority, those districts that gain from perpetuation of existing patterns of discrimination would be licensed to act without considering the costs. And if housing decisions that foster integration are to be implemented, the central City government must also retain the power to carry projects through to completion. Were the central City required to rely on individual districts to develop such projects, the possibilities for local stalling and delay would be immense.

Nor would decentralization ensure that benefits begin to flow to those groups that have failed to participate in the gains from federal and local redevelopment expenditures or housing expenditures. In a decentralized New York City, housing and renewal programs would be likely to serve the interests of more established middle-class and commercial interests, whether they be citywide or local, black, white, or Puerto Rican. The changes over the past five or so years in renewal and public housing philosophy—departure from massive clearance projects and curtailments of ghetto-based public housing—have been products of the pressures of spokesmen for minority groups and the poor through the courts and on the federal government, and not, by and large, directly on municipal government.

Lastly, decentralization could not be expected to yield substantial improvements in the efficiency with which individual projects were undertaken. Although large housing and renewal projects require substantial lead time and are almost universally unpopular with neighborhood residents, decreasing project scale does not seem to decrease project lead time or the amount of organizational energy required to assemble a workable project package. Perhaps, the intricate process of developing necessary administrative agreement over project location, design, and usage might be simplified in smaller districts with less cumbersome interagency bureaucratic relations. But the administrative skills available to thirty or more local districts would be bound to be less than those which can be afforded by a single central development agency like HDA, and the smaller size of each individual district would mean that there would be less opportunity for most districts to gain equivalent experience in working with federal housing assistance and renewal programs.

The major argument for a formal local role in housing and renewal decisions is not based on efficiency grounds or even on the hope of projects that are better designed or less destructive to the neighborhoods in which they are located. Instead, it is more overtly political. Even after decentralization of responsibility for personal and local environmental services, centralized housing and renewal decisions would continue to be seen at the local level as insensitive to the particular characteristics or needs of a neighborhood. In fact, local opposition to central projects might well tend to increase once there were active local district governments that could serve as focal points for local bargaining with central City agencies and officials.

Under those circumstances some sharing of housing and renewal decisions and responsibilities with local districts should increase the political stability of the system as a whole. If a large number of people feel it important to have a voice at the local level in at least some housing and renewal projects, for whatever reason, then it is appropriate to recognize this value judgment, even at the expense of less efficient project development. Furthermore, local district governments that had faced neighborhood demands about site selection, project design, relocation, and tenant choice might be more willing to work in a cooperative manner with central City officials than would local districts, which never had to bear the responsibility of choosing between action or inaction.

Providing for local district participation in housing and development decisions would be less easy than asserting the desirability of such participation. Mere consultative rights may not satisfy the predictable desire for some direct local district power to select the site and scope of projects of particular concern to the local district. In theory, such local district power could be provided through central City earmarking of housing and development funds for use within local districts according to local priorities. The responsibility for setting local priorities could perhaps be exercised by the local agency responsible for the local role in land-use decisions, as suggested in the previous section of this chapter.

But federal and state housing and redevelopment programs are not structured to facilitate earmarking of funds by the central City government to the local district. Under existing programs funds flow only to projects approved by appropriate state or federal officials, so that the central City could never guarantee a local district that its project preferences would actually be funded.

The obvious alternative would be the granting of formal legal authority to local districts to carry out their own housing and renewal efforts, including direct application and negotiation for assistance from federal and state funding sources. Authority could be divided so that major projects (defined in terms of dollar amount or geographic scope) would be the continued responsibility of the central City development agencies. Smaller projects, however, could be within the competency of the local districts. Because the central City would retain ultimate land-use decision authority (under the proposals of the preceding section of this chapter), local district projects would still be subject to substantial central influence or authority.

The major difficulty with this approach would be that it would require local duplication of the present relatively effective management capacity of the Housing Authority and the HDA. It might also involve less efficient relocation programs, if relocation were to be carried out by the local district, since the local district would have a much narrower market from which to obtain suitable relocation housing. Improvements in the quality of relocation might balance the more costly small-scale local relocation programs. But local district governments would be faced with the same conflict between careful relocation and the seemingly more important task of transforming project proposals into bricks and mortar.

A solution for both problems might be found in the application of the Los Angeles "Lakewood" plan approach to local district housing and renewal efforts. Local districts in a two-tier system of government in New York City could be required to contract with the Housing Authority of the HDA for the carrying out of their housing and renewal efforts, once the local district had accomplished the initial tasks of negotiating funding commitments, selecting a site, and determining overall project design. If such central City services were performed according to formal contracts with local districts, locally defined standards would govern central agency performance, whether in project construction or in relocation.

This approach would not increase local district government power to use projects to enhance the opportunities for local resident employment and local business participation in minority group areas. Minority-dominated local districts would understandably seek to translate political power into contracts that would favor minority firms or firms that employ minority group members. This, of course,

is a particularly touchy issue in construction, because of the dis-
criminatory history of the building trades unions and the difficulties
that have been faced by minority construction firms in getting bonding,
financing, and experience. Given the scant success of efforts to open
up the building trades unions, some local districts should perhaps be
given the responsibility for project construction, if they wished to
take it. Then, a local district would be free to decide for itself whether
it were willing to try to force the hand of the building trades by utilizing
nonunion firms and workmen.

The net result would be a housing development system in which
the central City and local districts would have certain parallel powers,
carrying out overall coordination primarily through exercise of central
land-use control powers. The goal would be to permit local units to
carry out projects in which they had a particularly strong and immediate
interest (replacement of a particularly ulcerous, but relatively small,
block of slums), while not terminating the role of the central City in
major housing and redevelopment efforts.

Criminal Justice System*

The criminal justice system offers a wider overlap of local and
areawide concerns than any other aspect of local government services.
The basic regulation of criminal conduct is statewide, through the
New York State Penal Code. Yet, to most people, the most important
aspect of the criminal justice system is the presence of a sympathetic,
understanding policeman in uniform on a nearby street corner. Few
people will stop to worry about how well the rest of the criminal
justice system is performing its tasks when the basic patrol function
of the police is felt to be inadequate.

There are five activities critical to the criminal justice system—
legislation, policing, prosecution, adjudication, and correction. The
outputs of each one of these activities are inputs of another. Legislatures define crimes and, thus, criminals whom the police are charged
with apprehending; police arrests lead to court prosecutions; court
convictions become penal cases; often exconvicts become police

---

*The material in this section, with the exception of the portions
on decentralization of patrol services, is drawn from a more lengthy
paper prepared for the Bar Association by Richard Danzig, who is
currently clerking for Mr. Justice White and will join the faculty at
Stanford Law School next fall.

problems; and the system recycles. Widening or narrowing the definition of crimes increases or decreases police, court, and correction business; changes in police techniques may overburden or free the time of judges and prison staffs; judicial exclusionary rules may force new police techniques or leave some laws unenforceable.

This interrelation means that one ought not to decentralize one component without considering fully the effects of that action on the rest of the system. For example, a community should not be able to legislate a severe program against drunkenness without having some of the opportunities and the responsibilities, or at least the cost, of handling the consequent enforcement and correctional problems.

Criminal justice decentralization, if otherwise feasible, offers the opportunity to make communities realize the problems of, and their responsibility for, the institutions of the criminal justice system. "Out of sight, out of mind" has long been society's main theme in relation to the inner workings of police stations, the "downtown" courts, and the isolated jails. Attitudes of irresponsibility assumed by both communities and civil servants are possibly as much a product of physical isolation as of legal or political organization.

Any decentralization proposal must also consider that, whatever the faults of the present system, there are some values that centralization fosters. Physical isolation and emotional detachment, for example, aid the prison system in holding—and giving City residents confidence that they will hold—those judged dangerous. These same characteristics insulate a court system from the passions and pressures of a community, thus enhancing the likelihood of due process and inspiring a sense of fairness in litigants. The disinterested restraint of the policeman and his nonphysical power as an embodiment of authority can be aided by the fact that he is not resident in the precinct in which he works.

These and related advantages should not be ignored in revising the existing system, even though the present institutions may be unsatisfactory in many respects. There is no virtue and much danger in decentralizing what can be done better centrally. Would we really want men to be compelled to stand trial before their close neighbors? Would citizens be safer if the authorized use of violence were delegated to community patrols of local residents? Does our commitment to reintegrating persons into society extend so far that we could want prisons located in our housing projects?

Criminal justice system decentralization might therefore take the form, at least initially, of a coexisting alternative system, supplementing and in some areas substituting for, but nowhere totally displacing, the existing apparatus. Under this approach the existing bureaucracy might find decentralization less threatening because of its more modest goals. In the following discussion only one element of the criminal justice system, the day-to-day police patrol function, is discussed as a potential candidate for relatively complete decentralization to new local governments of several hundred thousand people within New York City, and our conclusion is that this function should not be decentralized now.

Legislation

Society creates its criminals by using its laws to define crimes. Many think that we create too many criminals by labelling too many forms of conduct as "crimes."[11] This is an issue particularly relevant to decentralization. If street loitering is a social activity in a community whose streets are more hospitable than its tenement living rooms or if playing the numbers in a slum is no different from playing poker in the suburbs, why should the suburban concept of crime be imposed on innercity society? As long as externalities are minimal, it would be reasonable to allow each community some freedom to define its own crimes.

In New York City community life styles do affect the regulation of crime, but the process too often is governed by the discretion of individual civil servants.[12] When police overlook assaults in black areas that would produce arrests in silk-stocking districts or when judges vary sentencing patterns to conform to their vision of the mores of the complainant and offender, the resulting pattern of law enforcement is subject to neither community nor legislative control. Delegating some legislative power to define criminal misdemeanors to a neighborhood government could beneficially reassert the influence of local norms in local "street-level" law enforcement.[13] Communities would thereby be empowered to proceed legislatively in choosing the extent to which offenses like prostitution, gambling, homosexuality, drunkenness, loitering, vagrancy, and disorderly conduct would be deemed "crimes," subject to prosecution. (For this kind of localized establishment of rules of public demeanor to be effective, the local area must have some voice in patrol and enforcement decisions, as well as in prosecutorial decisions. These are discussed in subsequent subsections.)

But local power to define the boundaries of criminal conduct could be used to discriminate against the life style of local minorities or to enact local rules that would violate state or federal due process and civil rights standards. One way of keeping local discretion within reasonable bounds might be for the state legislature or the City Council to adopt a variant of the "model act" or "uniform code" approach. Such legislation might preserve the basic misdemeanor provisions of the existing Penal Code in relation to the kinds of crimes mentioned and would authorize local districts to adopt the code with lesser (but

not greater) penalties than those specified in the orginal document.
In this way a local district would be spared the cost and furor of
hammering out legislation and would instead be asked to make a
relatively simple choice, comprehensible to all neighborhood residents. State restraints on the upper limits of penalties and the definition of offenses would protect those who might be accused of crimes,
and the uniform nature of the act would facilitate the comprehension
of a district's laws by police (who might be transferred from district
to district), judges (who might handle cases from several districts),
travelers, and new residents. If the externalities from permitting
certain conduct should be greater than was at first recognized or if
some districts became bulwarks of organized crime, the City or state
could simply repeal its enabling ordinance.

Police

        The New York Police Department is the largest law enforcement
agency in the United States and the largest metropolitan police force
in the world. Its annual operating costs of $652.945 million (for 1970),
mostly devoted to paying the salaries of the 31,000 policemen, absorbed
77.5 percent of the City's criminal justice budget. This Leviathan—
the equivalent of two divisions and an armored brigade—is directed
by a commissioner, seven deputy commissioners, and a group of inspectors, operating out of police headquarters not far from City Hall.
Like the military, this command staff is generally overseen by civilian
authorities (the mayor and his assistants and, particularly, by the
Budget Bureau), but, at the same time, it retains considerable internal
autonomy and independent political power. As distinguished from the
military, however, the department is significantly constrained by employee organizations within its ranks (principally, the Patrolman's
Benevolent Association and the Traffic Safetyman's Benevolent Association).
        This police establishment is already subject to substantial
decentralization. New York City has fragmented the policing function
so that it is shared among different authorities: the New York Police
Department, the Metropolitian Transit Authority, the Housing Authority,
and the Port Authority—all patrolling different aspects of the City.
They are augmented by private guards, many of them licensed by the
City to carry arms. The following analysis is limited to the regular
Police Department.
        The Police Department is itself divided into specialized sub-
forces, the most notable of those being detectives and patrol. The
patrol function is further divided among seven borough commands and
subdivided among seventeen divisions and seventy-nine precincts. The
precinct, typically staffed by 1 captain, 5 lieutenants, 15 sergeants,

and upwards of 150 patrolmen, is the department's basic unit of operation, though it too is subdivided into beats and sectors. It is in the
precinct that most men develop their skills and attitudes (despite the
centralization of training in the police academy), it is in the precinct
that most important rewards and sanctions are invoked, and it is there
that most assignments and patrol patterns relevant to the neighborhood are decided. Yet, until the recent efforts of New York City Police
Commissioner Patrick Murphy to hold precinct captains more accountable for the effectiveness of patrol and detective activities, this concentration of authority at the precinct level was coupled with virtually
no responsibility for performance.

The critical question for those who would inject local governmental
authority into this already decentralized system may therefore be
phrased as follows: Assuming that precinct lines were redrawn so
that each precinct corresponded to a local government district, which
police functions could and should be delegated to a local district government and which left in the hands of the citywide department?

One type of plan would give the community some control over
allocative decisions within the neighborhood precinct. But community
priorities would inevitably conflict with those of central police headquarters. The precinct captain could either obey central orders and,
thereby, exacerbate police-community relations or he could go along
with community suggestions and disclaim any responsibility for the
consequences. Neither course of action would yield responsive or
responsible police performance.

Another plan would attempt to influence police decision making
by rewarding police officers who had made decisions of which the
community approved and by penalizing those who had done otherwise.
Two dramatic means of doing this present themselves. One would
provide for the selection of precinct captains by district vote—a system that survived in New York into the late nineteenth century—or
through selection by local district councils.[14] A second would create
a district commissioner or review board, capable of investigating
complaints and disciplining officers.

These proposals raise a fundamental difficulty in attempts at
partial neighborhood control of the police. Because quality of police
work cannot be directly correlated with crime levels, arrests, or
convictions, the community would have no yardstick by which to measure police performance and hold the police apparatus responsible.
In this respect neighborhoods could expect to have more difficulty
controlling their police than sanitationmen, doctors, or even teachers.

Each alternative, moreover, has its special problems. Community selection of the precinct captain would circumvent the present
civil service examination procedure for reaching this rank or, if the
community were confined in its choices to those who had already

become captains by examination, it would replace the judgment now exercised by the department's commanding officers in assigning captains to precincts. In addition to undercutting the authority of commanding officers, community discipline would clearly be unacceptable to those who run the police department, their men, and their civilian constituency and, hence, would be little easier to achieve than complete decentralization.[15] Using the results of the 1967 referendum on the Civilian Review Board as a yardstick, it is doubtful that this method of community control is politically viable in New York.

A third approach calls for the creation of a community patrol, paralleling the methods of the police crime prevention patrol, but manned by community residents, variously charged with preventing crime, detecting code violations, observing police conduct, calling the police, or escorting defenseless members of the community, depending on the plan. Often such patrol concepts involve too little or too much. To call the escorting of old ladies or the walking of beats without authority "community-controlled police work" is to miscast the function and underestimate the power of the police. Such low-priority activities might better be labelled adult boy scouting. At this level they might well be encouraged, but they should be viewed as what they are, not as a step toward community assumption of a police function.

When these programs are more ambitious, they often seek to superimpose a group on top of police attempts to perform their professional function. As such, experience suggests they usually alienate the police and disquiet the community; neither constituent is pleased at the prospect of laymen running stop lights while chasing "suspects" or being equipped to exercise force at their own discretion.

A quite different kind of community patrol effort offers more promise. Such a local patrol might perfrom some of the functions of maintaining order that do not involve the use of force, such as detention of, or aiding, drunks; conciliation or at least dampening of family disputes; lecturing, and perhaps making referrals or keeping records of, juveniles who have disturbed the peace; and similar activities. Those activities are almost entirely local in impact and are also closely related to the legislative decisions that could most easily be delegated to a community. The volume and difficulty of on-the-street order maintenance activities would be partly determined by a community's definition of order. Furthermore, police training and professionalization has least reached this "social service" aspect of police work. Finally, these police-community contacts call for insight into the mores of a community, sensitivity to the personalities involved, and the human relations skills necessary to secure voluntary cooperation.

Carefully controlled experiments in New York City have shown that civilians who persuade alcoholics to accept treatment are at least as effective in minimizing vagrancy on the Bowery as police using the tactics of arrest,[16] and that specially trained response teams answering only family dispute calls improve upon regular police handling of these problems and at the same time reduce their own injury rate to zero, despite the fact that more police are injured while intervening in family disputes than in any other line of duty.[17]

There are a number of reasons, however, for expecting that widespread additions of such community forces might not be completely satisfactory. A local district with such a force still would not be able to determine the priorities to be fixed in combatting serious crimes, so community relations with the regular police would not necessarily improve. Furthermore, it might be difficult to ensure that the two forces followed consistent or complementary law enforcement and public order strategies; the likely differences in emphasis could result in more time spent in mutual recrimination than in productive law enforcement. Finally, in today's climate of fear, most local districts would seek to use any community patrol as a deterrent to violent crime, not as a social service agency. And experience in Chicago suggests that any widespread delegation of family dispute intervention functions to nonpolice employees ultimately results in requests for police escorts.

Reasons such as these make it seem sensible to consider going beyond the notion of the community force to true decentralization of police patrol functions. Some of the objections that are sure to be raised to any such radical change in the structuring of the City's Police Department are of little merit. Hiring and training of personnel, for example, would not have to be turned over to each individual local district. Quality training programs could be operated by the central City for local police forces, just as they might be for sanitationmen. If minimum citywide hiring standards and background investigation were required and carried out by such a central unit, it should be possible to control entry-level competence.

Nor would the problems posed by the creation of new jurisdictional boundaries be insuperable. Such boundaries would be no greater a barrier to "hot pursuit" in the City than they are at present in adjacent suburban communities. The possible loss of flexibility and ability to shift manpower about the City would be of greater importance, as would the impact of decentralization of patrol on the ability to perform detective functions. A central force of significant size would be needed for such things as visits of heads of state, major parades, the control of large disorders and demonstrations, and the provision of police services to territorial areas that might remain the responsibility of the central City government (perhaps the central business district or the major waterfront industrial areas of Queens and Brooklyn). A single citywide service might also be better adapted to patrolling the City's arterial highway system and its large parks.

Such central police manpower could be provided by retaining a predominantly centralized detective force and a relatively small centralized patrol force. The central City could also be given the right to call up local police for central City purposes. If the central City had to pay local districts at least the out-of-pocket costs of such a call-up, the power would not be likely to be abused. Some unity and maintenance of common understanding between the local and central forces could be retained through central force hiring procedures that stress prior service on local district forces.

New York would actually have a great advantage in developing a two-tier police patrol system, which a group of historically autonomous smaller cities would not have: the power to avoid decentralization of functions not essential to the success of decentralization and more costly to operate on a decentralized basis. In a suburban county each town would have developed its own communications system, its own equipment purchasing operation, its own motor pool facilities, and its own record-keeping and information system. Although the town officials might recognize that joint operation of facilities would be more efficient and effective, it would be difficult to overcome the existing investment in bureaucratic power of those providing such services in each individual town. New York City would have no such problem. It would start with a central communication system, a record-handling system that is not perfect but is still structured to provide a citywide information flow, and vehicle- and equipment-purchasing operations that could be converted or adapted to district cooperative efforts.

There are, however, a number of serious issues that must be faced before opting for any substantial police decentralization. They include the probability of hostility to such changes by present police department personnel, increased difficulty in control of police corruption, and the danger to respect for individual civil rights in each of 30 or so local districts. In addition any period of gradual transfer of responsibility to local districts would raise many issues similar to those that rocked the City's school system in 1968 and 1969.

It is difficult to predict whether decentralization would increase or decrease police susceptibility to corruption. The answer would lie beyond the size and internal organizational structure of the police force. If new local district governments were unstable and failed to arouse the continued concern of local residents, it would not be only the police that would be susceptible to illicit influence and the abuse of privileges. The greater risk with decentralization would be that senior officials in all departments might become less visible to their local publics and, hence, might feel more able to take advantage of their positions. But the incidence of such behavior again would depend upon what local residents were prepared to tolerate, how easily

they could organize, and what kind of assistance they would receive
from the media.

Under decentralization, the character of local district law enforcement might well be determined by the content of dominant local
prejudices. Areas that feel that present enforcement practices are
unsympathetic to local standards might appreciate such change. But
minority groups in many districts might find the new standards op-
pressive, whether the minority were black, Puerto Rican, or white,
middle-class or poor. Differing police standards and attitudes
might also increase the feelings of visitors that they are unwanted in
many City districts. And such polarization might also hurt the City
economically.

There are two additional reasons why any initial transfer of
powers to local district governments ought not to include significant
police powers—one valid only for the next several years and the other
likely to be permanently valid. The first relates to the current efforts
under Police Commissioner Murphy to transfer substantial authority
and responsibility for performance to the City's existing precincts.
If these experiments are successful they ought to undercut some of
the arguments for police decentralization advanced above. The employment of increased numbers of minority group policemen may be
of similar utility in reducing the number of abrasive citizen-police
contacts.

More importantly, the controversy certain to accompany any
efforts to decentralize the political responsibility for police management and performance could easily generate enough uncertainty and
dissension to cause the whole experiment to fail. Accordingly, police
decentralization should be considered a longer-term goal, to occur, if
at all, only after there have been some successful transfers of power
and responsibility in less controversial services. The political institutions and affairs of the new local district governments should
have time to stabilize before they are forced to cope with the strains
of police decentralization.

Once decentralization of other services has occurred, there
might be less pressure for police decentralization. The coercive
power of the police is qualitatively different from the other services
and responsibilities of local government. Before there had been any
decentralization, it would not be politically expedient for prospective
political leaders in areas supportive of the concept of decentralization
to oppose police decentralization. But once local units of government
exist, local leaders temporarily out of power might realize that retained central control of the police could be to their advantage. The
natural reaction of a politician in power is to use any means at hand,
including the police, in order to maintain his position. We know all
too well, in this country's experience with black-white relations, just

how potent and one-sided this ability to use the police can become.
For those already concerned with the potential power and lack of adequate public exposure of the proposed new local officials, avoiding the
decentralization of police might be one way of keeping local government power in check.

On balance, then, police responsibilities should not be transferred to local district governments. At least at the outset increased
administrative decentralization would seem the more prudent course.
Precinct lines should be made congruent with local district government boundaries, and precinct captains should be delegated substantial
authority and held accountable for the performance of their men. Under
those conditions precinct officers would be under considerable pressure to respond to district priorities and to respect district life styles.
The precinct captain should also be able to cooperate to help other
decentralized criminal justice experiments work. Districts could be
permitted to experiment with various forms of community patrols,
using their own tax receipts or a portion of any federal, state, or City
grants not earmarked for other purposes. The whole issue of police
decentralization should then be reviewed after a few years' experience
with local district government.

The District Attorney Prosecutorial Function

In New York City the district attorneys' offices are organized
on a county basis. The dominant aspect of the district attorneys'
work is criminal prosecutions. In Manhattan, for example, the district attorney is responsible for prosecuting all violations of local and
state criminal laws by its 1.7 million residents. Toward this end he
employed, in 1970, 128 assistant district attorneys, divided into two
general and six specialized bureaus. The general bureaus (the Supreme
Court Bureau, responsible for felony prosecutions, and the Criminal
Court Bureau, responsible for misdemeanor prosecutions) each absorbs
more manpower than all six specialized bureaus taken together (appeals,
complaints, frauds, homicides, indictments, and rackets). The breakdown is not substantially different in the other large boroughs. The
Staten Island district attorney, by contrast, employs five full-time and
four part-time assistant district attorneys.

Within the broad range of criminal prosecutions, the serious
crimes, not surprisingly, get most of the attention. The district attorneys are elected officials and, therefore, cannot appear to skimp
on prosecution of those accused of the serious crimes that attract
media attention and raise citizen apprehensions. As a result the district attorneys' offices are dominated by criminal prosecution responsibilities and tend to remain aloof from the nonviolent-crime
problems of the typical lower-middle-income or poor City neighborhood.

When it does intrude in the lives of these constituents—particularly
ghetto dwellers—it typically does so as a prosecutor.

Furthermore, because of the district attorneys' heavy criminal
burden and low funding (their 1970 five-borough budget was about
$13.3 million, or 1.6 percent of the City's annual criminal justice
expenditure), a significant number of legal initiatives, which an aggressive "attorney general" (i.e., an attorney not primarily occupied
with enforcement of the criminal code) would undertake on behalf of
a community, are overlooked amidst the flood of criminal business.
Thus, a useful innovation in a decentralized system might be a community attorney with the powers to take legal initiatives in criminal
matters of community concern except criminal prosecutions for more
severe crimes. The latter would be handled as a matter of course by
the appropriate district attorney, who would also have the power to
take up other prosecutions that the community attorney had waived.
This safeguard, akin to those discussed with relation to local legislative powers, would be desirable in order to protect the residents
of other areas from local laxness.

Such an attorney should also have the responsibilities of the
City's corporation counsel to prosecute violations of local housing,
health, and sanitation code regulations. The responsibility of the
corporation counsel for the whole City can too easily downgrade the
importance of single code violations to the lives of neighborhood residents. (To be fair, code enforcement laxness may ultimately be partly
attributable to the judiciary: manpower may better be used elsewhere
when the courts give "wholesale prices" to serious code offenders.)
The switch to administrative enforcement of such violations recommended earlier would not alone provide sufficient change. It would
not increase the responsiveness of enforcement officials to the needs
of individual neighborhoods within the City. Nor would it help to bring
about the necessary unification at the local level of the investigations
and inspections involved in finding violations of health, sanitation, and
housing codes. A community attorney specially charged with code enforcement in a relatively small geographic area, working with the
local environmental services inspection force, would be likely to give
this duty greater priority, whether it involved the prosecution of violations in the courts or in an administrative tribunal.

The Courts

At the outset of this section, it was noted that there are some
things for which the existing centralized system seems well designed
and that these functions should stay centralized. The courts may not
give as many defendants the benefits of a due process trial as they
should, but this points primarily to a need for more courts or for

improving the workings of the courts. If distance, professional objec-
tivity, a "blind" treatment of all individuals as if they were alike, and
a highly controlled procedural system are the underpinnings of due
process, then reformers attempting to expand the opportunity for a
due process trial should be cautious in calling for decentralization of
the court system.

As commonly conceived courts also seem irrelevant to decentralization because each case involves so little policy input, once a legislative code has been framed, and each case (except for the most spec-
tacular) yields so little of consequence to the political arena when it
is resolved. This perspective changes, however, if we stop thinking
of courts as adjudicators and view them as parts of a therapeutic process aimed at conciliation of disputants or reintegration of deviants
into society. The arguments for abandoning the adjudicative model
have most merit in two of the functional areas of the court work that
more localized institutions might assume: those related to juveniles
and to family disputes. New York's present Family Court, reorganized
in 1962 and again nominated for reorganization in 1969, retains the
trappings of the adjudicative model.[18] Judges, thirty to forty years
older and of an entirely different social level from those who typically
appear before them, preside over cases involving assaults between
family members, juvenile delinquency, divorce, and nonsupport. The
social and psychological distance between such a judge and the citizens
before him is difficult or impossible to overcome. The circumstances
of a case cannot be penetrated in the limited time available. Decisions
by fiat rather than conciliation, therefore, become the norm.[19]

A neighborhood conciliation-oriented court might handle segments of this case load in a different manner. Again, we are dealing
with activities such as assaults between family members, juvenile
delinquency that does not reach the level of felony, and marital relationships other than divorce, none of which have significant externalities. There are cases in which adversary due process proceedings are least successful. Here also the existing system is overburdened and undermanned. If a less elaborate alternative could assume a portion of the case load, it would leave the regular court time
to function in cases where its professional skills were relevant.

Such a conciliatory community court might come to be an entry
point for family disputes and some marital issues, such as paternity,
support, and separation; juvenile delinquency; landlord-tenant relations;
small torts and breaches of contract involving only local residents;
and misdemeanors affecting only community members. Typically,
however, it might draw its business from referrals by social agencies,
the community police, the municipal police, the existing court system,
or from voluntary submissions by individuals who wished the services
of the body.

If parties refused to attend, the community court would simply refer the case to the municipal law enforcement agency responsible for proceeding through the existing criminal justice system. This latent threat should often secure the cooperation of those who would be defendants in the court system. A significant attraction to complainants would be that the local institution would be more conveniently located, more considerate, and much faster in processing cases than the municipal system. Moreover, there is evidence that a number of would-be complainants do not proceed through the regular police and court system because they do not want the offender to be "harmed" or think that the incident is a private, not a criminal, matter.[20] For such people an informal, private, noncoercive style might be very appealing.

Correction

The two most salient characteristics of the 13 facilities operated by the City's Department of Corrections are that they are overcrowded and undercorrective. A system with a rated capacity of 7,993 prisoners held 12,238 accused and sentenced adolescents and adults on a typical day in August 1970.[21] In 1970, 68 percent of the department's budget was used to keep its inmates prisoners, 21 percent indirectly supported this operation, and 7 percent was expended on inmates' health needs. Only 4 percent ($2.518 million) was allocated for rehabilitation, or about 0.3 percent of the City's criminal justice budget.

Decentralization of the custodial portion of the corrections system would not be feasible, nor is there any reason to believe that local prisons would be any improvement. But local district governments might take responsibility for a district-based parole and probation system, perhaps coupled with a "prison-alternative" program, like the employment project conceived by the Vera Institute.

In such a program a defendant or a released prisoner would receive assistance on two fronts. A job placement bureau would locate a job offering immediate financial independence and the prospect of permanent employment, while the community representative would assist with personal problems, either associated with the situation that led to the allegation of criminal conduct in the first place or arising from the unprecedented demands of regular employment.[22] The program could be considered to be part of the over-all local district personal services responsibility, able to draw on various aspects of local government services when necessary.

SUMMARY

There is no "right" allocation of responsibility for governmental services between the new local districts and the continuing central City

government. In any process of developing a decentralized government
structure, the initial transfer of responsibility should cover only those
services with respect to which the potential benefits of decentralization
are most clear, as long as the new district governments are given
enough authority to make them important to district residents. Enough
personal and local environmental services would seem to be appropriate for decentralization to assure that local districts would command the active attention of their residents. And there would seem
to be useful roles for the districts to play in planning and housing
programs. Over the longer run local district governments might be
given control over other services, including even police patrol and
fire services, but any such transfers of responsibility should be deferred until the capability of the district governments and the response
of district residents become more clear.

CHAPTER

5

**FISCAL AFFAIRS
AND BUDGETING IN
A DECENTRALIZED CITY**

The system of raising and spending money for a two-tier system of City government must try to balance three somewhat inconsistent goals. First, the second tier, or local units, should be given substantial control over their own expenditures, as a means of fostering local initiative, responsibility, and incentive for economizing. Second, the fiscal arrangements should permit the central City to raise taxes on the basis of ability to pay and to distribute funds on the basis of need. Third, the City must be able to balance its budget. These fiscal and budgeting considerations are of critical importance to the success or failure of any decentralization effort. Variations in ways to raising revenues and allocating expenditures to different City services will often have a greater effect on the lives of New Yorkers, for better or worse, than will new approaches in social work, elementary education, or other local government program activities.

Nevertheless, the opportunities for great changes in fiscal policies and procedures in a decentralized system will be limited by the general urban revenue "crisis." City financing and budgeting are increasingly geared to day-to-day fiscal survival. Mayors strive to maintain a cushion of funds for the inevitable emergencies, cost overruns, and adverse wage settlements. Budget personnel feel compelled to second-guess proposed program changes and operating agency purchasing and staffing decisions in order to limit short-run costs, even at the expense of long-run program effectiveness. Since decentralization will not affect the nationwide urban fiscal squeeze, these tendencies will persist and must be taken into consideration in any two-tier system of urban government.

THE CITY'S PRESENT BUDGET PROCESS

New York City is required by state law to maintain separate capital and current expense budgets. The expense budget is the larger of the two by a factor of four or five and must be balanced on an annual basis. The New York State Constitution limits the amount of real property taxes the City may collect to cover current expenditures to 2.5 percent of the full value of taxable real property located in the City. Other taxes, such as the City's income and sales taxes, supplement the real estate tax, but the imposition of, and rate changes in, these taxes normally require the consent of the state legislature.

The capital budget is financed by borrowing. The state Constitution limits the City's indebtedness to 10 percent of the full value of taxable real property located in the City, except for indebtedness for certain exempt purposes. The City collects real property taxes outside the 2.5 percent limit to pay interest and amortization on this capital debt.

The annual expense budget process begins with the estimation by each operating agency of what it will cost to maintain existing services for the coming fiscal year. The agencies take into account regular salary increases for seniority, salary increases arising from union contract changes, materials and supplies price increases, changes in client population, and changes in federal and state requirements. This preliminary projection, typically put together solely on an aggregate basis without regard to geographic distribution of expenditures, is known as the agency's "mandatory budget" for the coming year, because if funds for these activities are not found, people will have to be laid off and services cut back. The items included in this budget are commonly called "mandatories." In addition each agency also submits its request for new or additional funds, either for expansion of existing programs or for addition of new programs. Such requests are known as "discretionaries."

The Budget Bureau aggregates "mandatories." If the revenue estimates for the coming year are sufficient to fund all mandatories plus some discretionaries, the political barriers to layoffs or service diminution mean that no agency is likely to be cut back. Requests for discretionary funds then will compete for any estimated revenue surplus above the amount needed to cover the mandatories. Budget management becomes tense when estimated revenues will not cover estimated mandatories or, more rarely, when a new or increased program is deemed by the mayor to be of greater urgency than some existing programs.

If cutbacks become necessary, they are rarely made in the open. Instead, the Budget Bureau will try to control agency expenditures—

which are typically 80 to 90 percent wages, salaries, and associated fringe benefits—by stretching out the inevitable delay in filling positions vacated by termination or promotion. The term "accruals" is applied by the Budget Bureau to the savings that are achieved by taking advantage of the gap between actual payrolls and the paper cost of filling all budgeted jobs for 365 days a year. In times of fiscal austerity, the Budget Bureau will simply order an agency to allow for greater-than-normal accruals in the coming fiscal year. The agency is thereby forced to delay longer than it normally would in filling vacated positions, thus cutting its total personnel expenditures for the fiscal year. By imposing increased accruals on agencies, the mayor and his budget staff can lower the rate of expenditure on personnel without appearing actually to have decreased the number of City employees, since the authorized number of employees appearing on the official budget schedules is formally unchanged.

Once the agencies, the Budget Bureau, and the mayor agree on what discretionaries are to be included and on the extent to which any agency is to be required to allow for greater-than-normal accruals, the budget goes to the Board of Estimate and City Council for approval and possible modification and then back to each agency's headquarters budget staff. It is not customary for agencies even to attempt a breakdown by geographic areas until after the Budget Bureau and the mayor have acted. Even then the Budget Bureau tends to limit explicit geographic considerations to decisions about whether to begin, expand, or cut back on specific programs—such as the decision to begin concentrated code enforcement in Brooklyn or terminate a neighborhood health facility in the Bronx. The present budget system includes no formal methods for considering the individual agency or cumulative geographic distribution of expenditures for ongoing citywide programs.*

Once the fiscal year is underway, agency adherence to the defined targets for accruals and to authorized expenditure totals is enforced by Budget Bureau monitoring of the rate of expenditure of each agency. If there are unanticipated expenditures or revenue shortfalls during the fiscal year, the Budget Bureau may return to each agency to negotiate for increased accruals. The bureau obtains cooperation through its power to refuse permission for individual personnel

------

*This is no longer true for the new community school districts. Under Section 2590-i of the New York State Education Law, Board of Education requests for funds for local school purposes are built up from requests submitted by each individual local school district, and appropriated funds are required to be allocated to the local districts on a formula basis.

appointments. To circumvent this power an agency must be able to convince the mayor to reverse the Budget Bureau—a task that only agencies with significant autonomous political power can contemplate.

When revenues lag badly or expenditures swell, as in fiscal years 1970/71 and 1971/72, agencies may be forbidden to fill any vacancies without specific approval from the bureau. In addition, the Budget Bureau may also control nonpersonnel expenditures by requiring that all orders for certain kinds of goods or contractual services pass through the Budget Bureau for prior approval.

The Office of the Comptroller is a second source of fiscal power in the City. The comptroller makes all of the City's payments. Before a check is issued, the comptroller's staff conducts a preaudit to make certain the City's obligation is valid; they also conduct widespread postexpenditure audits to make certain that funds were properly spent. Much of the comptroller's power stems from the City Charter requirement that no salary be paid by the comptroller unless there is a scheduled position (a "line") for that salary recipient.[1] The official City expense budget, therefore, must include a massive set of supporting schedules listing each separate personnel position: formal amendment of these schedules is required before a new job position may be created, even if the agency is willing to trade off an existing position. In addition the comptroller requires a certificate that the payee is qualified for, and appropriately appointed to, the position. In theory the Department of Personnel provides that certificate, but in practice even this notification passes through the Budget Bureau, thus reinforcing the Budget Bureau's power to enforce required accruals.

The present concentration of decision-making authority in the Budget Bureau probably reduces the incentive for individual City agencies to develop their own program plans and budgets or to evaluate the effectiveness of their programs. Agency heads know that their decisions in budget preparation and budget administration will be second-guessed in detail by relatively low-ranking budget examiners. The frequency of budget reallocations during the year among the divisions in an agency, or even among agencies, further limits administrative initiative in City agencies, because no one will ever believe that fund allocations can be counted upon for planning purposes.

In spite of the recognized adverse impact of the existing system on agency initiative and planning capacity, City budgeting officials consider the present centralized system essential. They argue that major City services—fire, police, sanitation, schools—have to be provided, come what may. If an agency uses up its annual budget allotment before the end of the fiscal year, the Budget Bureau and the mayor will be under great political pressure to find the necessary dollars to keep the police cars rolling or the children in school. Moreover, there are emergency expenditures and unanticipated labor contracts that cannot be allowed for in the annual budget cycle. Because increasing taxes in the middle of the year is an unpalatable alternative, the mayor and the Budget Bureau feel they must have tight controls over agency rates of expenditure and must also have plenary power to reallocate funds within and among agencies.*

This inescapable concern over solvency is the source of one of the three goals of a two-tier urban fiscal system set forth at the beginning of this chapter. If new local units depend in any way upon the central City for funds, the relationship must be one that gives the central City mayor either the legal and political capacity to refuse requests for additional funds by local districts that run short or close and continuing control over the rate of local district expenditures from the beginning of the fiscal year.

Some other caveats about fiscal aspects of decentralization may appropriately be noted at this point. Whatever the system chosen, real property assessment should remain a central function as long as real estate taxes form an important part of central City revenues. Otherwise, individual districts could affect the taxes imposed to finance central City responsibilities simply by varying their assessment practices. Nor would it make sense to decentralize the ministerial task of tax collection. Tax administration is susceptible to substantial scale economies. Efforts to administer tax collection on a decentralized basis would probably lessen the number of tax dollars collected per dollar of administrative costs.

Lastly, decentralization is unlikely to have a positive impact on the supply of funds available to the City, at least in the short or medium run, and is likely to result in an actual increase in administrative, or "overhead," costs. If local districts were given some marginal taxing capacity, they might be willing to raise funds to be spent locally for increased services when they would not consent to an equivalent increase in central tax rates. But they would not be enthusiastic about raising funds locally if this meant that central City funds would be diverted away from them for use elsewhere.

----

*In the spring of 1972, Mayor Lindsay authorized some of the City's operating agencies to hire, promote, and transfer employees without Budget Bureau approval. It is too soon to tell whether this form of horizontal decentralization will increase efficiency as hoped or to tell how completely or for how long the Budget Bureau will in fact relinquish its review authority. The New York Times, March 20, 1972, p. 33, col. 1.

FISCAL ALTERNATIVES
IN A TWO-TIER SYSTEM

Several approaches for financing a system of two-tier government in New York City are theoretically possible. The four major possibilities summarized in the following paragraphs assume a mixture of central and local district service delivery responsibilities, such as that set out in Chapter 4.

Autonomy

The most far-reaching approach would be complete fiscal autonomy for new, local, second-tier government districts, with each district relying on local property, income, and sales to generate taxes to pay for its own services. The closest American analogy would be the relationship between municipality and county in those states where the counties have retained the responsibility for important municipal services. The municipality is fiscally and politically independent of the county. The municipal resident pays both municipal and county taxes and looks to the municipality for some services and to the county for others.

Under such a division of powers and responsibilities, each local district in a two-tier government for New York City would deal directly with the state and federal governments for grant-in-aid funds in programs over which it had service delivery responsibilities. The central City would not be in the business of allocating or channeling state or federal funds to local districts.

Multipurpose Block Grants

A less-complete fiscal division between central City and local districts would provide for block grants from central City to the local district governments to cover all services and activities for which they are responsible. These grants would be supplemented by any revenues raised by local district taxes or received by local districts through state on federal transfers. Such block grants would be an intra-City analogue to state and federal revenue sharing.

With this approach, local districts could still maintain direct relations with federal and state grant programs in areas of local district program responsibility. Block grant transfers from the central City to local districts would leave the choice of program priorities and delivery methods to the local districts, within limits

imposed by state and federal law. Grant amounts would vary from
district to district, depending on district wealth, population, and general
need factors. This would be somewhat similar to the system used in
Greater London. There, the boroughs levy their own taxes and receive
grants and transfers directly from the national government. At the
same time the poorer boroughs receive real property tax equalization
grants from the GLC.

Function-by-Function Formula Grants

A third approach would give local districts substantial freedom
in their choice of program methods and program goals, but would
concentrate basic resource allocation decisions in the central City
government. Under such an approach the central City would grant
funds to local districts for each program category for which responsibility had been transferred to the local districts. The amounts of these
functional grants in each program category would vary from district
to district in accordance with a formula based on factors indicating
relative district needs. Federal and state grant-in-aid funds for
services performed by local districts would be allocated among local
districts by the central City, much as the present Title 1 education
funds are allocated among the community school districts by the
central school board. The annual City budget would therefore consist
of a number of appropriations to retained central City functions (e.g.,
fire, water supply, waste disposal, and transportation) and other
appropriations for transfer to local districts (e.g., elementary education, social services, health services, and parks and recreation).

Inclusion in Present Budget System

The least fiscal independence would exist in a system in which
all City taxation and federal and state grants were centralized and in
which the local districts would have to come to the central City with
budget requests, just as citywide agencies now must present annual
budget requests. There would be no direct relations between local
districts and federal and state funding sources, and there would be
little room for autonomous local district decisions on program priorities and program goals. All significant local district program and
fiscal decisions would be subjected to central scrutiny. Although
budgetary detail might not be the same for local districts as it is for
central City agency budget submissions, budget examiners, or their
successors at the central level, would be able to set local priorities
by being able to control local reallocation of existing funds and to
control the programs to which new funds are applied.

Advantages and Disadvantages
of Possible Models

The fourth of the alternatives presented above would not offer
sufficient local district autonomy to satisfy such goals of decentralization as local capacity to tailor services to local needs. Policy control
is inseparable from control over money, and in this alternative local
district money control would be less extensive than the power of the
present community school boards. The districts would have no more
autonomy than federal regional officials have from central agency
offices in Washington—an autonomy that is formally asserted to exist
but that is cut back whenever regional decisions pose any likelihood
of embarrassing the Administration.

The first alternative would be unsatisfactory on equity grounds,
because of the uneven geographic pattern of receipts from property
and nonproperty taxes in the City. This pattern bears little relation
to the concentration of most of the City's social service, health, and
welfare expenditures and of its greatest public education challenges
in perhaps 25 percent of the City's area. These mismatches of revenues
and expenditures are at the root of current proposals to federalize or
otherwise remove from local governments the bulk of the income-
redistributive health, welfare, and poverty program expenditures and
to elevate fiscal responsibility for schools to the state level. Until
such changes come about there is no case for local unit fiscal autonomy
in a two-tier pattern of government in New York City. Even now, the
City is admittedly not a very appropriate base for income-redistributive
taxation. But fragmentation of the City's tax base would make the
situation worse by increasing the disparities between the capacities
of wealthy and poor districts to support governmental services. Fiscal
autonomy would be feasible, therefore, only if the federal and state
governments collect a much larger proportion of all taxes and either
assume financial responsibility for a far greater proportion of services
now provided by local government or make very large block grant
transfers to even out funds available to local governments, regardless
of their own tax base. Until such a reordering takes place, any fiscal
system should involve central City government retention of primary
responsibilities for tax assessment and collection on a uniform citywide basis and for distribution of tax revenues as needed throughout
the City.

This leaves the second and third approaches (or some combination of them) as possible fiscal patterns for a two-tier structure of
government in the City. To begin with, any system of central distribution of funds to politically autonomous local units of government with
the responsibility for ongoing programs probably ought to provide for
the determination of relative district shares on some kind of a formula

basis. There are two reasons for this assertion. First, a formula
system would inhibit the use of the central budget process as a tool
for fiscal retribution against currently unpopular local district governments. Second, difficult-to-change principles for determining district
shares would help prevent the budget process at the central level from
deteriorating into a bastard version of the fourth alternative model.
Without fixed formulas for evaluating relative local district entitlement
to funds, the central City would be likely to evaluate competing local
district claims to funds based on needs and priorities as determined
by central officials.

For both the multipurpose block grant model and the functional
allocation model, use of formulas would mean that the issue of the
allocation of funds among districts would be largely separated from
the question of determining the total funds to be allocated by the central
City for the use of the local districts as a whole. Once the total allotment of funds were determined for all district activities or for any
functional area, the taking away of funds from an unpopular district
would require the considerable effort of rewriting a formula or formulas
in terms that would penalize the offending district but no others.
Whether the basis of the allocation formula were per capita income or
number of children in school, this would be a difficult task.

The annual budgetary process at the central level, in either of
these two models, would require an initial fundamental decision: How
much money should be transferred to local districts to pay for services
they deliver and how much should be spent on programs and activities
for which the central City government remains responsible? In the
multipurpose block grant model, the decision would be phrased in
terms of whether the net demands of local districts outweigh the
demands of central City-provided services. In the functional allocation
model the decision would be similar to the present budget process:
Should more money be made available for schools, or police, or
recreation?

This comparatively simple approach is complicated by the
tendency for the costs of providing a given level of service to increase:
in New York City parlance, "mandatories" increase from year to year
at constant service levels. The budget process must decide which, if
any, functions (at which level of government) are to be augmented,
which are to receive only enough funds to maintain the prior service
level, and which are to be cut back.

Program cost changes that arguably constitute "mandatories"
arise in four principal ways: (a) through increases in workload under
circumstances in which the government cannot choose those who will
receive services (more persons eligible for welfare), so that the
services received per service recipient would drop if resource inputs
remained constant; (b) through increases in the costs of materials

and supplies; (c) through changes in the quality or quantity of services required to be supplied by law (e.g., state-mandated higher welfare levels); and (d) through increases in public employee wages and salaries.

Annual budgets must reflect these changes, whether they have already occurred or are to be expected from the next round of price increases or collective bargaining agreements. But the system should be structured to encourage central agencies and new local district governments to respond to cost increases as economically as possible. By explicitly reflecting increases in each of the four categories, the existing budget system fails to encourage agencies to economize by shifting from rapidly rising cost items, such as, for example, wages of municipal employees, to less rapidly rising alternatives, such as, perhaps, audio-visual teaching equipment or use of contracts with private enterprise to perform government-financed services. In a two-tier system in which the bulk of local district funds represent transfers from the central City to local districts, budgeting techniques that made it easy to pass on all local district cost increases could destroy the system. If it became normal for the central City to pick up all local district cost increases on a dollar-for-dollar basis, the central City would soon be compelled to control local district expenditures in a detailed manner inconsistent with local budgetary freedom and flexibility.

Therefore, in either a multipurpose block grant or a formula allocation model, the budgetary system should seek to reflect cost increases only in a relatively generalized manner, rather than on a person-by-person or item-by-item basis. This would mean, of course, that compensation for cost increases (through increases in block grants or increases in specific functional grants) would always seem to penalize or benefit some districts more than others. For example, if general labor costs should increase, a roughly offsetting percentage increase in the multipurpose block grant would be of relatively greater benefit to those districts that utilize less labor-intensive ways of providing municipal services. While superficially this result might seem inequitable, it makes sense in terms of effective resource allocation. If one input becomes more costly relative to other inputs, continuing to use the same amount of the more costly input should not be a painless decision.

THE BUDGET PROCESS UNDER
A MULTIPURPOSE BLOCK GRANT SYSTEM

Under a multipurpose block grant system, the annual central City budget process might take the following form:

1. The Budget Bureau would determine whether there were changes in the workload for central City-operated programs and would estimate the enlarged or reduced resource commitments that would be necessary were those programs to be maintained at their present level.

2. The bureau would determine whether the variables in the formula that determined relative local district entitlement to a central City multipurpose block grant had changed over the preceding year. Since there are unlikely to be significant pressures to reduce the total amount distributed through multipurpose block grants to the local districts (particularly if welfare transfer payments remain a central responsibility), the Budget Bureau would probably take as a starting point the total grant amount for the preceding year and see how it would be distributed among the local districts in the light of the changes in relative entitlement produced by changes in population, relative poverty, and other variables in the distribution formula.

3. This preliminary budget would form the basis for political negotiations among the mayor, the central City legislative body, central operating agency administrators, and the local districts. The ultimate decision on whether more, less, or the same amount of funds would be allocated to each central City program and to the multipurpose block grant fund would be a political decision and not a rule-based decision defined in terms of cost increases or workload increases.

4. The final budget submitted to the central City legislative body would then include the following: (a) a section for programs that remain as central City responsibilities, probably quite similar to the present City expense budget, except that budget information ought when possible to be broken down in terms of administrative districts covering the same geographic areas as are covered by the new local district governmental units; (b) a lump request for an appropriation to the multipurpose block grant fund, providing a breakdown of how that total amount will be allocated among the local districts and a narrative justification of changes from the preceding year's total; and (c) recommendations on any taxation changes needed to finance increases in the block grant fund or in appropriations to central City agencies.

THE BUDGET PROCESS UNDER
A FUNCTIONAL ALLOCATION SYSTEM

The major substantive difference between the multipurpose block grant and the functional allocation alternative is that, under the latter scheme, the allocations to local districts would be made in terms of broad program categories, such as education, health services, social services, or environmental services. In addition federal and

state funds would be channeled almost exclusively through the central
City, and the local districts would be less likely to be given taxing
authority.

Once a functional allocation system were underway, a series of
formulas would determine the proportions in which total City allocations
of funds for each program category would be divided among the local
districts. The total amount of funds available to each local district
would be the sum of the categorical allocations from the central City,
plus any revenues generated by the local district government from
local taxes or user charges.

Even under a functional allocation system, some revenue should
probably be locally generated. Community Action and Model Cities
experience suggests that funds raised exclusively by other levels of
government are not treated as seriously as local tax funds and that
local residents do not seem to hold their officials accountable for 100
percent grant funds, particularly when there is no requirement that
the funds be used to accomplish any particular objective. It is probably
true that pressures for accountability would increase were local
officials responsible for a full range of local services rather than the
kind of marginal services provided in Community Action and Model
Cities, regardless of the financing methods used. But economy in the
use of public resources and local concern over the performance of
local officials should both be heightened if at least part of the dollars
spent at the district level were extracted from local pockets in a
traceable manner.

The annual budget process would then be similar to that outlined
for the multipurpose block grant model:

1. The Budget Bureau would determine whether there were
changes in the workload for central City-operated programs and the
enlarged or reduced resource commitments that would be necessary
for such programs to be maintained at their present levels.

2. The next step would be to determine the extent to which
factors in the allocation formulas had changed since the preceding
budget season. Since the formulas by themselves would not define
any particular level of expenditures but only the relative entitlement
of each district to a total pot, a reasonable starting point in the absence
of clear political pressures for an increase or decrease in public
service levels would be to use the current year's total appropriation
for each program category as the initial estimate for the upcoming
year. If there were no relative changes among the local districts in
the variables that make up a particular formula, then the district
distribution in that category would not change. If the variables had
changed, then the distribution among districts would change.

3. As in the multipurpose block grant model, the overall budget

recommendations for the total appropriation of each category would
be determined by political judgments. The political judgments would
reflect the relative demand for central and local services, the tolerance
of City residents and businesses for tax increases, and the complaints
that would surely come from any district in which the application of
the formula resulted in a substantial grant reduction.

4. The preceding balancing process would be more difficult than
it would be in the block grant model, because in that model the mayor
would assess the overall demand for additional local funds versus
the overall willingness of the City to settle for increased citywide
taxes. He would not need to decide whether he was supporting the
local school lobby or the local sanitation lobby when he requested an
increase in the block grant appropriation. In the functional allocation
model the mayor would find it necessary to respond to pressures for
increasing specific kinds of funds (school dollars) at the expense of
other funds (parks and recreational dollars).

5. The central City budget document that resulted would thus
include allocations to central City services, a series of appropriations
for the program categories in which central City extended support to
local districts, and a revenue proposal explaining how the necessary
revenue to support the proposed expenditures and transfers would be
realized.

Although the last two items look similar to the parallel items
for central budgeting in the block grant model, they would be considerably more complex, because central transfers to local districts and
central revenue-raising proposals would have to take into account
state and federal transfers and grants-in-aid to the City. The formula
allocation to an individual district would not be a lump sum of City-
raised tax funds, but rather a mixture of federal and state funds with
varying degrees of restriction on their uses, City-raised funds that
were required to be spent for various purposes, and unrestricted
City-raised funds.

CHOOSING A MODEL FOR A NEWLY
DECENTRALIZED CITY

For a city that is moving from a unitary to a two-tier form of
government, the choice between these two fiscal models should not be
governed only by the considerations laid out in the previous outline.
Also relevant are the kinds of performance demands that would be
made upon the institutional capacity of second-tier, local units of
government. In a unitary city, such localized institutional capacity
by hypothesis is rudimentary or nonexistent: there are no governmental

powers at the decentralized unit level and, hence, no local experience in fiscal management and budgeting procedures, relations with state and federal funding sources, or labor-management relations. Because the functional allocation method would be simpler for local districts to manage and would spare them from most or all of the problems created by direct relations with state and federal funding sources, it represents a more appropriate initial pattern for structuring fiscal relations in a two-tier city government system.

ISSUES IN CREATING A FUNCTIONAL
ALLOCATION SYSTEM

Shifting to any kind of a two-tier system would involve transition problems, unless the prechangeover allocation of public expenditures fortuitously happened to coincide with the allocation produced by the formula chosen for the initial year. This is unlikely to be the case, so that the first few years of any transition to a two-tier governmental pattern would be likely to involve the gradual reduction of gaps between actual allocations and formula allocations for each local function.

In addition to the difficulties raised by the disparities in physical plant or capital equipment in different parts of the City, a major transition hurdle in any formula grant system would be the fact that under the existing system, equal dollar allocations buy different amounts of services in different sections of the City. Teacher salaries, for example, are a function of seniority, so that a district with relatively young employees could purchase more hours of employee time per budget dollar than a district with a heavy concentration of high seniority employees. Work rules also would differ from area to area, because, for example, teachers get more preparation periods per week in ghetto schools and more firemen ride trucks in inner-City areas than in outer Queens. Equal dollar expenditures would therefore purchase different output in different districts. In addition some costs, either by necessity or by union contract, are not proportional to workload. Sanitation garage superintendents and school principals are not paid in direct proportion to the payroll and workload of their facilities, but rather on a roughly uniform basis across the City. An elementary school principal, costing $22,500 per year, adds $45 to per/pupil cost in a 500-student school, but only $18.75 in a 1,200-student school. Moreover, rules that specify maximum workloads per employee will restrict reallocations of the existing labor force according to need. If a contract requires four men per truck, resources cannot be redistributed away from a low-need district.

There are more fundamental questions about the viability of a two-tier fiscal system based on central allocations of funds to local

units of government for specific service categories. Is it possible to
construct fair formulas with the data that can reasonably be expected
to be available? How can the notion of formula allocation of funds to
specific service categories be reconciled with the desire to give local
districts significant discretion in the choice of methods of service
delivery and in the choice of services supplied? How would funds be
channeled to local districts once they were appropriated? How, or to
what extent, would the central City monitor the use of funds by local
districts? Could federal and state grant programs be channeled
through the central City government to local districts without imposing
burdensome accounting and reporting requirements?

Creating Formulas
for the Allocation of Funds

The simplest formula would be an equal per capita allocation.
Annual budget decisions then would be made in terms of the dollars
per capita to be devoted to each public service in the City. But public
services are not consumed on an equal per capita basis: school-age
children, the poor, and the aged place the heaviest burdens on local
government. Nor can a per capita distribution of funds easily compensate for the highly uneven distribution of goods and services
generated by the private sector of the economy.

Allocations of funds to local districts for the performance of the
services transferred to them thus would have to take into account
factors other than population, if there were to be fair formulas in
light of contemporary standards of entitlement to public services.
For each service category for which there were a separate fund allocation, it would be necessary to identify the variables that provide a
fair approximation of local district need for that service and to translate differences into measures of local district need and then into
different dollar allocations.

The second part of this task is likely to be more difficult than
it sounds, particularly for personal service programs, where goals
are defined in terms of knowledge, or skills, or client satisfaction.
Deviation from national average reading levels might be accepted as
a suitable measure of relative local district educational need. But
there is no way to predict the relationship between giving additional
dollars to the district and district movement toward average reading
levels. Therefore, there would be no objective way of assigning weights
to interdistrict differences in reading levels in order to determine the
relative dollar entitlement of each district. It would be a political
rather than a technical decision that said a district with reading levels
two years below normal should receive twice the bonus of a district

with reading levels one year below normal, as distinguished from four times the bonus or one and one-half times the bonus.

Moreover, in areas such as sanitation or preventive health care, where one might be able to determine relationships between costs and goal achievements with some confidence, extreme deviations from per capita average distributions for a given service might not be politically acceptable. At the least each district might have to receive some minimum amount of funds for every program area, even though most residents of that district relied little or not at all on some public services. The actual dynamics of any shift to a two-tier structure of government for New York City would probably yield formulas that represented relatively closely the distributional status quo at the time of decentralization. Changes in the formulas thereafter would be incremental and would be justified in each instance by specific allegations of inequity in the existing formula, rather than by comparison to some ideal formula.

There are several general principles of economy in identifying and using measures of comparative need. Insistence on accuracy of measurement of need should not be pursued at the cost of forgoing more readily determinable measures of need or measures that can be taken to apply to several different program areas. Some rough measures of need are already available through the data collection operation of City, state, and federal government agencies; the cost of obtaining more accurate data might well outweigh any gains in increased accuracy. Also, the more detailed and precise a measure or index of need purports to be, the more room there would be for ultimately fruitless debate over the weight assigned it in creating an allocation formula.

The difficulty of measuring need in a specific service category is illustrated by education, where the decentralized community school boards have brought a general urgency to the question of defining comparative district need. As long as educational attendance is required, the basic workload can be defined in terms of the number of students to be provided with physical facilities and teaching staff. Minimum facilities and staffing requirements may be defined by state law or union contract. But most people think that such simple calculations are poorly related to educational need if the purpose of education is to equip students to earn a living and to understand something of the world about them. When students must not only be contained but also taught, the comparative ease or difficulty with which students can be coaxed, coerced, or encouraged into learning becomes relevant in determining the necessary commitment of resources to educational purposes.

One way of determining the comparative difficulty of the educational task among different groups of students would be to define an educational goal, such as national average reading levels, and determine the deviations from that goal. Another system would be based on the "culturally deprived children" hypothesis and assume that educational difficulty is a function of the incidence of broken homes, poverty, lack of parental education, malnutrition, and crowded housing.[2] These two ways of evaluating comparative need differ substantially. Use of performance measures, such as deviation from average reading levels, seems to reward poor performance and to encourage cyclical fluctuations in resource allocation to individual districts. Use of predictive measures, such as poverty or housing quality, depends on data that cities often do not possess with any accuracy and on uncertain hypotheses about the relationship of home environment to educational achievement.

A complicating issue is the probability that alternative measures of comparative need would produce quite different rankings of need. A study done for the New York City Board of Education in 1970 investigated the need rankings produced by three separate measures of need: (a) participation in the free school lunch program (measuring local district poverty); (b) English-language difficulties; and (c) reading retardation levels. If the rank order of the 31 local districts for any two of these variables is compared, individual district positions vary by 5 or more places in from 9 out of 31 instances (free lunch versus reading retardation) to 15 out of 31 instances (free lunch versus English language difficulty).[3] When there are a number of readily ascertainable variables deemed relevant to measuring program need, it might therefore be politically expedient to utilize a combined, equally-weighted index despite uncertainty as to the magnitude of the contribution of any of the variables to overall educational need.

The ultimate decisions on the formulas to be used in education and in other areas would, therefore, require political judgments, based in part on shorter-run considerations of political feasibility and expediency and hopefully also on longer-run social goals and principles of equity and fairness in the distribution of public expenditures. There would be little of the "scientific" about formula distributions, and no particular formula for allocating resources among local districts would be defensible as <u>the</u> logically correct formula.

Local District Flexibility
in Program Choice

One of the common arguments for decentralization is that it permits local districts to substitute their priorities for expenditure priorities forced upon them by the existing citywide government. If local districts could and would do a more accurate job of reflecting local priorities than a more distant central government, central allocations of funds among program categories would appear to inhibit the capacity of local government to be responsive.

The same dilemma is at the heart of much of the present controversy over federal revenue sharing. Many fear that unrestricted federal revenue sharing would be used by states and localities simply to reduce their own tax loads or, in the alternative, would not be used to benefit those most in need of increased public services. Current proposals of the Nixon Administration for both general and special revenue-sharing programs recognize this concern by requiring that large blocks of transferred federal funds be spent in defined program areas rather than simply at local discretion. But to the extent that these federal funds come with program strings attached, they would not really be revenue sharing or block grants but very broad categorical program grants—analogous to the kind of formula-based functional allocations we have been discussing for a two-tier government in New York City.

One way of resolving the conflict between central allocation and local priorities at the City level would involve a combination of the functional grant and block grant approaches. Local districts could be given some unrestricted funds in addition to their functional grants or local districts could be allowed to reallocate some percentage of each functional grant to use as they chose. Flexibility would also be enhanced by ensuring that the functional grants from the central City are broadly defined: "elementary and secondary education," not "salaries," "educational materials," or "bilingual education." Finally, local districts could be permitted to raise some taxes locally or to impose user charges.

One could also resolve the contradiction by continuing to determine local district fiscal allocations on a function-by function basis but giving local districts complete discretion to spend the funds as they saw fit. But complete flexibility at the local district level would cause local districts to claim increased allocations from the central City in those programs or services in which their proportionate shares of the total City appropriation were the largest, as determined by the applicable distributive formula. If a particular district wanted more money for sanitation and received 2 percent of the sanitation appropriation but 4 percent of the parks and recreation appropriation, it would make more sense for that district to lobby for an increase in the parks appropriation. This incentive to a revenue-maximization bargaining strategy in the annual budgeting process would have two undesirable results. It would turn the annual budget process into a shell game, in which the public would find it extremely difficult to separate real district needs from shadow needs, asserted because of their favorable revenue consequences. It would also make it much easier to use the

annual budget process to aid and penalize districts. The mayor or
City Council could increase appropriations in functional areas in which
the fiscal allocation formulas favored influential districts and cut back
on appropriations in functional areas that favored unpopular districts.

The difficulties attributable to complete local district flexibility
in a formula-based program allocation system would seem, therefore,
to outweigh the philosophical arguments for complete deference to
local priorities, at least in the early years of any decentralization.
If such deference were deemed of overriding importance, the appropriate move would be to the multipurpose block grant system. That
system focuses attention on the total level of resource transfers from
the central City to local districts and would avoid the kinds of juggling
of the annual budget process that would occur if central appropriations
based on program need could be used without restriction by local
districts. If this jump to the multipurpose block grant approach were
not made, flexibility should be limited to that which could be achieved
through keeping the functional grants broad, by including small, supplemental block grants to the local districts and by authorizing local
districts to raise marginal funds through supplementary local taxes
and user charges.

Earmarked Federal and State Grants

The City is fortunate in that few of the receipts from City-
imposed taxes are earmarked for specific uses. On the other hand
many of the federal and state programs that support City expense
budget outlays specify the purposes for which funds may be used or
otherwise limit the freedom of discretion of the City in spending the
funds. These limitations and conditions would complicate a two-tier
system in which state and federal funds flowed to local districts
through a central budget process.

Fortunately, it seems to be the rule that the larger the federal
or state grant, the less restrictive it is. The 1970/71 expense budget
included about $1,316 million of federal funds. But over 75 percent of
this was in direct or indirect payments to individuals for welfare and
medical expenses. The City plays no role in selecting recipients of
Medicaid and Medicare funds. It simply joins the state and federal
government in reimbursing health professionals and health institutions
that render services to eligible or poor patients. While the City does
process applications for welfare assistance to the aged and disabled
and to families with dependent children, the proposed decentralization
plan would not delegate this function to local district governments.
Hence, decentralization would have no effect on the $1 billion of federal
Medicaid, Medicare, and welfare funds.

Of the remaining federal funds, $117 million were Title 1 elemen-
tary and secondary education (ESEA) grants, $65 million were Model
Cities grants, and $44 million were poverty program grants. All of
these grants are earmarked for areas of the City where needs are
greatest, and all may be used to pay for a wide variety of activities.
The City already successfully allocates ESEA funds among 31 school
districts, poverty program funds among 25 community corporations,
and Model Cities funds among three model neighborhoods. Decentralization would not materially change this allocation process or the rules
under which these federal funds are used.

About $1,446 million of 1970/71 state categorical funds were in
decentralizable program areas.* In addition there was another $424
million in the City's 1970/71 expense budget in unrestricted state
grants, primarily under the state general revenue-sharing programs.
The total $1,446 million included $552 million in net support state aid
to the Board of Education, $43 million in urban poverty school aid,
$111 million in the charitable institutions budget, $77 million in
Medicaid contributions, and $489 million in the Department of Social
Services budget. All of these were relatively untied funds, were
intended for direct or indirect transfers to individuals under state or
federally established eligibility criteria, or were available without
significant strings across a broad program area, such as education.
They constituted 88 percent of the total state categorical aid.

Thus, there were only about $170 million in state aid and $50-
$75 million in federal aid that could cause substantial problems in
trying to adjust to a two-tier governmental system. This does not
mean that coping with a two-tier system under the existing maze of
state and federal assistance programs would be easy. Permissible
allocations probably would not conform precisely to City estimates
of local need. And it might be difficult to make the local districts
directly responsible to the federal government for the use of those
funds, even if the central City were allowed by the federal government
to allocate them among local districts.

With the small federal demonstration grant programs, it might
even prove easier to allow local districts to negotiate directly with
the appropriate federal agencies. Many of the small planning and
demonstration programs for which funds are available involve grants
that range from $100,000 to $1 million per year, with local matching
requirements ranging from 0 to 50 percent. Local districts could

---

*Another $175 million of state funds are earmarked for programs
not suggested herein as amenable to decentralization—largely involving
courts and correction systems and higher education.

provide the requisite local matching contribution if they had access even to small amounts of untied resources through the kind of local taxation discussed below or through small, supplemental block grants from the central City.

Alternatively, in many of the small programs, the City could be directly responsible to the state or federal funding agency, as it is today. A retained, innovation-oriented HRA or Board of Education could serve primarily as a vehicle for gathering small grants for experimental and innovative purposes from the Department of Health, Education, and Welfare or other funding sources and apportioning those grants to various local districts. Even if local districts demanded to go directly to the funding source, such a central agency staff could be retained to help prepare or review applications. Such a central role might be more efficient than the development of "grantsmanship" capacity in each of 30 or 40 local districts.

Moreover, if the Nixon Administration's proposals to combine and reduce radically the number of federal categorical aid programs were carried out, funneling federal aid through the central City to local districts would become much simpler. The broader a category, the less room there would be for detailed scrutiny and review by a state plan agency or federal officials. Need-based allocation principles should make it relatively easy to pass funds through a central City budget office and remain in compliance with federal requirements— as with present Title 1 education assistance, with its relatively simple grant calculation formula and maintenance of effort requirement.[4]

ISSUES IN BUDGET ADMINISTRATION

In any system of government there must be some rules about the way in which payrolls are drawn up, the identity of the officials responsible for actually writing checks, the rate at which funds can be expended, and other budget administration matters. In present centralized New York City, the Budget Bureau and the comptroller between them hold all the fiscal aces: materials and supplies, contracts for services, and the hiring of new employees can be held up practically indefinitely by the budget director and the comptroller.

The web of controls exercised by the Budget Bureau and the comptroller, and outlined at the beginning of this chapter, is intended to prevent misappropriation of public funds and to ensure that appropriations are not exhausted before the end of the fiscal year. Unless these controls are loosened as part of any decentralization, local district budgetary freedom to set program priorities and choose techniques of providing services would be rendered meaningless. Central authorities could not be permitted to second-guess hiring, materials, or contract decisions for services that were nominally a local district responsibility. If central review power existed central officials would feel it politically necessary to exercise that power because they could expect to be held responsible for the inevitable dishonesty or disaster that would occur in some new local district.

A desirable and perhaps even essential corollary of not giving central City officials expenditure and hiring controls over decentralized local district governments in the formal legal recognition that personnel or purchase contracts concluded by an individual local district would not constitute legal obligations of the central City. Otherwise, the central City would be in the position of having to make good any local district fiscal default or mismanagement. If local district obligations could be enforced against the central City, it would never consent, and never should be expected to consent, to any considerable local fiscal autonomy.

In theory, the shift to a two-tier system in which services were being provided to discrete subsections of the City should reduce pressures on the City as a whole to make up shortfalls in local district budgets. The existence of a series of local sanitation budgets, for example, rather than a single citywide budget, would isolate the effects of overexpenditures. A district that exhausted its sanitation allocation might come crying for more money to the central City. But it would be unlikely to get a great deal of support from other districts that had been more careful with their expenditures.

Nevertheless, the central City would still have substantial concern over the rate of local district expenditures. If most or all districts overspent, pressure on the central City government to come up with more money would be as great as in today's system, in which the more-or-less unified community school districts could convert deliberate appropriation overruns into a successful campaign for more money. Furthermore, City tax receipts are stretched out over the fiscal year, so that the annual transfers to local districts would have to be stated in terms of time-phased transfers rather than lump-sum, start-of-the-fiscal-year transfers. Central transfers to local districts thus would most likely be in terms of monthly allocations, stated as part of the budget document. Individual districts that wished to spend in a different time pattern might be permitted to do so by requesting the central City to utilize tax anticipation certificates, but the cost of such acceleration should be charged to the local district.

Under either fiscal grant system it would be possible to make local districts entirely responsible for their own fiscal management and payroll administration. It would also be possible to retain at a central level the ministerial task of writing checks and accounting, while leaving policy control over expenditure decisions in the hands of local districts. This second alternative would permit the retention of the scale economies in centralized payroll and accounting services and allow local district officials to concentrate on organizing the provision of services rather than on the provision of honest, efficient local paymaster and accounting operations. More practically, it might overcome some of the initial fears of people who feel that decentralization offers too much risk of fiscal abuse and mismanagement.

But if the comptroller were to have any accounting and paymaster responsibility for local districts, he could not be given the same power to second-guess local districts that he has with respect to central City agencies under the present City Charter. This means that the comptroller should not be empowered to look behind the local district payment vouchers or payrolls before paying against them. Any audit role left with the comptroller over local districts should be a postaudit responsibility, like that possessed by the state comptroller.

If a local district submitted payrolls and vouchers for nonpersonnel services that exceeded funds alloted to it, the comptroller should have the authority to refuse to pay more than the total specified in the expenditure plan. As a sanction against excessive payroll requests from local districts, the comptroller could be required to pay the lowest salaried persons first and then proceed upward along the salary scale until the available funds were exhausted. Such a rule would make the responsible local district senior administrative officials bear the burden of appropriation overruns. The comptroller would not be in the position of making discretionary decisions about who does and who does not get paid at the local district level.

The placing of fiscal- as well as program-management authority at the local district level would create a concomitant need for local district fiscal-management capacity. Someone would need to authorize payment of salaries and expenses. Each district would need to allocate its expenses over the period between monthly or quarterly draw-downs from the central City or would need to balance expenses against its own tax revenues. If funds were to be transferred from one function to another, some local agency would have to keep track of the changes and ensure that restricted state or federal categorical funds were not wrongfully shifted. If programs were to be planned as well as carried out at the local level, there would have to be some capacity to evaluate program alternatives and to display them in a manner permitting rational choice among them. This means that there would have to be a miniature budget bureau at the local district level, with the capacity to control accruals and expenditure rates, ensure compliance with personnel ceilings, and serve as a general fiscal-management watchdog.

If cutbacks in expenditures became necessary, the cutbacks would have to be apportioned between central City and local district programs; then, the local district share would have to be apportioned among the local districts. The task would be complicated by the existence of state and federal categorical grants with local matching requirements. A $500 cut in City funds for a program that is one-third local and two-thirds federal money means a $1,500 cut in expenditures and a possible irretrievable loss of $1,000 back to the federal treasury.

Decisions on the allocation of cutbacks in expenditures could not be made by the application of formal rules. The mayor and the Budget Bureau would have to consider the impact of cutbacks on the level of City funds going to various services in terms of the total fiscal loss generated by a cutback in City fund expenditures and then estimate the amount of political opposition in the City to cutbacks in various services. Cutbacks in programs carried on by local districts would then be apportioned among the local districts in accordance with the applicable allocation formula. Thus, a district entitled to 4 percent of the funds under the allocation formual would bear 4 percent of the cutback. The process of apportioning cutbacks would be simpler in the multipurpose block grant model. The central decision would involve only one figure—the size of the multipurpose block grant fund. The local district would then be free to allocate cutbacks among its services.

In such a negative budgeting process, the City Council should have a chance to pass on a mayor's cutback provisions. Yet delay could not be tolerated if a budget deficit were in the wings. Delay could be avoided by providing that the mayor's fiscal cutback provisions became effective when filed with the council and would remain in force until such time as they were amended by the council to redistribute the burden or until more funds were found to cover the deficit.

LOCAL DISTRICT TAXES

Under a multipurpose block grant system, the central City's grants would probably be supplemented by significant local district tax receipts, so that local district residents could decide to what extent they wanted to increase local government expenditures by taxing themselves. Some local authority to raise taxes and impose user charges would permit greater local flexibility in setting program priorities under a functional allocation grant system. It would also encourage local initiative and experimentation and should increase local responsibility and prudence. Under either system it would be necessary to determine how much of the funds to be spent by local districts could and should be raised by taxes imposed by the district government and what kinds of taxes would be suitable for local control.

Determining the appropriate level of local taxes under a multipurpose block grant system requires balancing the desirability of encouraging local independence against the danger that too much local taxing authority might reduce the City's capacity to provide for its

poorer neighborhoods. Local initiative, pride, and pressure for local
fiscal prudence should increase as the proportion of locally raised
taxes to total local expenditures increases. But as the more affluent
districts came closer to being able to raise enough funds by local taxes
to pay for all local services, their representatives in the City Council
would become more inclined to vote against citywide taxation, which
could be used for local services in needier districts. And the broader
the authority for local district taxation, the greater the limitation on
the tax options of the central City, either because the districts would
preempt some taxes or because of practical limits on the combined
central and district tax rates.

Under a two-tier system of taxation, therefore, no local district
should be allowed to raise enough taxes to pay for all services for which
it was responsible. Some portion of the multipurpose block grant funds
should flow to every district, and every district would need its share
of those funds to provide necessary services. This could be accomplished by limiting the taxes that would be subject to local district
control and limiting local tax rates. But the residents of even the
poorest districts should be subject to enough local taxes to give them
a substantial stake in keeping their local government honest and efficient and to give them some options for improving their own services
out of receipts of local taxes or user charges.

Local taxing authority should be granted only with respect to
those taxes that would generate significant revenues in all districts
of the City. Decentralization of taxing authority over property or
transactions that are concentrated in only few districts or are virtually
nonexistent in some of the poorer districts would provide little or no
independence to the poor districts, would tend to highlight inequalities,
and would further encourage conservative, affluent districts to seek
fiscal self-sufficiency and vote against citywide taxes.

Table 1 shows the distribution throughout the City of various
classes of real estate. The assessed values of taxable property have
been broken down by community districts. As discussed in Chapter
3, not all community districts would be appropriate for local districts
in a two-tier system. For example, the downtown and midtown Manhattan districts have small populations and large concentrations of
valuable property. Except for these districts, however, the community
districts are representative enough for purposes of this analysis of
local district taxation potential.

Residential property assessments are significant in amount in
all districts. They range from an average of $332 per capita to $1,152
per capita, even in the fifteen poorest districts. All except the nine
poorest districts contain residential real estate assessed at an average
of more than $1,000 for each resident of the district. If each district
were given taxing authority over local residential real estate to the

TABLE 1

Amount and Distribution of Property Tax Assessments by Classes of Property

Class of Property	Total Assessed Value Citywide	Assessed Value Per Capita Citywide	Assessed Value Per Capita in 15 Districts with Lowest Per Capita Assessment	Assessed Value Per Capita in 15 Districts with Highest Per Capita Assessment*	Assessed Value Per Capita in 30 Middle-Range Districts
All property	$37,123,000,000	$4,700	$1,213	$9,150	$2,706
Office buildings, hotels, and theaters	5,481,000,000	694	15	1,633	43
Utilities	7,819,000,000	990	0	3,172	0
Other commercial	1,453,000,000	184	57	367	145
Industrial ware-houses and garages	3,375,000,000	427	64	1,133	182
Residential	17,352,000,000	2,197	752	3,364	2,042
Miscellaneous	1,642,000,000	208	43	477	153

*Community districts 1 and 5 in downtown and midtown Manhattan have been excluded because they both have very small populations and very high concentrations of valuable properties.

Source: Tabulated from worksheets provided by New York City Finance Administration.

extent of $1,000 times the district population, all except the nine poorest districts would have the same per capita tax base. For those poor districts the multipurpose block grant from the central City could be increased to compensate for the property taxes the district failed to receive because its total residential realty tax base was less than $1,000 times its population.

Such a sharing of taxing authority between the central City and the local districts would work as follows.* The City would still be responsible for assessing all property. Each year the City would divide the total assessed value of residential property in each district by $1,000 times the district's population to determine the percentage of the residential property tax base allocable to the district government. Each district would be authorized to set the rate, perhaps up to 7 percent or even higher, on its portion of the property, and the City would set the rate for its portion. Every residential property owner's tax bill would be broken down to show the percentage of his property subject to district tax at the district rate, as well as the percentage subject to City tax at the City rate. In wealthy districts most of the residential property tax rate would be set by the central City and most of the receipts would go to the central City. In the poorer districts the district government would be responsible for most or all of such tax. And in districts in the middle range, the City and the district would share about equally.

Under such an arrangement a district of 150,000 population would have a residential property tax base of $150 million, against which it could assess a tax of up to 7 percent, yielding up to $10.5 million. The City would be foregoing the right to collect real estate taxes citywide on some $7.5 billion of the $37 billion of assessed value of real estate subject to City tax. (In order that "local" property tax receipts would keep up with total receipts from taxes on residential real estate, the initial $1,000 of local tax base should be increased each year in proportion to the increase in average citywide residential real estate assessments.) The local districts would have substantial leeway as to how heavily they would tax their residents to make local variations in services. This should stimulate some competition among local districts. At the same time the $1,000 per capita ceiling on local tax base and the 7 percent ceiling on tax rate would result in a local

---

*Such a dual system of real property taxation would probably require amendment of Article IX of the state Constitution. Separate limits could be set for citywide real property taxes and for district taxes, not unlike the constitutional arrangements for upstate counties and cities within those counties.

property tax ceiling of $70 per capita, even in the wealthiest districts. City councilmen from those districts would still need to vote for substantial central City taxes to supplement locally raised funds to provide needed services through multipurpose block grants.

Unfortunately, taxation of residential real estate is a relatively regressive form of taxation. In addition, high taxation of residences discourages new residential construction and rehabilitation of old tenements and drives middle-class taxpayers out of the City. But until the federal and state governments assume a larger share of the City's fiscal burden, property taxation will continue to be a necessary evil. Its regressive and uneconomic effects would not be materially greater if the tax were levied by local districts than when it is levied by the central City. Furthermore, it is possible to vary the rate of property tax in fine gradations without undue administrative inconvenience, so that rates can be varied to fit local preferences without increasing the expense of central tax collection. The residential real estate tax does then lend itself to decentralization; nevertheless, the City should be careful to ensure that local districts do not become too dependent on use of property taxes, because the long-range tax policy objective should be to reduce reliance on real property taxation.

Delegation of authority to tax commercial or industrial properties would not make sense. Office buildings are highly concentrated in a few affluent districts. The range of assessed values per capita for other commercial property runs from an average of $15 per capita in the poorest district in central Brooklyn to $764 per capita on Manhattan's East Side, and the average assessment per capita for such commercial properties in the 15 poorest districts is $57, while the average assessment per capita for such property in the 15 most commercially developed districts is $367. The disparities for industrial property are even greater, with the average for the 15 least industrially developed districts being $64 per capita, as against $1,137 per capita in the most industrially developed districts. Thus, poor districts with the greatest need for government services could call upon only 5 to 10 percent of the tax base per capita available to wealthier districts. Furthermore, local tax authority over commercial or industrial properties could have detrimental economic consequences. Some local districts might impose very low taxes to attract stores or industry and, thus, start a tax rate war. Or some districts might seek to exclude stores or industry by unduly high tax rates. Either course of action would be damaging to the economic well-being of the City as a whole.

Table 2 shows the distribution of federal income tax collections among the City's community districts, again excluding the unrepresentative downtown and midtown Manhattan districts. City income tax collections closely parallel federal income tax receipts, so that these

TABLE 2

Amount and Distribution of Federal
Income Tax Collections

Tax Collection	Amount
Total tax collections in the City as a whole*	$2,500,000,000
Tax collection per capita	320
Tax collection per capita in 15 poorest districts	110
Tax collection per capita in 15 wealthiest districts*	670
Tax collection per capita in 30 middle-range districts	280

*Community districts 1 and 5 in downtown and midtown
Manhattan have been excluded because they both have very small
populations and high concentrations of wealth. In addition, many
nonresidents file their returns in the downtown Manhattan office of
the Internal Revenue Service.

Source: Tabulated from Internal Revenue Service data on
federal income tax collections by zip code.

federal figures are appropriate for comparison purposes. The disparity between the average income tax bill of the residents of the 15
most affluent districts and the average bill of residents of the 15
poorest districts is just about the same in relative terms as the
disparity between these two sets of districts for residential property
tax assessments. Thus, the federal government collects some $670
from the average residents of the 15 most affluent districts and some
$110 from the average resident of the poorer districts. Federal income
tax collections in the 30 middle-range districts average approximately
$280 per capita. While a local right to add a surcharge to the City's
individual income tax could encourage local initiative, experimentation,
and competition, any such surcharge should be strictly limited because
it would benefit affluent districts so much more than it would benefit
poorer ones.
    Local authority over sales taxes or general business taxes does
not seem feasible. We were not able to break down sales tax receipts
by community districts, but many districts, including most of the
poorest ones, have no major shopping facilities and would benefit little

from a delegated sales tax authority. Furthermore, any extra local
district sales tax would drive customers away from that district.
Indeed, substantial disparities in sales or general business tax rates
among districts in the City could well distort commercial and industrial
development, to the detriment of the City as a whole.

A different approach to local district taxation is suggested by a
recent proposal for equalizing local school-taxing power.[5] The major
objectives of that proposal were to encourage local commitment and
initiative by letting school district residents determine how much they
would tax themselves for educational purposes, while at the same time
equalizing local educational taxing power throughout an entire state,
so that any given rate of tax would produce the same amount of money
per pupil, regardless of the wealth of the school district. Under the
proposal the state would determine how much money per pupil any
given tax rate would produce but would permit school districts to set
their own rates. For example, the state might permit local tax rates
ranging from a 10-mill rate yielding $500 per pupil to a 30-mill rate
yielding $1,500 per pupil. The state would assess all property and
collect taxes at the rates set by the school districts, but would grant
funds back to the districts in accordance with the formula described
above. The funds per pupil available to the school districts would
vary only with the local millage rate, and not with the amount of local
property assessments. In effect, the state would be supplementing
the property taxes of poor districts and redistributing some of the
taxes collected from more affluent districts.

Essentially, the same arrangement could be used in New York
City for financing part of the cost of the services to be delivered by
local district governments. Thus, the City could assess all residential
property and permit local district governments to set residential
property tax rates at between 5 and 7 percent. The City would collect
all such taxes but would grant the proceeds back to the districts on the
basis of a formula reflecting the locally set tax rate and the population
of the district, but not the assessed values of the residential property
in the district. Since the assessed value of residential real estate
averages almost $2,200 per capita (see Table 1), the City could safely
grant back $100 per district resident if the district set a 5 percent
rate, $120 at a 6 percent rate, and $140 at a 7 percent rate. In the
poorest 15 districts assessments per capita of residential property
average only $752 per capita, so that at the 6 percent rate the City
would be collecting $45 per capita and would in effect be making a
supplemental grant of $75 for each district resident. In the 15 most
affluent districts (excluding midtown and lower Manhattan), the average
per capita assessment is $3,364. At the 6 percent rate the City would
be collecting $202 per capita and would in effect be redistributing
$82 per capita on the average from those districts to the poorer dis-
tricts.

If the affluent districts as a group and the poor districts as a
group both set the same tax rates, the equalizing grants would just
about equal the excess collections from affluent districts. If the
affluent and poor districts as groups set different rates, the taxes
collected and grants distributed would not match. This possible
mismatch can be illustrated from existing New York City assessment
figures. For purposes of comparison it will be assumed that the 15
affluent and the 15 poor districts as groups both have aggregate populations of 2 million (in fact, the poor districts are on the average somewhat larger than the affluent ones). If the affluent districts all set a
5 percent rate, the City would collect $340 million from those districts
and grant back $200 million, thus generating $140 million for distribution to the poor districts. If the poor districts all set a 7 percent rate,
the City would collect about $106 million from those districts and
grant back $280 million, leaving a gap of $174 million, or $34 million
more than the surplus from the affluent districts. If the affluent districts all set a 7 percent rate and the poor districts all set a 5 percent
rate, the problem would be reversed, and the City would have a surplus
of some $66 million. In order to guard against too large a deficit, the
City could set up its grant formula so that the total to be granted back
would be somewhat less than the total taxes that would be collected if
all districts set the same tax rate. Or the City could set up a reserve
from other sources to cover any deficit. After a few years of experience with the system, the City should be able to develop a formula of
per capita grants under which total grants would come very close to
equalling total tax receipts.

This equalizing system could also be applied to the City income
tax. But such a system of equalized property or income tax probably
should not generate all of the funds needed by local districts. Per
capita equality would not reflect differences in needs among districts,
which probably should be taken care of through the multipurpose block
grant system. And at least some block grant funds should go to all
districts, to increase the likelihood that representatives of affluent
districts would vote for the centrally controlled taxes that would fund
multipurpose block grants, as well as centrally managed programs and
activities.

Districts could also generate revenue by adoption of user charges.
Local districts could charge for trash collection, street cleaning, use
of parks and recreational facilities, use of health facilities, and even
use of some educational facilities. User charges can be an efficient
mechanism for local government to learn the kinds and amounts of
services people really want. In addition, a user charge system makes
it possible for government to avoid taxing individual residents for
services they do not want. Hence, local user charge authority would
not only generate local revenues, but could also be an effective tool
for responsive resource allocation.

On the other hand the central City government and local district governments might well insist that certain basic services be maintained, whether or not some (or even the majority) of the residents of the district chose to pay for those services. Twice-a-week street cleaning and trash collection might be deemed minimally necessary and be paid for out of tax receipts. But block associations or even individual property owners might order and pay for extra service. Similarly, parks might be tax supported, while tennis or swimming facilities might be financed by user charges. Similar differentiations could be made for other services.

The City should also make sure that user charges to not have the effect of highly regressive taxation and are not used to facilitate segregation of services. If user charges were imposed for necessary services, such as immunization shots or textbooks, the poor would have to pay as much as the rich and the City's effectiveness as a redistributor of wealth would be diminished. If district residents had to pay the full cost of special educational, health, or recreation programs, the poor, and, in most cases, minorities, would be unable to participate, and such programs would become economically, and possibly racially, segregated.

Under a functional allocation grant system, there would be advantages to be gained by authorizing local districts to add a small amount to the tax rate on local residential real estate or to add a small surcharge on the City's individual income tax. Local districts could also profitably experiment with user charges, particularly if the district government could retain any savings for use in improving other services. Furthermore, some taxing experience should increase the residents' participation and popular concern for local government efficiency and should smooth the transition from the functional allocation grant fiscal system to the multipurpose block grant system.

THE CAPITAL BUDGET

The City's present annual capital budget process begins with an estimate by the comptroller of the funds that will be available for capital projects during the next fiscal year. Then, the Planning Commission holds hearings, at which department officials and members of the public speak about their needs. The commission adopts a budget, which typically is a long list of specific building and construction projects (for example, a new elementary school for Crown Heights). That budget goes to the mayor, although he and his staff will have already been working closely with the Planning Department staff. The mayor, acting through the Budget Bureau, prepares a new budget, which among other things occasionally responds to the public outcries

that follow the Planning Commission's version. The mayor submits
this new budget to the City Council and the Board of Estimate. They
hold hearings, and the Council Finance Committee and members of the
board meet privately for many hours, negotiating over inclusion or
exclusion of projects. Finally, the council and board adopt a budget.
If the mayor signs it, it becomes law. If he vetoes it, he can be over-
ridden by a two-thirds vote of both the council and the board.

But inclusion of a project in the capital budget does not mean
it will be built. Sometimes, inclusion is little more than a political
gesture to local sentiment. Construction occurs only when the agency
that will use the structure, plus the various overhead agencies, especially the Budget Bureau and the Department of Public Works and the
Real Estate Department, act to pick and obtain a site, choose an
architect, and take other preparatory steps. And they take those
steps for only some of the projects that get included in the capital
budget. Again, an ability of those who want the building to make noise
or to exercise other kinds of political influence is very helpful.

Neither the functional allocation nor the multipurpose block
grant approach to allocating expense budget funds among local districts
would be easy to use for capital budget items. The technique of formula
allocation, while theoretically applicable to the capital budget, is more
difficult to envision, because capital expenses are, by nature, not a
steady flow but a discrete series of lump-sum outlays. A renewal
project is completed, and another may or may not begin ih that district.
Schools last many years, and a district with a stable school population
may have long periods in which neither major rehabilitation nor new
construction is necessary.

Nor would it be as easy to develop reasonably simple indices
of comparative need within a single program area. If one district
has a sixty-year-old school without a cafeteria and another has a new
but overcrowded school, which one is in greater need of new investment?
A valuation of past investment in an area is not a valid measure of
present comparative need, at least for capital outlay items that are
needed only at irregular intervals. The relevant variables in measuring
need are numerous and would tend to change over time for each functional area, whereas the expense budget formulas, though equally controversial, probably can be based on fewer variables of more general
applicability.

Furthermore, in the expense budget, only marginal changes are
possible in program allocation in any given year. Commitments to
salaries and community objections to drastic changes in the levels of
service provided make it impossible, for example, to cut education
in half and devote the now free resources to health services and police
protection. By contrast, much more of the capital budget is up for
grabs each year. Sanitation truck replacement can be accelerated or

delayed; this year's emphasis can be school construction, while next year we rush to build neighborhood health centers.

Allocating capital funds by function and on a formula basis would not be the only possible approach. Districts could receive formula grants of expense budget funds but continue to go to the central City for individual capital projects, at least for major ones. Districts could be fiscally autonomous for capital budget purposes or they could receive block grants of capital project funds, perhaps based on population and the district level of expense budget outlays.

The fiscally autonomy approach would be as unsatisfactory for capital funds as it would be for current expense funds. Autonomy in capital budget matters would mean that each local district would have to have a sufficiently broad-based and strong set of revenue sources to be able to float bond issues, which would not do much for the South Bronx or for blighted waterfront industrial areas. Moreover, any suggestion of central guarantees for local district bonds without a mathematical formula allocating guarantees to districts would require central review of local financing decisions. No central government would guarantee the bonds of a subordinate unit unless it could control the amount and, to some extent, the purposes of the local expenditures.

The multipurpose block grant approach, for reasons discussed in relation to the City's expense budget processes, would be more likely to be a long-run goal of any commitment to decentralization than a method of financing during any transition period or initial years of decentralization. During at least the early years of political decentralization, the more feasible capital budget process would be similar to present capital budgeting, with most capital funds being allocated on a project basis by the central City. Capital budget allocation decisions would remain primarily in the hands of the central City government, based on capital project requests from the operating departments of the central City and from the local districts.

At the time of submission of budget requests, project costs would not be capable of precise estimate, since detailed plans would not yet have been prepared, sites not acquired, nor estimates obtained. The central City agencies or the Budget Bureau would need to produce general cost indices for repetitive projects, like schools or health and social service centers, to permit comparisons of local district budget requests and to allow a ready means of translating statements of service need (for example, elementary school space for 900 children on one site) into preliminary cost estimates. Site and site preparation costs would have to be separately estimated in each case. As long as local district requests were within centrally established cost indices, central agencies should not interfere with the local cost estimates, but should be limited to accepting or denying the local request.

Making a local district list of priorities binding on the central

City probably could not be made to work, because of the tie between
capital budget funds and expense budget commitments needed to operate
completed facilities or new equipment. There is some risk that in
cases in which local and central priorities honestly differed, stalemate
might occur without such a rule. But leaving disagreements to negotiation rather than defining absolute rules in advance would be more
sensible.

Even in a system that placed primary capital funds allocation
responsibility in the central City, it would be advisable for there to
be some capital funds over the use of which local districts had full
discretion. The political capacity of local units would be likely to be
improved if they could make small local "luxury" expenditures and
local environmental improvements or could provide special facilities
not normally within the ongoing operations of local government.

This might be accomplished through an allocation each year of
a small portion of the unencumbered margin of the City's debt-incurring
powers to the local districts. Local districts could spend these funds
for any lawful capital project purposes, with prior approval by the
local district legislative body and subject to City postaudit. Budgets
for the specific projects should be on file with the central City Planning
Commission, not the central budget office, before expenditures began,
to provide for the corrective of publicity, ensure that the central City
has not allocated funds for the same purpose, check land-use appropriateness, and serve as notice to City agencies or other local districts
that might be affected. Also, any local district tax revenues could be
used for purposes normally classed as capital rather than expense
budget outlays.

Another issue is the challenge of ensuring that expense budget
funds would be available to operate and maintain local district capital
projects. In most cases a new facility would either be offset by the
phasing out of an old inefficient facility or would reflect increases in
need that would show up in the districts' share under either the functional or block grant formula. But there still might be transitional
problems. In schools, for example, addition of a large new facility
might require a sudden increase in staffing and maintenance. Perhaps
the simplest kind of review of the availability of operating expenses
would be to require that each capital budget request from the local
district demonstrate how manpower and maintenance funds would be
available in the requisite amounts at the time of scheduled completion.
This demonstration could be based on anticipated normal growth in
expense budget funding, on transfers of staffing and maintenance
outlays from facilities presently overutilized or scheduled to be shut
down, or on outside funds, such as local district taxation or foundation
grants that would be available.

SUMMARY

The City could give local district governments enough budgeting authority to make local program control effective without losing its capacity to keep the citywide budget in balance. The central City should continue to assess and collect substantially all City-level taxes, though district governments could be authorized to set part of the rates for taxes on residential property in their districts and to add small surcharges to the City income tax. Most of the funds for the services delivered by district governments would come from City grants distributed among the districts in accordance with formulas based on population and relative need. At first the central City might make separate functional grants for each broad category of decentralized service. But as soon as the districts developed administrative capability, City funds should be distributed to each district in one multipurpose block grant, so that district programs could be made responsive to local needs and so that district governments would have both capacity and incentive to economize.

The districts would develop their own budgets, which would not be approved in advance by any central City agency. But having relinquished budget control, the central City could not be responsible for district government obligations and could not be expected to bail out any district that ran out of money before the end of the year. While the City Comptroller might handle local funds, his only review power would be to postaudit district accounts.

Development and approval of the capital budget should probably be a central City responsibility, though local districts would propose capital projects in program areas for which they were responsible. But each district could have the right to spend perhaps $1 million a year for special capital projects of its own choosing.

APPENDIX TO CHAPTER 5:
EDUCATION FISCAL ALLOCATION FORMULAS

At the time this study was being carried on, the central Board of Education was still managing the entire budget for New York's school system, but the new education law mandated some budget decentralization and, in particular, required the development of a formula or formulas for allocating funds to the new community school districts. The Board of Education commissioned McKinsey & Co. to develop alternative patterns of allocation. This appendix summarizes McKinsey's findings and analysis.

At the start, Mckinsey found that, under existing union contracts,

the existence of varying seniority levels in different districts meant
that equal dollars bought different numbers of teachers in different
districts. Furthermore, even where district average salaries were
the same, differences in the number of teacher preparation and administrative periods between poverty area and nonpoverty area schools
meant that ratios of pupils to teachers and district average class size
varied. These three variables—dollars per teacher, pupil/teacher
ratio, and average class size—are interdependent because under present rules, district average salaries and the number of nonteaching
periods in a district are determined independently by past teacher
transfer decisions and the union contract. Therefore, if funds were
allocated to a district to place any one of these variables at a given
level, the values of the other two would be fixed at the same time.

Given the kinds of contract restraints and seniority differences
that existed, and using the 1970/71 budget figures, the following results
were obtained from equalizing among the 31 districts any one of the
three measures—dollars per student, pupil/teacher ratio, or average
class size:

1. With equal dollars, pupil/teacher ratio would vary by 28
percent and average class size by 15 percent.
2. With equal pupil/teacher ratio, dollars per student would
vary by 25 percent and average class size by 13 percent.
3. With equal class sizes, dollars per student would vary by
14 percent and pupil/teacher ratio by 13 percent.

Thus, before one began to worry about need-based allocations, it is
clear that it would be difficult to agree on an appropriate way of
allocating resources among local districts.

In developing need-based formulas, the initial decision is how
need is to be measured. The scanty data available to the Board of
Education made three choices seem possible: (a) reading retardation
rates, a performance measure; (b) participation in the school free-
lunch program, an indication of family poverty as a predictive measure;
and (c) English-language difficulty, also a predictive measure. As
indicated in the main text, district need rankings would vary widely,
depending on the measure of need chosen. District 23, for example,
is the most needy district in terms of numbers of pupils with significant
reading retardation, and only the sixteenth most needy when measured
in terms of English-language difficulties.

A practical decision in such circumstances is to use a combined
need index, giving equal weight to each if no more obvious choice
exists. Beyond this decision, however, a second decision has to be
made before measures of need can be translated into an index that
determines how much needier one district is than another. Are

degrees of need to be measured under each index or does one simply distinguish between the needy and the nonneedy districts? The latter approach has one big advantage. It avoids argument over how much additional compensation should be given for a child who is two years behind in reading ability, compared to the child who is only one year behind. Moreover, if funds are distributed in proportion to the total number of needy children in each district, in effect, an averaging process occurs. Needy children in each district will range from somewhat need to very needy. Distribution of extra funds to each district based on the number of needy children will then be unfair only if there are significant differences among districts in the distribution of needy children along somewhat needy to very needy range.

Whatever the method of allocation and measures of relative need used, the least-needy district must always receive enough resources to maintain an average class size of no more than 32 students under the existing union contract. Thus, if equal dollars are given to each district, "each district must receive the number of dollars per student that the highest average salary district requires to meet its average class size requirements."[6] And if equal teachers are allocated to all districts, "each district must be given enough dollars to purchase the number of teachers required to ensure that average class size remains below 32 students."[7]

The equal dollar allocation technique ends up giving more money, and hence more teachers, to those districts with lower average teacher salary levels. But in New York City in 1970, the districts with the lower average salaries are by no means the districts with the highest levels of need. Moreover, the least-needy district happens to have the highest average salary levels, so that an allocation of equal dollars based on the amount that the least-needy district needs to stay below the 32 students per class limit leaves very little money that can be allocated specifically in accordance with local district need.

By contrast, if each district receives only enough money to ensure that it has an average class size just below the maximum, there is much more money left to allocate among local districts according to need. Low-average salary districts would receive a base allocation measured in terms of teachers, rather than in terms of dollars.

Specifically, the differences are as follows, assuming 1970/71 budget totals, union contract provisions, and average salary levels and assuming that the compensation for a needy child is some fixed percentage of the compensation for a nonneedy child:

1. With a compensation for need added on to the equal dollar-based formula, only about 7 percent extra dollars could be allocated to each needy student before the average class size in the least-needy

districts rises to the maximum level permitted by the union contracts.

2. With an allocation in terms of average class sizes, as much as 32 percent extra teachers could be given to needy districts before the least-needy-district average class size approached the upper limit.[8]

This difference occurs because the allocation of funds to equalize maximum permitted average class size in each district leaves a much larger pot of funds after each district's minimum is met than is left unallocated when the allocation equalizes district dollar flows at a level high enough to permit the highest-salary district to meet the minimum class-size requirement.

Not surprisingly, class-size-based formulas produce class-size patterns that parallel the need ranking, but vary rather widely in dollar allocations per capita. Dollar-based formulas allocate dollars per capita according to need but yield very irregular class sizes. Thus, if average class size is considered to be a suitable measure of equity in relation to need, then class-size-based formulas should be used for distribution. If dollars received by districts are considered to be the best measure of equity, then dollar formulas should be used. For example, if the seniority-caused differences in average teacher costs among districts were to disappear rather rapidly under decentralization, dollar allocations might be preferable, since progressive variations in teaching techniques among districts might render class-size measures progressively less meaningful as a way of comparing resource inputs to needs. Moreover, under a district-based system, class-size restraints might begin to vary from district to district, thereby eliminating class size as a reasonable starting point for allocation.

The major reason in favor of the class-size-based formula is that, at this time, it would permit the board to allocate discretionary dollars on a need basis. That is, once each district were allocated the funds necessary to meet the class-size limit, the remaining funds would be unencumbered by contract restrictions and could be allocated solely according to relative need. Discretionary dollars would not be allocated in proportion to need with the dollar-based allocation formula, because that formula, in granting equal dollars per student as a base measure, makes no distinction between high-need districts with low average salaries and low-need districts with low average salaries. Both would get substantial amounts of discretionary funds.

However, this apparent reason for favoring the class-size-based formula is weakened by the impact of state and federal special education funds, which are required by law to go to needy children, although the measures of need are not necessarily those used in the hypothetical allocations discussed in the preceding paragraphs. These funds

permit the granting of far more "discretionary" dollars to needy
districts than would be possible under either the dollar or the class-
size formula at present appropriation levels for local state and federal
funds. The federal and state funds, in 1970, added about $230 per pupil
in discretionary funds to the amount given to the neediest district; the
class-size-based formula permitted a transfer of only about $115 in
discretionary dollars, and the dollar-based formula, only $80 in
discretionary dollars. If one could count on federal and state transfers
remaining at a high level, it might make more sense to wait out the
period of seniority adjustments than to adopt the principle of basing
resource allocation upon class-size constraints. Furthermore,
dollar-based allocations are probably easier to sell politically, given
the above-demonstrated complexity of explaining the alternative.

6

**CIVIL SERVICE
AND
MUNICIPAL UNIONS**

The City's employment system regulates the performance of the 380,000 civil servants who work for City departments and public authorities that govern the City and serve its residents. The structure and operations of that system determine the level of City taxes and the quantity and quality of City services. Any increase in salary level or pension contributions, any relaxation of working conditions, or any change in the ratio of municipal employees to the equipment they man or to the clients they serve directly affects either the amount of taxes that must be collected or the level or quality of services. The incentives and disincentives the system provides for vigorous management and employee productivity materially affect the costs and effectiveness of governmental services. The quality of services also depends greatly on the attitudes of City employees toward their jobs and toward the City residents they serve. The City's employment policies significantly affect the job opportunities of its residents, particularly its minority residents, who have had great difficulty finding stable, well-paying jobs in the private sector. For all these reasons the ability of decentralization to make governmental services more efficient and more satisfactory will depend on how well the City's employment system can be adapted to serve the purposes of decentralization.

THE CITY'S PRESENT
EMPLOYMENT SYSTEM

The City's employment system is a mixture of civil service law, Department of Personnel practices, operating agency procedures, Budget Bureau regulation, union agreements, and state and City political relationships. Informal practices and understandings are frequently as important as formal rules. And the system is sufficiently complex to allow almost all the participants to find others to blame if something goes wrong.

The City's civil service rules are based on the seventy-five-year-old Section 6 of Article V of the state Constitution, which provides that appointments and promotions in the civil service shall be based on merit and fitness, to be ascertained as far as practicable by competitive examination. Civil Service rules were enacted to prevent politically motivated favoritism or reprisal and to ensure that hiring and promotion were based on merit. A basic premise of the civil service is that all personnel actions should be based on standards that are sufficiently objective to permit administrative and, ultimately, judicial review.

In New York City, the civil service rules are administered by a Civil Service Commission, consisting of two mayoral appointees, who serve for six year terms, and the chairman, who serves at the mayor's discretion and also serves as director of the City's Personnel Department. The commission and the department set standards for hiring, promotion, disciplining, and firing of City employees; classify and grade civil service jobs; recruit new employees; design and administer tests for hiring and promotion; and carry out a number of personnel service functions. The commission also hears and disposes of employee complaints against personnel actions by line agencies.

The constitutional requirement for competitive hiring and promotion has meant that most hirings and promotions are based on ranked lists of qualified applicants. The hiring or promoting agency usually must select one of the top three persons on the list. In the case of new employees who enter the civil service at the bottom of a career line, the rankings are usually based almost entirely on written tests, sometimes supplemented by physical exams or personal interviews. Usually, applicants must also meet education and experience requirements.

Civil service rules technically permit City agencies to open the competition for higher-level jobs to outsiders, if they can show that such open competition would be in the interests of the City. But line agency heads rarely take advantage of this opportunity, because they want to avoid offending their employees, because they feel it is not worth the time and effort to obtain a commission ruling, and because of union pressure. As a result almost all higher-level jobs, including administrative positions, are open only to persons who are already employed at a lower echelon in the same agency. Applicants for promotion are usually ranked on the basis of scores on written tests, plus a 15 percent seniority factor, which can be quite important, since test scores tend to be bunched. Job performance was until recently a factor, at least in theory, but agency supervisors have rarely given much consideration to performance evaluations. In 1971 when union leaders asked the commission to amend the civil service rules to delete any reference to job performance as a necessary factor in promotions, City officials raised no serious objection. The change was made;* there is now even less management opportunity for motivating extra effort or recognizing superior ability.

The Civil Service Commission also determines what positions are exempt from merit competition because competitive selection would be impractical. Positions requiring broad discretion, policy setting, and the handling of confidential information could be exempted. While several thousand jobs of this type are exempted from merit competition, in most departments and agencies, all jobs except commissioners and their deputies are part of the competitive system. Civil service rules affect transfers only through commission review of interagency transfers. The commission also reviews contested disciplinary actions and firings.

Civil service rules theoretically allow the City's operating agencies substantial flexibility in personnel matters and encourage wide management initiative. Agencies can develop their own rules for merit increases, intra-agency transfers, training, and discipline, as long as the rules provide for objective standards, fair procedures, and opportunity for appeal. The commission has also tried to help agencies build up management cadres by authorizing them to create entry-level management intern positions with relatively high salaries and college degree requirements. As a practical matter no agency takes advantage of these opportunities to build management capacity because they are too time consuming, because the Budget Bureau provides no funds or discourages expenditures for management development or for selective employee benefits, or, more recently, because union pressure inhibits such management activities. Indeed, the Department of Personnel has discontinued its program for recruiting generalists directly from colleges and has reverted to recruiting only specialists.

As guardian of the City's solvency, the Budget Bureau has always monitored personnel actions closely. As discussed in Chapter 5, the Budget Bureau exercises its strongest influence on personnel matters by reserving the right to pass on the filling of all vacancies. In tight budget years the bureau may prevent implementation of any

---

*Rule 5323 of New York City's Civil Service Regulations formerly required that performance be given 15 to 30 percent of the weight in evaluating candidates for promotion. That rule was amended in the summer of 1971 to make consideration of performance optional.

new personnel actions and even freeze all replacement hiring. Furthermore, since training, merit increases, and other management development efforts promise pay off only over the long term and carry high
risk of failure, the bureau has generally given such programs low
priority at budget-cutting time each year. All New York mayors have
discovered that the Budget Bureau is the only office under their control that can monitor all plans and expenditures. The Budget Bureau,
therefore, is encouraged to maintain a closer and closer control over
all personnel actions. As a result the Civil Service Commission, the
Personnel Department, and the operating agencies have all been
discouraged from personnel program initiatives because they can
expect them to be vetoed or second-guessed by the Budget Bureau.

The other major factor in New York's employment system is
the unionization of most of its employees. Until the decade of the
1950's, few municipal employees had collective bargaining rights.
Some civil servants belonged to fraternal organizations, and some
joined together to support lobbying activities. Only the transit workers
were represented by a full-fledged union with collective bargaining
rights—an inheritance from private ownership of bus and subway
lines. By the early 1950's, however, a series of factors coalesced to
foster the rapid growth of union power. Civil servants had become
dissatisfied with their low compensation in comparison with private
sector employees, and, increasingly, public employees were performing
the same jobs as employees of private companies that had unions.
With most of the easily organizable private sector already unionized,
attention began to focus on public agencies. By that time organized
action, including boycotts and picketing, had become more widely
acceptable, even among professionals such as teachers and social
workers, many of whom had participated in civil rights efforts.
Municipal employment was then ripe for organization, and civil
servants in New York City embraced the union movement with increasing enthusiasm.

Civil servants were interested primarily in better wages and
pensions, more holidays, shorter hours, and more pleasant and
less-arduous working conditions. They also wanted even more protection against arbitrary discipline, transfer, and dismissal. Many
professional employees also wanted to participate in program decisions
concerning such matters as case load, class size, and even textbook
selection. Moreover, they were willing to fight to secure their objectives.

In most states, including New York, there was no requirement
that public employee unions be recognized, there was no provision
for collective bargaining, strikes were illegal, and strikers were
punishable by immediate dismissal. Decisions affecting the terms
and conditions of employment were made unilaterally by the employing

government. In the mid-1950's, New York's Mayor Wagner recognized municipal unions and established procedures for negotiations administered by a reconstituted City Department of Labor. As employee unions gained strength they became dissatisfied with this arrangement. As a practical matter the City retained exclusive power over final determination of the terms and conditions of employment. The City did not allow arbitration of grievances, and there was no provision for written collective bargaining agreements. The unions wanted arrangements more like those in the private sector. A series of costly strikes in the early and mid-1960's persuaded Mayor Wagner and, later, Mayor Lindsay that new arrangements were needed.

During the same period the state was also revamping its procedures, and in 1967 the Taylor law was enacted, mandating recognition of unions statewide and requiring collective negotiations, while continuing a uniform prohibition of work stoppages.[1] The Taylor law also provides for strong penalites against striking individuals and their unions.

As permitted by the Taylor law, New York City has been developing its own collective bargaining procedures. The Office of Labor Relations represents the City in bargaining. In 1967, by executive order, the mayor created a tripartite Office of Collective Bargaining, with two labor members, two City members, and three public members, to assist in resolving collective bargaining disputes.[2] Its public members also certify bargaining units, supervise union elections and resolve questions of the scope of negotiations. The mayor recommended in 1969 that the Office of Collective Bargaining have final authority to impose settlements of unresolved issues. The City Council approved his recommendation in December of 1971.[3] The effects of this form of binding arbitration have not yet been assessed.

These new agencies carry an enormous work load, as the City works with some 50 unions, which represent about 200 separate employee bargaining units. Those of New York's public employees who work for mayoral agencies are covered by the City procedures. Although the City has asked for jurisdiction over the rest who work for independent authorities or nonmayoral agencies, including teachers and transit workers, these workers still come under state procedures. But the City, as a principal source of financing for education, mass transit, and other nonmayoral agencies, plays a critical role, even in bargaining with these workers.

Collective bargaining agreements not only cover wages, hours, and other economic benefits, but also frequently prescribe procedures for transfers, discipline, and dismissal. By executive order the City has agreed that a wide variety of issues can be raised as grievances and settled by arbitration, including the propriety of opening positions to lateral entry.[4] The unions also influence promotion policies through

informal pressure on the mayor and his top staff. While the City is
not required to negotiate about policy issues, employee selection, and
other matters within management's theoretical prerogatives,[5] issues
such as equipment-manning ratios and deployment of personnel are
in fact negotiated, are frequently covered by written agreements, and
thereby become immune from unilateral change by the City.

State and City politics constitute the last element of the employment system. The City government passes on most collective bargaining agreements, but the state legislature maintains continuing jurisdiction over all of the terms and conditions of employment in the civil
service. The legislature must approve pension agreements, it is constantly modifying the sanctions for illegal strikes, and it can broaden
or circumscribe the scope of collective bargaining, union employer
relations, and even the right of unions to exist.

Before employee organizations were recognized for collective
bargaining, their only leverage was through lobbying activities.
Municipal union leaders have not lost their touch in Albany. The
larger unions with stable memberships are well financed by dues
collected through check-off, and their members are vitally concerned
and are thought to constitute an effective voting block. Union professionals are skilled at lobbying and public relations. Until 1971
the unions never had any problems in getting approval of rapidly
escalating pensions or in preserving civil service protection and
collective bargaining rights. Most importantly, they were almost
always successful in shaping substantive legislation to suit their interests. For example, the teachers union was able to dictate almost
all of the personnel provisions in the school decentralization legislation and even won added protection against involuntary transfers.
District 37 of the American Federation of State, County, and Municipal
Employees, the principal City union for employees outside the schools
and the uniformed services, was able to block the creation of the City's
new Health and Hospitals Corporation until it secured all existing
rights of hospital workers plus a special new hospitals corporation
civil service system arranged to assure heavy union influence.[6] The
unions have not been able to eliminate or even modify the state's
Taylor law, but they have tempered efforts to increase the penalties
for illegal strikes.

The municipal unions have been even more effective in City
politics. While there are large ideological differences among the
unions, they are united in their desire to build up wages and fringe
benefits for City employees and to reduce the area of management
discretion in employment matters. As representatives of the 380,000
best-organized votes in the City, the key union leaders carry tremen-
dous weight with the mayor and the City Council. This political influence, together with City indifference, has discouraged management

from any vigorous efforts to influence employee performance. At
contract negotiation time, the influence of the votes of thousands of
union members and their families and friends, combined with the
very credible threat of a strike or crippling slowdown, has been
yielding agreements that have caused the City's labor costs to rise
much faster than receipts from existing taxes, forcing the City to
seek new sources of revenue each year.

Union political and bargaining power may have reached its peak.
Partially because of their bargaining successes and partially because
of greater unemployment generally, there are now many more applicants than openings for most City jobs. The media have been publiciz-
ing the relatively high City wages and pensions. Additional sources
of City revenue are becoming harder to find. The 1971 state legislature
for the first time refused to ratify negotiated pension improvements
and enacted other restrictive legislation.[7] In response the teachers
union has approved a tenfold increase in state dues for lobbying. The
next few years will see intensive political as well as bargaining
activity, but the public employers are now experienced and seem more
confident.

In the present City employment system, however, the union
leaders are still in strong bargaining positions on economic issues
and in terms of leadership of the bulk of the City's employees. Their
influence reinforces the tendency of civil service and the Budget
Bureau to cut down management discretion and to preserve municipal
employment as a closed system, with little lateral entry of personnel
or ideas. Agency heads exercise little control over their employees,
and middle management has little incentive to manage aggressively.
The system does, however, work with relatively little friction; and
the dullness, danger, or drudgery of most jobs is offset by good pay,
the prospect of early retirement, and loyalty to the system, if not to
the City.

Blacks and Puerto Ricans hold relatively few of the higher-
paying City jobs that have pleasant working conditions. Most blacks
and Puerto Ricans do not meet the educational or experience requirements for these jobs or score relatively poorly on the competitive
written tests. Since none of the City's job requirements or tests
has been validated by comparing applicants' educational backgrounds
or test scores with subsequent job performance, there is little or no
evidence that the screening process selects the most capable people.
While some unions have on occasion encouraged recruitment of
minorities, others have prevented relaxation of job qualifications for
City jobs designed to encourage black and Puerto Rican applicants.
Minority groups claim that the whole selection system is discrimina-
tory. And, as suggested in Chapter 2, few blacks or Puerto Ricans
even seek employment in the uniformed services, which have
traditionally been the preserves of other ethnic groups.

Even fewer blacks or Puerto Ricans hold high-level supervisory jobs. Since it takes years to rise through the ranks and since blacks and Puerto Ricans have held City jobs in significant numbers only during recent years, few minority persons have sufficient employment seniority to qualify for high-level competitive jobs. Blacks and Puerto Ricans also complain that they are discriminated against for appointive jobs that are exempt from competition.

DECENTRALIZATION AND CIVIL SERVICE

In order for elected local district officials to be accountable for the quality of the services rendered in their districts, they should have substantial control over classification of positions that are peculiar to the district and over selection, promotion, disciplining, and firing of local employees. At least those districts that would have a majority of black or Puerto Rican residents might also want pre-employment educational requirements and tests to be modified to assure that their residents would qualify. No district would want its employees to be able to transfer out of the district at will, and no district would want to be obliged to accept transferees from other districts. All districts would want some flexibility to bring new people into supervisory jobs by lateral entry. They would want as few as possible restrictive work rules covering such matters as job assignments, class size, manning tables, and case loads. Finally, they would want district program managers and staff directors and, at least, their deputies to be subject to dismissal without cause.

Such increased local control and flexibility would involve substantial modifications in the City's civil service regulations, substantial reduction of the authority of the Budget Bureau, and wholesale changes in collective bargaining structure and in current union contracts. Collective bargaining issues and potential union and employee reactions to these changes will be discussed later. Here, we will discuss the advantages and disadvantages of such increased flexibility, the changes that would be necessary in civil service rules and City overhead agency procedures, and the feasibility of such changes.

Administrators and politicians everywhere complain that they have inadequate flexibility and control over their employees, and civil service systems have become popular whipping boys. But the basic principles behind civil service are still valid. Consistency of policy and practices and some central processing can increase efficiency, and even the most dedicated elected officials need to be protected from the patronage demands of their supporters.

Under the present system of centralized personnel testing and hiring, a job applicant need meet only one set of requirements and be qualified only once. Under a completely decentralized system a person seeking a job might have to apply to each local district, going through the separate application and qualifying procedures of each district and creating 10, or 20, or even 40 different personnel records in as many different local districts. Such a procedure would not be in the interest of economy in government or in the interest of those who wish to become government employees. It would probably be a real burden on poor persons, who could not afford the time to pursue employment opportunities in several districts. Accordingly, for most common employee categories—teachers, clerical personnel, social workers, sanitationmen—there would be substantial continuing benefits from maintaining a centrally located organization to pass on the qualifications of applicants for jobs throughout the City. Some districts might accept applicants with less education or different test score profiles to make it easier for their own residents to qualify; tests should be offered at places convenient to residents of poor neighborhoods. But applicants should have to go through only one set of examinations and one stage of credential certification in order to be eligible for appointment by any local district.

Political realities also argue for some independent organization for classifying and qualifying applicants for hire or promotion and for policing disciplinary actions and dismissals. Even the most conscientious local elected executives would need to be able to justify refusal to hire the proteges of political backers or to fire their enemies. The mere existence of such a classification and qualification system would usually be enough protection. Furthermore, there would always be some elected officials who were more concerned with patronage than with quality personnel. Until locally focused media, alert opposition parties, and informed and vigorous local electorates develop in all districts, some civil service protection would be desirable, to keep down corruption and favoritism regardless of other factors.

An independent job classification and qualification system need not involve ranking all candidates in order of merit. Ranked lists not only cut down flexibility, they are also unfair. Commonly used tests probably have little value in predicting job performance, certainly not in any strict rank order. Instead, the independent civil service system could determine whether or not applicants are qualified and let each district pick those it wants from among those qualified. If qualification rosters were kept open at all times, district managers or politicians could send persons they wanted to hire to civil service. Once these preselected persons were qualified, they could be promptly hired instead of other persons who had qualified earlier and who might have ranked higher had there been a traditional ranked list.

Complete elimination of competitive lists would violate Article V, Section 6, of the state Constitution. Many believe that Section 6 of Article V should be changed to eliminate mandated competitive lists, but when this change was sought at the last state constitutional convention, civil service representatives were able to stop the effort. An apparently constitutional alternative would be a rating system with only four grades (outstanding, well qualified, qualified, and unqualified),[8] like the system recommended by the Hoover Commission for the federal service.[9] If the "well qualified" rank encompassed the great bulk of applicants, local districts should have plenty of freedom. While such an arrangement might be challenged as violating the constitutional requirement for a competitive system, the arrangement could be defended on the ground that tests do not predict performance precisely and the broader grouping and rounding off of test scores reduces the chances of unfair discrimination. This argument is supported by recent federal court decisions in employment discrimination cases that have questioned the use of tests and other job requirements, the validity of which have not been demonstrated.[10] In addition, ranked lists would be much less practicable with 30 to 60 separate district employing agencies than with one citywide employer.

The same principles could apply for promotions, though this is a much more sensitive area for unions. Again, present employees and potential lateral entrants could be ranked in four grades. If the "well qualified" grade proved to be a large one, districts would have adequate flexibility. Hopefully on-the-job performance evaluations would be instituted in some districts, perhaps through simple assessments of promotability by relevant supervisory personnel. At least some judgment of supervisory capacity should be brought into the promotion equation.

Such increased flexibility in the system of qualifying entry-level job applicants and applicants for higher-level jobs would be especially significant for minority applicants and for local government districts controlled by minority elected officials. Since blacks and Puerto Ricans tend to receive relatively low written test scores, they have fared particularly badly in the strict ranking system. The scarcity of "qualified" blacks and Puerto Ricans is particularly acute for supervisory positions, and minority-controlled districts might well have difficulty filling key jobs with satisfactory persons unless the present system were changed. Under the proposed system a sufficient number of black and Puerto Rican applicants for jobs at all levels could be expected to achieve the "well qualified" rank, so that officials who wished to hire blacks or Puerto Ricans could do so. In this way more minority persons could be expected to obtain high-paying, interesting, policy-making, and supervisory jobs more quickly than under the existing system, and elected officials in minority-controlled districts would find it much easier to recruit blacks and Puerto Ricans for policy-making and supervisory positions.

But hiring and promotion flexibility cuts both ways. White-controlled districts would also find it easier to select only whites for positions at all levels. Unless some system of quotas were established, the loosening of employment standards might well mean increased segregation in public service employment.

In addition to needing greater flexibility in selecting employees, local district governments would want substantial control over other employment matters, such as job classification; training and management development programs; transfer privileges; lateral entry; and exemption of senior positions from civil service protection. There are a wide variety of ways in which the civil service system could be modified to increase such district government independence. At one extreme formal authorities could be left as they are, but substantial personnel powers could be delegated to the new local district governments. At the other extreme the civil service system could be abolished, leaving government-employee relations to collective bargaining, as in private industry. In between the rules could be changed so that local district governments and their local operating agencies become the basic employer units instead of the existing citywide operating agencies; local governments could be given somewhat greater personnel authority than existing central operating agencies. The central City Civil Service Commission could be retained to review local actions and render technical assistance and to classify and grade positions, set hiring and promotion standards, and administer tests. Because the local districts would be separate employer units, the commission could vary job classifications and entry and promotion standards to reflect differing local district needs. Another version of this intermediate arrangement would substitute separate, new, local district civil service commissions for the existing central commission.

The first and least disruptive adaptation of civil service rules would leave existing citywide departments intact for personnel purposes, so that only the central staff of each local district would technically work for the district government. But the citywide line agencies would delegate to the districts their powers to select among qualified candidates for hiring or promotion, to recommend changes in local position classifications, to drop or retain probationary employees, and to assign supervisory employees. Each district program unit could be made a separate unit for promotion rights; transfer into a district could require local approval. While this option would require relatively little statutory change and would induce less employee opposition, it would not be consistent with the transfer of program and fiscal authority described in earlier chapters as necessary for workable decentralization. As a practical matter most employees would continue to identify with the central functional departments, as they would still have the real power with respect to promotion, transfer, discipline, and grievances. Local district governments would usually find their efforts to change service delivery methods opposed by the formidable coalition of the central line and overhead departments and the unions, all of which would value citywide political accommodation over specific local changes. Finally, the central government departments would always have the bargaining edge, because they could always withdraw or modify the delegation.

At the other extreme abolition of civil service would greatly simplify the municipal employment system and might have widespread initial appeal. Unions and collective bargaining are already performing many of the functions over which the Civil Service Commission used to have sole responsibility. Municipal employees do not need two parallel systems for setting standards for promotion, lateral entry, discipline and dismissal, for settling grievances, or for protection against arbitrary political action. Such a dramatic change might well attract public support as a way to get rid of the civil service bureaucracy. State legislators might be pleased to find an alternative to tinkering with the Taylor law and a way to get civil servants off their backs. Municipal union leaders would like to achieve full parity with industrial unions, including the right to an agency shop.

But the defenders of civil service reform are still devoted and influential, and the state Constitution is hard to change. Furthermore, the civil service does still perform essential functions, including carrying the major responsibility for setting hiring standards and for qualifying applicants, as municipal unions concentrate their efforts on enhancing the rights and privileges of employees after they are hired. If civil service were abolished, the setting of hiring standards and qualifying of applicants, as well as classification and grading of positions, would become the responsibility of the district executives and their program and staff aids for decentralized activities and the responsibility of the mayor and his staff for programs that remained centralized. Thus, the City would be losing all of the advantages of citywide uniformity and citywide processing of personnel actions, as well as losing most of its protection against undue pressures for political patronage.

Under either intermediate model the principal function of the Civil Service Commission (whether it be one central commission or a series of separate ones for each district) would be to set standards for entry-level jobs and to test and qualify job applicants. Unless the state Constitution were amended, the Civil Service Commission would also officially perform the same functions for promotions, but, as a practical matter, collective bargaining would continue to determine

most procedures for promotion, including limits on opening up jobs
to lateral entry. Beyond these functions the authority of the Civil
Service Commission would depend on how substantial a stabilizing
influence one feels a relatively independent commission should have
over such personnel matters as classification and grading of positions,
how much one wants civil service surveillance to continue to parallel
union grievance procedures with respect to such matters as transfers,
discipline, and dismissal, and whether an independent source of advice
and technical assistance is desired for such matters as training, community relations, safety, and employment of the handicapped.

The choice between a central Civil Service Commission and a
series of local district commissions depends upon a balancing of the
values of citywide uniformity and some economy of scale as against
local initiative, flexibility, and local variations in job classifications
and in employment and promotion requirements and procedures. It
would be possible to assure continuing local influence on a central
commission by providing for two citywide commissioners, with each
local district personnel director serving as the third commissioner
for matters affecting his district. On the other hand there could be a
central City representative on each local district commission. A
central commission with local representation would tend to be more
independent of local politics and would tend to maximize uniformity
but might also operate more slowly, reflect central City political
needs, and more frequently stand in the way of local changes.

Personnel management, like fiscal management, is complex
and time consuming, and skilled personnel managers will be hard to
find. As long as the City were operating under a functional allocation
grant fiscal system and as long as collective bargaining remained
basically a centralized function, it would probably make sense to
keep a central Civil Service Commission and to give it jurisdiction
over classification matters, as well as job entry standards, recruitment, and testing. The central Personnel Department could also
furnish technical assistance to the districts or even perform district
personnel functions by contract. Civil service protection for those
already employed, however, would seem to be redundant now that
collective bargaining is established, and the role of the Civil Service
Commission in promotions, discipline, transfers, and dismissals
should be phased out as soon as collective bargaining agreements
provide comprehensive coverage, to the extent allowable under the
state Constitution.

Under such a compromise arrangement local districts could
establish new job classifications without fear of being overruled by
central departments, but the Civil Service Commission and the courts
still could review whether the positions were really new and different.
Separate promotion lines and limits on interdistrict transfer would

build local staff cohesion. Some districts would impose residency requirements or reinstate performance evaluations as part of the promotion procedure, even though others did not. Somewhat differing standards could be adopted with respect to lateral entry, discipline, and dismissal, but those would be largely matters for collective bargaining. Under decentralization senior district supervisory positions should be exempt from competitive selection procedures, because they would require exercise of discretion, policy making, and access to confidential information.

When and if the City moved to a multipurpose block grant system, each district should have the option of creating its own civil service commission. By that time, the local governments should have developed the necessary stability and expertise. Such a move would also be more compatible with full decentralization of collective bargaining responsibilities. But the local districts should continue some kind of common arrangement for qualifying and processing job applicants.

In summary, civil service rules could probably be changed enough to fulfill the needs of decentralization within existing constitutional provisions. Separate district civil service jurisdictions could hire from central lists of "outstanding" and "well-qualified" but otherwise unranked candidates. Promotions could operate the same way, but only those employees already within the district should have preference over lateral entrants. Districts could set different job qualifications, so long as they were truly relevant to potential job performance; new classifications could be established for positions with new demands. Discipline and discharge would become entirely a management-union matter. There is no constitutional reason why appropriate top-level jobs could not be exempt from civil service appointment or dismissal rules. An appointee to such an exempt position from civil service ranks could be given the right to claim any open civil service job for which he was qualified at his old level and salary, if he were dropped within a specified period from his political, policy-level job.

Such adjustments to civil service rules would have little effect, however, if central operating agencies maintained substantial control over program standards and procedures. The break from citywide functional departmental direction to local district direction must be as complete as possible. Otherwise, local district professional workers would constantly be torn between loyalty to central City professional mentors and loyalty to the district government and its residents.

Continuation of the authority of the Budget Bureau and the comptroller to second-guess or preaudit personnel actions would also thwart achievement of decentralized personnel objectives. The Budget Bureau now has more personnel power through control over filling vacancies and establishing new positions than does the Civil Service Commission or Personnel Department. As discussed in Chapter 5, this power could be given up without undue danger of City fiscal collapse. Under decentralization new or replacement hiring decisions and management-development programs could be given final approval at the district government level, so long as the district kept its expenditures within monthly allotments filed with the comptroller. But for fiscal or personnel decentralization to work, the mayor, the state and federal governments, and the citizens of the City must recognize that responsibility stops at the district level and that City Hall will not bail out local district improvidence.

DECENTRALIZATION AND COLLECTIVE BARGAINING

As New York City moved toward school decentralization, relations with the teachers and supervisors unions presented immense difficulties. Accommodation with the unions was important because the quality and attitudes of teachers and principals are critical to school performance, and teachers and supervisors rely heavily on their powerful, well-organized, and determined unions. Accommodation was difficult because the aims of decentralization seemed more at odds with the aims of the unions than with those of any other interest group.

The proponents of school decentralization sought increased management authority and flexibility for community school boards in selecting, promoting, assigning, disciplining, and dismissing teachers and supervisors and in determining the mix of equipment, teachers, paraprofessionals, guidance counselors, and other personnel. The new school boards also wanted authority to experiment with such new techniques as team teaching, ungraded classes, and varying class size and generally to control all matters of educational policy. While wages and fringe benefits were not explicit issues, it was naturally hoped that the community schools could purchase as many teaching hours as possible with the funds available.

The unions were equally interested in these matters, because they involved the working conditions of their members. These were professional issues, which the unions felt could best be resolved by bargaining between the professional unions and the professional staff of the Board of Education, who are almost all former teachers. Over the years the unions had succeeded in bringing most of these "condition-of-employment" matters within the terms of collective bargaining agreements, and they had no intention of relinquishing control to inexperienced, lay community school boards. The unions and their members were particularly interested in preserving the standards and procedures that almost guaranteed that supervisors would be selected from within the system and in continuing the opportunities for experienced teachers to transfer to schools near their homes or to schools in attractive neighborhoods. And the unions were vitally interested in continuing to improve salaries, pensions, and fringe benefits.

Decentralization meant change in structure, change in procedures, and change in relationships. The unions had been doing well under the old centralized system on economic issues and in terms of working conditions and educational policy. They understood the procedures and had developed satisfactory relationships with the staff of the central board. They felt reasonably in control of matters of vital interest to them. Change would mean uncertainty and might mean transfer of control to new local institutions with unfamiliar leaders and unreliable procedures and standards. Moreover, decentralization of the structure of the school system might foster development of local employee power centers from which insurgents could challenge existing centralized union leadership.

Many institutions and interests participated in the school decentralization movement. The mayor's office, other City elected officials, a series of City boards of education, a wide range of parent and civic groups, experimental local school district boards, and the unions all had their own agenda and their own lines to the state legislature. As the movement developed the unions came to fear that the other participants were not paying adequate attention to matters of vital interest to them and to their members. The unions dug in their heels and persuaded the state legislature to give the community school boards almost no authority over personnel matters. The new central board and chancellor were given control over almost all personnel matters, leaving relatively little scope for local variations or experimentation. Many of the goals of community control, therefore, may be difficult to achieve. Continuing conflict between the community school boards and the unions was probably inevitable, because their interests and objectives diverge, but the statute providing for decentralization provided no structure or procedure for resolving these conflicts.

Accommodation of the interests of municipal unions with those of new decentralized local district governments would be just as important as was such accommodation in the school decentralization effort and might be just as difficult. The attitudes, incentives, and loyalties of sanitationmen, health and social workers, building inspectors, and policemen are as critical to effective, satisfactory service as are the attitudes, incentives, and loyalties of teachers. And in many respects the objectives of the several relevant unions could be just as much at odds with the objectives of a multipurpose decentralization effort as was the case in the school decentralization effort.

Any broad, over-all decentralization effort would seek to increase the power and discretion of management; it would seek to facilitate differences in program and personnel practices throughout the City; it might well seek to cut down employee mobility among the districts; and it would seek to increase employment opportunities for blacks and Puerto Ricans at all levels—at least in districts with majority black or Puerto Rican populations. As suggested earlier in this chapter, municipal employees and their unions seek to limit management discretion by providing objective standards in their collective agreements; they seek protection against arbitrary action, which means protection against discretionary power that might be exercised arbitrarily. In addition many professional employees want to participate in, if not control, program policy decisions. Most unions draw much of their strength from their power to secure equal treatment for all members, which militates against variations in conditions of work among districts. Senior employees are usually the most loyal union members, and they have always wanted priority to transfer to better jobs in more pleasant neighborhoods. Finally, unions would naturally resist any move to displace union members to make room for blacks and Puerto Ricans.

These differences in objectives do not make decentralization impossible, but they must be taken fully into consideration in designing any new collective bargaining structure. They also suggest that changes should be negotiated, not imposed. The teachers union's experience with the experimental local school boards in Ocean Hill-Brownsville and Harlem and the long and bitter fight between Newark teachers and that city's new black-controlled school board in the spring of 1971 may well have made all municipal unions especially resistant to change. In both cases the unions and their senior members felt threatened and felt that the new employer representatives were not abiding by the "rules." If change is to be achieved, it must be carefully and scrupulously negotiated. Bargaining authority and responsibility must be clearly allocated between the central City and the local districts, and bargaining procedures must be clearly defined and comprehensive. In an atmosphere of suspicion and with such broad differences in objectives, unclear authority or procedures could be fatal.

There are four possible models for collective bargaining in a two-tier system: First, citywide bargaining could be retained, but provision would be made for district representation on the City's bargaining committee. The union's role would be unchanged, but the Office of Labor Relations, as the City's bargaining agent, would have to resolve differences among central City agencies and district representatives. Agreements would continue to be citywide and cover all negotiated issues.

Second, bargaining authority could be divided between the central and district governments. The central City could have authority over certain matters such as pensions, and agreements in those matters would be effective citywide for all employees and all unions. The City could also be responsible for bargaining on a citywide basis with functional bargaining units, such as teachers or sanitationmen, with respect to wages, holidays, and other economic matters. Issues such as work rules or assignments to shifts could be bargained separately in each district for each functional bargaining unit. The question as to which matters would be bargained at each level could itself be a subject for negotiation in the bargaining between the various unions and the City, with participation by representatives of the local districts.

Third, as a variation of the second model, the division of bargaining authority between the City and the local districts could be determined by state legislation or City executive order. Fourth, bargaining with respect to all terms and conditions of employment could be decentralized for employees who would be working in decentralized programs. Each district would be a separate bargaining unit. Local employees would be represented by a local of one of the citywide unions or even by a separate organization. Each district would have its own bargaining representative to carry on the functions of the City's Office of Labor Relations. The central City's Office of Collective Bargaining might be retained to administer the system.

Full citywide bargaining would be the easiest to administer and would be the most acceptable to the unions. If the districts were operating under the functional allocation grant system, they would have little fiscal flexibility and could not pay for any substantial wage increases out of their own resources. Thus, the central City would be the logical level of govenment for collective bargaining, because it alone would have authority to carry out any bargain involving substantial funds. But it would be hard in such a system for district governments to have a real voice in setting nonmonetary terms and conditions of employment. And substantial variations among districts would be difficult to achieve.

Complete decentralization of bargaining would be conceptually more consistent with multipurpose political decentralization, because it would substantially increase the opportunities for districts to adjust the terms and conditions of employment to their own priority needs. Under the multipurpose block grant system, there is no reason in theory why local district governments could not assume full responsibility for collective bargaining, as well as for program policies and budget balancing.

But complete decentralization of bargaining would create enormous problems, even if this arrangement were acceptable to the unions. Public sector bargaining has been so controversial and so costly to cities, in large part because the cities have been much less experienced as bargainers than their union adversaries. It would take years for 30 to 60 New York City districts to build up the competence the City as a whole is beginning to demonstrate. Unions would be able to win costly settlements from weak district bargainers and then insist upon equal terms throughout the City—much as the Teamsters now do for certain categories of truck drivers whom they represent nationwide. The main thrust of public sector bargaining reform today is to create consolidated regional bargaining units precisely to counter this whipsaw tactic. Moreover, a union could afford a strike in one or two districts when it might shrink from a citywide strike. In addition the administrative burdens of certification, determination of bargaining units and scope of bargaining, impasse resolution, and grievance proceedings in 30 to 60 districts would be expensive and debilitating to government. Finally, despite these potential tactical advantages for the union side, present union leadership would probably fight such decentralization. They also would feel these administrative problems. More importantly, they are likely to fear that decentralization would foster development of local insurgents who might challenge the uneasy hold many leaders have on the reins of union power.

Full decentralization of collective bargaining could therefore be disastrous in practice in the early years of any decentralization program. If and when decentralization should mature and the districts assume broad fiscal powers and civil service responsibilities, they might then be in a position to assume full collective bargaining responsibilities as well. But at least for the first few years, the central City should probably retain a substantial role in collective bargaining.

Under the intermediate options, bargaining responsibility would be allocated between City and districts by statute or by agreement. Leaving allocation of responsibility to agreement between the City and the unions would have the advantage of flexibility. Bargaining with social workers should not necessarily parallel bargaining with clerks or sanitationmen. Some districts might be willing to have the City handle most matters, while others might want broader responsibility. But, as a practical matter, the decision as to what if any matters would be bargained locally would probably be made by representatives of the central City and the unions, with the local districts having little influence. The central City representatives might well be more interested in City budget matters and political accommodation with the unions than in increasing local district autonomy. If the goal is local district control over many of the terms and conditions of local employment, the only safe course would involve statutory allocation of bargaining authority, at least in general terms, with room for negotiation of the scope of local district bargaining power at the margins. Individual districts that did not want to exercise their power could always contract for representation by the central Office of Labor Relations.

Allocation of bargaining responsibility between the City and the local districts should be consistent with allocation of fiscal and management responsibility. Wages, pensions, and fringe benefits should therefore be centrally bargained, at least until the City adopted a multipurpose block grant system, because a local district with negotiating power but with no substantial taxing power could not fulfill its bargain. The City would have to ratify any local bargain and would inevitably dominate the negotiation. Central bargaining would also avoid the problem of whipsaw tactics by strong unions under any fiscal system. Some districts might want authority to make supplemental merit or incentive payments; districts with recruitment problems might want to offer bonuses or such inducements as shorter hours to attract talented teachers or other professionals. But strong unions might take advantage of open-ended authority for local supplements by negotiating selective increases and then seeking to impose their gains citywide. The safer course would be to include any merit or bonus arrangements in centrally negotiated agreements.

Local districts would want to control bargaining over personnel practices, such as standards and procedures for hiring, transfer, promotion, and discipline; such local control would be necessary to complement decentralization of civil service responsibilities. But these are also sensitive matters for unions; local districts would have to bargain carefully to avoid costly misunderstandings. It is in this area that district inexperience might be most damaging.

Control over bargaining with respect to work rules would have high priority for districts that sought to adapt services to their local needs. But changes in work rules can be costly. The local districts would have to be prepared to commit what little flexible funds they might have, if they were to avoid central review of work rule negotiation.

District governments would also need to control bargaining over matters of professional policy, such as educational innovations, social service policies, and case loads. While the districts could in theory insist that these matters were within their management prerogatives and refuse to bargain, such a policy would increase bargaining tensions and would be a poor way to develop a sense of community service from professional civil servants.

In all three areas—personnel practices, work rules, and professional policies—local districts might have difficulty wresting union concessions if they had no control over major money matters. Work rules concessions might be traded for more flexibility over professional policies, but the range of maneuver would be limited. As a result local district bargaining should be tied into the central negotiations, so that money benefits do not take effect until local contract clauses are set.

Such simultaneous bargaining arrangements at central and district levels would be complex and difficult. Trade-offs among wage levels, fringe benefits, work rules, and personnel practices, for example, would be difficult to coordinate when the employer interests were divided between central and local governments. If all sides refused to tip their hands until the last moment, bargaining could be impossible. But multilevel collective bargains are accomplished in the steel and automobile industries and for many groups of technical workers who belong to the omnibus District 37 of the municipal employees union in New York City itself. In all these cases good faith and careful work compensate for the complexity of multilevel bargaining.

Another way of giving local districts bargaining room would be to provide in the central negotiations for a fund of perhaps $200 per employee, which the local districts could use in local negotiations. Some districts would "buy" changes in work rules or modifications of professional policies. Others might bargain for the opening of more supervisory jobs to lateral entry or for pay differentials based on productivity. A few might simply increase wages. But local variation would be possible with little danger of whipsaw effects.

Radical or rapid change could not be achieved, in any event, in such areas as transfer rights, restrictions on lateral entry, or preferences for local district residents. The costs of taking privileges or protection away from existing employees would probably exceed any benefits of management flexibility or increased employment of blacks and Puerto Ricans; the important objective of increased cooperation between civil servants and district residents would be lost. In order for unions to accept decentralization, such changes would have to be introduced gradually. Existing employees would have to be protected by grandfather clauses, which, for example, would continue the right of senior employees to transfer at least one more time to a more attractive job or location. In some cases early retirement might be more economical than the conflict that might arise if a district insisted on cutting back on privileges on which senior civil servants had come to rely.

Administration of two-level employment contracts would also be complex. As a general rule the level of government with authority to comply with an arbitration award or court order should represent management in any grievance proceeding and in any subsequent arbitration or court proceeding. If a grievance involved wages and the central City were responsible for wage bargaining, it should be the respondent in any wage arbitration. If the issue involved a work rule for which the district government was responsible, the district should control the employer side of any arbitration. But the central City government's labor relations officials should be organized on a geographic basis, so that the district and central representatives can work together and avoid burdensome duplication or conflict for the employees and their unions and, also, to prevent the unions from playing one level of government against the other.

On balance, a sharing of collective bargaining between central and district governments would seem the best course, at least until the local districts develop considerable experience and fiscal auto- nomy. But any such division of responsibility would invite confusion and buck-passing, both of which would hamper effective collective bargaining and responsible decentralized management, as well as confirming union apprehensions. The only short-term answer would be extraordinarily careful work by the government officials at all levels. In the long run if local districts grow in competence and take on larger fiscal and budgeting responsibilities, they should probably assume increasingly broad collective bargaining responsibility as well.

SUMMARY

The City's employment system could be adapted to decentraliza- tion, but not without substantial difficulties and risks. Civil service rules would present no insurmountable problems, and local district governments should be able to tailor job qualifications and classifica- tions for their employees to the special needs of their districts. Civil service rules would also not prevent districts from controlling the right of employees to transfer in and out of districts or setting standards for promotion, recruitment for management jobs, or discipline and dismissal. But all those matters are considered to be "conditions of employment" by the powerful municipal unions and would, as a practical matter, be the subject of collective bargaining.

Collective bargaining arrangements would be hard to adapt to a decentralized governmental structure. As long as the central City continued to be responsible for raising most of the funds to pay dis- trict employees, it should not relinquish control over collective bargaining. But the local districts would have to have substantial control over personnel policies, work rules, and professional policies, if they are to assume effective control over delivery of services. The only possible arrangement would appear to be to keep bargaining over wages and fringe benefits as a central function but to allow districts to control bargaining over other matters. Any such arrangement would be complex at best and could not work without union cooperation. Thus, the difficulties of collective bargaining process underline the importance of achieving a broad favorable consensus before any major change in governmental structure is made.

This analysis of New York City's institutions and of the changes necessary to transfer substantial authority and responsibility to new local district governments leads us to believe that multipurpose political decentralization could provide a framework for the solution of many of the City's serious and pressing problems.

Such a two-tier decentralized system of government would involve some 30 to 40 new governmental units with approximately equal populations. Local district boundaries should reflect natural and man-made barriers to communication, existing patterns of neighborhood identification, and the distribution of commercial, recreational, and public facilities. Each district would elect a chief executive officer; each would have a legislative council elected from subdistrict areas of equal populations. Local district governments would have their own budgetary, personnel, purchasing, and legal staff offices. And each would be responsible for carrying out significant service and regulatory functions.

The central City government would continue to be led by a strong mayor. The central City Council would be elected from districts coterminous with new local governmental districts. The Board of Estimate would continue to be a hybrid policy-making and administrative agency. While a number of presently centralized functions and a number of central personnel would be transferred to the new local district governments, the central City government would retain responsibility for all decisions of substantial citywide or interdistrict significance and would represent the City as a whole in dealings with other local governments, the state, and the federal government.

Each local district would take over responsibility for furnishing a wide range of personal services, including social services, some health services, and housing-management services. As soon as practicable, elementary and secondary education districts should be

183

aligned with local government districts and local district governments given substantial, if not complete, authority over broad educational decisions. The local districts would also become responsible for local environmental services, including solid waste collection and street cleaning, code enforcement and housing maintenance, small parks and recreation programs, local street maintenance, and local parking control. District-level planning and zoning commissions could decide local land-use issues, subject to central City override with respect to decisions with impact beyond district boundaries. District governments could also develop their own small-scale renewal and housing projects, but the central City would retain the power to disperse subsidized housing and control major projects. District governments could experiment with supplementary criminal justice programs, but the existing criminal justice system would be retained, including all major police functions. All other regulatory and service functions would remain centralized at least for the first few years of the new two-tier system.

The central City government would continue to be responsible for tax assessment and collection, debt management, and most pay-master and auditing functions. At first funds to pay for locally managed services should be distributed among the districts by annual grants in each major functional area, allocated according to formulas based on population and relative need. Later, as local competence develops, functional grants should be replaced by single block grants, covering all local activities, also allocated among the districts by a formula reflecting population and need. Each district would budget its own programs, and the central City would control expenditures by refusing to pay invoices in excess of local district balances, but not by pre-audit of personnel actions, purchases, or program planning. As soon as feasible each district should have the power to set tax rates over a limited portion of its residential property and of its residents' incomes—enough to permit some local initiative and to encourage local pressure for economizing, but not enough to permit local fiscal autonomy. The central City would continue to allocate and manage the capital budget.

Local districts would be given almost complete control over classifying, hiring, promoting, disciplining, and firing personnel in programs for which they were responsible. The civil service system would be changed to permit hiring and promotions from large group-ings of qualified candidates rather than from ranked lists, and most civil service decisions would be made by local district commissioners. Collective bargaining over wages and fringe benefits would continue to be central responsibilities, at least until it were reasonably clear that local districts would be able to hold their own in negotiations with municipal unions. But local districts would take the lead in

bargaining over personnel practices, work rules, and professional
policy matters.

Decentralization of program authority along those lines should
facilitate improved management of personal service and local environmental programs. Closer employee identification with neighborhoods
and their residents could restore dignity to municipal employment and
increase productivity and consumer satisfaction. Local district governments should be able to tailor government services to local needs and
desires, to make substantial improvements in program coordination,
and to induce greater cooperation from landlords and tenants in maintaining neighborhood environments. New Yorkers could find out what
resources were being spent in their neighborhoods and what these
resources were producing. And they would have far readier access
to local government officials with knowledge and authority over important services.

Such a restructuring of the City's government should not detract
from the City's capacity to deal with citywide matters. A balance
between central and local political power could be struck. Indeed, the
mayor and top central officials should be able to concentrate on citywide matters of importance. Service delivery and regulatory responsibilities could be apportioned between central and local governments so as to assure local governments enough authority to become
viable, while maintaining scale economies, avoiding undue spillover
costs, and preserving citywide values. Fiscal and budgetary arrangements could allow local districts the necessary freedom of action,
without destroying the City's capacity to distribute taxes and benefits
fairly and to balance its budget. With reasonable union cooperation,
civil service and collective bargaining rules and procedures could be
adapted so as to benefit both City employees and City consumers.

But these improvements in the quality of government services
would occur only if New Yorkers cared enough about their government
and its services to inform themselves and vote at local elections, to
communicate their insistence on effective services through their
choice of candidates and through year-round monitoring efforts, and
to step up their cooperation with municipal programs and municipal
employees. The case for decentralization depends, ultimately, on a
judgment that many citizens who are now only disgruntled recipients
of government service would become part-time participants in the
auditing of government output and the making of government choices.
Decentralization would not require participation by everyone; but unless many more citizens take up municipal roles than are active now,
decentralization would only mean the replacement of citywide interest
groups with local groups who would be even less visible and even more
impervious to change. Decentralization should be supported only by
those who feel there is such a pool of latent government participants,

whose involvement today is deterred by the massive citywide municipal structure and the apparent lack of accessible pressure points.

Successful decentralization would require thousands of new participants in government; the successful change to a decentralized system would need the approval and support of millions of New Yorkers. Therefore, no legislative commitment to decentralization should be made unless and until it is clear that a broad consensus of the City's population and of its major interest groups understand just what decentralization would mean to them and support it with some enthusiasm.

POSSIBLE COSTS OF
DECENTRALIZATION

Even assuming such an informed, supportive consensus, the City should still balance the possible gains in the quality of government services against the possible costs of such a radical change. The costs of decentralization might take three forms. First, the new government structures and the shifts in service district boundaries would require new capital facilities, new district government staff personnel, and perhaps additional staff in decentralized operating agencies. Second, if powerful interest groups opposed decentralization, it might be necessary to make concessions to them or assure them compensating benefits—either of which might be expensive. Third, scarce top management talent and political capital devoted to achieving decentralization would not be available for other efforts to improve City life.

Capital and Operating Costs

This study has not tried to develop cost figures for the capital facilities or personnel needed to create effective local district governments or to shift personal and local environmental services from central to local control. But the new government headquarters staffs would surely be expensive. New capital facilities should not be built merely to accommodate decentralization, and district governments would be encouraged to share facilities with each other. But replacement of inconveniently located station houses, garages, and even schools would probably be accelerated if relocation seemed to promise more manageable local district control. Local program officials would have more responsibilities and be better paid than existing middle management. Staffs of central City operating agencies being decentralized would have to be largely dismantled if central City second-guessing and delays were to stop. But bureaucrats seem almost infinitely capable of delaying change, and central savings would not be as great as they should be. Finally, no matter how careful the selection of services to be decentralized, there would be some losses of economies of scale. (See, for example, the discussion of sanitation reserve squads in the Appendix.)

For the first few years, decentralization would probably mean that existing levels of service would cost somewhat more. Thereafter, economies arising from greater management incentives, better planning and coordination, and, hopefully, increased employee productivity should mean more efficient as well as more satisfactory services. Regardless of decentralization, the City will soon be forced to curtail its annual 11 percent escalation in the costs of government services. Hopefully, the City would be able to economize more rationally if its residents had a better understanding of program costs and trade-offs.

Concessions to Opponents of Decentralization

Almost all institutions resist change, and New York has more than its share of powerful interest groups who could block decentralization or could insist on such costly concessions that decentralization could never improve service effectiveness. The municipal unions, for example, could demand substantial wage, fringe benefit, or work rule concessions as a condition to limiting transfer rights or opening supervisory jobs to lateral entry. Borough presidents could insist upon duplicative staff increases or intermediate planning or review power that could be costly in time and energy as well as dollars. Even if no such obvious compensatory benefits were exacted, unions could sabotage decentralization by persuading employees not to cooperate, and politicians at all levels could slow down or stop the process of bargaining out the details of a decentralized system. The concerns of all interest groups will need to be taken into account. But a workable two-tier system cannot afford costly concessions or compromises. Such concessions would probably be avoidable only if it becomes clear that a broad consensus of informed New Yorkers want decentralization to work. Without such a consensus, these indirect costs would probably be too great to justify the decentralization effort.

Diversion of Management Talent

While this study has not examined alternative approaches to resolving the City's major dilemmas, each such other approach

should certainly be carefully assessed to determine whether it is
more promising than decentralization and whether it would be compatible with decentralization. Development and implementation of
any program of decentralization would involve an extraordinary commitment of the City's scarcest resources: experienced, vigorous
administrators and influence with such powerful interest groups as
the unions, the political parties, and the state and federal governments.
Changing the organization, work habits, and loyalties of a bureaucracy
is a formidable task anywhere; in New York City it would be Herculean.
Before the City bets all its chips on decentralization, therefore, it
should be sure that decentralization is the most promising approach
and would enhance the chances of achieving other important objectives.

A major City objective must be to close the gap between the
quantity and quality of services the City is able to deliver and the
perceived needs of its residents. While the size of this gap could be
affected by changing the mix or character of services or by persuading
residents to be more realistic in their demands, it will also be necessary to face up to the basic issue of efficiency in terms of the quantity
of goods or services received for each dollar spent. This must involve
increasing, or at least stabilizing, the productivity of the City's employees, since payroll absorbs the bulk of service expenditures. Cur-
tailing wage and fringe benefit increases should be a substantial part
of the answer, but wage increases negotiated at the start of the current
Phase II wage freeze are still running at more than 7 percent a year.
Production increases apparently could be achieved by rescheduling
employees' work weeks to coincide with the times of greatest need—
Mondays and Tuesdays for sanitationmen and the evening hours for
firemen and policemen. Job requirements rather than employee
convenience could be emphasized in personnel deployment and equipment-manning tables. For example, not all squad car patrols need
two policemen and not all fire alarms require the same initial response. Employee incentive might be increased in some service
areas by provision for pay differentials based on production-ton-mile
collections per hour, for example, for sanitationmen.

But analysis of City services to determine how productivity can
be increased is new, complex, and controversial—particularly for
services other than police, fire, and sanitation, where changes in
work rules and incentive pay differentials are easier to conceive.
Negotiation of necessary work rule changes would entail substantial
management energy and use up substantial political capital, which
could not be used at the same time to carry through a decentralization
program. And it is by no means clear that local district governments
would be as competent or have as much bargaining power as does the
central City in such negotiations. But for the City employees productivity will depend on the incentives and capacity of management

and on employee attitudes as much as on work rules or even incentive pay plans, and decentralization would seem the most promising route to improving municipal program management and employee attitudes. For that reason, decentralization and increases in productivity would appear to be mutually reinforcing.

Regionalization, rather than decentralization, might well be the only solution for some of the City's worst problems and would also provide a better framework for the delivery of some services. The trends toward concentration of low-income minority persons within the City and toward exodus of the white middle-class to the suburbs can only be reversed if lower-income housing becomes available in the counties surrounding the City. No substantial increase in such suburban housing opportunities seems likely until regional institutions control land-use planning and zoning and housing and renewal programs. Regional authority may also be a necessary prerequisite to any significant improvements in mass transit and highway development or in pollution control or waste disposal.

Suburban resistance to sharing the City's burdens or giving up any local autonomy might well be insurmountable, even if the City were to direct all of its energy to the goal of regionalization. Simultaneous efforts for decentralization and regionalization might then appear to be unrealistic. But suburban towns and counties will never voluntarily submit to domination by an all-powerful New York City government, and City representatives lack the influence to force state legislative action. A decentralized City, with Riverdale, Bayside, and Canarsie having almost as much power as Mount Vernon or Great Neck, might appear much less formidable to suburban leaders. As suggested in Chapter 1, decentralization of power within the City itself could well be a prerequisite to any substantial movement toward regional government.

No matter now successful the City is in devising and implementing schemes to increase employee productivity and in developing regional institutions, the City's tax base will almost surely become less and less capable of supporting the services that its residents need. New York City has many advantages over Newark, Cleveland, and St. Louis, for example, in the size, diversity, and stability of its population and of its economy, but the long-range outlook for New York is probably the same as for all older cities. Commerce and industry and middle-class families will almost surely find that central City tax demands increasingly exceed those of alternative locations. Once a net exodus of taxpayers starts, it could rapidly snowball, with City bankruptcy the likely result.

Radical change in the system of financing City expenses, therefore, must be at the top of the City's agenda. Acceptable new systems could take several forms. The state or federal government could equalize

local property or income tax capacity, regardless of the level of local
property tax assessments or local incomes, along the lines suggested
for City equalization of local property tax. As an alternative, or
complementing such an equalizing scheme, the state or federal government could assume full fiscal responsibility for education, health, or
welfare expenses. Or the state and federal government could substantially increase revenue transfers to city governments, either for broad
functions, such as education, or better still as general purpose block
grants. In order for any of these systems to benefit New York City,
the state and federal government would have to recognize that the
needs of the City's residents for governmental services are greater
than those of suburban or rural residents and that its costs are also
greater.

But no matter how much importance the City ascribes to state
and national fiscal reform, the City alone has very little influence.
Decentralization would neither increase nor decrease that influence.
But regionalization of important responsibilities might well make
possible alliances with the suburbs that would tip the balance. Thus
decentralization alone would have little or no effect on solving the
City's fiscal problems, except as it diverted top management attention.
But if decentralization should pave the way for development of broad
regional governmental institutions, the net effect might well be positive.

POSSIBLE SOCIOPOLITICAL
CONSEQUENCES OF DECENTRALIZATION

While the main purpose of decentralization should be to improve
government services, the creation of new semiautonomous units of
City government would, as suggested in Chapter 2, have other important sociopolitical consequences, which should be weighed carefully
before irrevocable decisions are made. Decentralization would certainly affect racial and economic housing and educational patterns
and, perhaps also, patterns of employment, shopping, recreational
activities, and even social intercourse. Decentralization might also
affect locational and employment decisions of the City's business,
industrial, and financial community. Once increased local autonomy
is accepted, fragmentation might go further than intended, particularly
in fiscal and budgetary matters. The new local districts might be
more parochial and less tolerant of minorities than the City as a
whole. The mayor might have less bargaining power in Albany and
Washington, and the state agencies might gain greater influence over
City programs.

Even though the central City would keep control of zoning and
planning decisions and of the power to locate subsidized housing and

to set housing and building code standards, and even though housing and employment discrimination would continue to be a citywide concern, decentralization would inevitably stabilize the character and the ethnic, racial, and economic populations of the City's neighborhoods. The priorities and operating styles of some neighborhoods might be inhospitable toward the poor, minority groups, or aged persons. As a general rule racial and ethnic groups—white, black, or Puerto Rican—would tend to move out of districts in which they were small minorities. Racially balanced districts would certainly have no better chance of survival than do racially mixed neighborhoods in the existing centralized City's structure. On the other hand white emigration from the City might well decline significantly, if whites could have almost as wide a range of choices within the City as they would by moving to a suburb. The net result might be a more stable, better-integrated City as a whole, but with greater segregation within local districts. A stabilized City, with a checkerboard pattern of neighborhoods largely segregated on racial and ethnic lines, would facilitate development of political and management leadership among groups that are minorities in the City as a whole but majorities in their own districts. But such a pattern might well freeze segregated school conditions for years to come and could reduce all kinds of social and economic intercourse across racial and economic lines.

If regional housing and zoning commissions or even regional general government bodies develop, such a checkerboard housing pattern might evolve in the metropolitan area as a whole. While far from the ideal of a unified society, such a pattern of development should be more conducive to economic and political equality of opportunity than the alternative of an all-minority, all-poor central City surrounded by white, middle-class suburbs.

Decentralization should not make the City less attractive for commerce or industry. Business regulation and business tax decisions would remain central responsibilities, as would mass transit. While some broadening of the City's tax base might be needed to keep businesses in the City, in the short run decentralization should not result in any additional fiscal pressure on the business community. Indeed, stabilized neighborhoods might well pull middle-class individuals back into the City and slow the growth in the percentage of City residents requiring expensive services. Major office buildings and stores already provide much of their own service, but as suggested in Chapter 3, it might make sense for midtown and downtown Manhattan to be constituted as a special district, under the control of the central City government.

One of the strengths of New York City has been its cosmopolitan outlook and its relative tolerance of minority cultures, life styles, and political views. Because no racial or ethnic group has ever

constituted a majority of the City's population, ethnic and racial groups
have usually had to form alliances to achieve their objectives. As
these alliances shift from time to time, it has rarely been politic to
disregard the interests of any minority group. With decentralization
particular ethnic or racial groups might become absolute majorities
in some districts, and minority groups might find it impossible to
form coalitions to protect their interests. While federal, state, and
City program standards would protect minorities against overt discrimination, some of the more subtle forms of majority favoritism
or even racism could well evolve. The danger of majority tyranny
can be exaggerated, but some parochialism would certainly be part of
the price of increased local autonomy.

     An important factor in a successful decentralization effort would
be an increase in the quantity and quality of program information.
District voters should be better able to find out the cost of resources
being made available to each district, what programs were accomplish-
ing in each district (in terms of reading levels, for example, as well
as numbers of teachers or class size), and what trade-offs were
possible between municipal employee wage increases and tax increases
or program reductions, for example, or between savings in one program and expansion of another. Such information would be necessary
for effective resident voting and program monitoring. But the availability of such information would also make it much more clear that
taxes collected in relatively affluent neighborhoods paid for services
in poor neighborhoods. While local district taxing power could and
should be strictly limited so as to make local district fiscal autonomy
impossible, representatives of more affluent districts still might
oppose citywide taxes and favor local district taxes or user charges,
which would not have to be shared with other districts. Hopefully,
no such tax revolt would succeed, and hopefully residents of affluent
districts would be satisfied if allocation formulas were based on
clearly demonstrable need factors. But formulas would not be completely scientific, and representatives of more affluent districts
could easily seize upon the inevitable disclosures of waste or even
dishonesty in some of the poorer districts to oppose redistribution
of tax proceeds and gain favor with constituents who found it hard
enough to maintain satisfactory living standards without contributing
to the support of residents of other districts. Such self-interest
could well assert itself, but the alternative of withholding such information and relying on the wisdom and benevolence of professional
government officials is no longer acceptable, if it ever was. The
price of an informed electorate will always be decisions with which
some disagree, including liberals who favor equalization of wealth
and income.

Decentralization would probably reduce the power and influence of the mayor and of the central City government and increase the power of the governor and of state agencies. Many City health, education, social service, and housing programs are larger than all of the other programs in those fields in the rest of the state put together. As a result, the City has been able to carry on its programs with little interference from state administrators and has maintained direct lines to a number of federal funding agencies that normally work only with state-level officials. As responsibility for citywide programs is transferred to district governments, state officials should become able to exercise the same monitoring authority within the City as they now exercise for programs in other parts of the state. This probable increase in state influence might improve local program quality or might mean simply another layer of regulation and delay, but its likelihood should not be ignored.

The local district election process would probably dilute the mayor's power. Many local officials would not be members of the mayor's political party, and others would represent dissident factions of the mayor's party. Officials of some districts might feel more at home with representatives from Nassau or Westchester County. And a number of local officials would develop their own lines to Albany. As a result the mayor would be even less able than he is today to speak for the whole of New York City or to control the votes of the whole City delegation in the state legislature.

The City as an institution would, therefore, probably be less influential after decentralization. But as the City's share of the state's population decreases, the City is becoming less and less able to carry the state for the Democratic Party or to influence Republican state administrations or legislatures. Sooner or later the City will have to develop new alliances if City residents are to be assured of fair treatment. If decentralization sped up development of a common City-suburb cause, the City's residents might be gainers, even if the City as an institution became less significant.

TRANSITION TO DECENTRALIZATION

If it were decided that the potential advantages of political decentralization outweighed its costs and that the possible sociopolitical consequences were acceptable or at least worth risking, the next issue would be how the City should move toward decentralization. If the objective were to make certain that decentralization occurred and that it not be sidetracked by its opponents, the best course might be to press for passage of a new City Charter providing for immediate decentralization. In that way the new local district governments would be in existence and exerting political influence while the snags in the system were being worked out.

Such a course of action would involve high risks. Conflict would be inevitable, not only because those who opposed the change would feel that decentralization had been rammed through without regard for their views but also because the City Charter would be full of ambiguities and outright mistakes if it were not preceded by a period of testing and experimentation. The argument for immediate decentralization is that controlled experiments in government rarely succeed because political forces always demand instant impact or premature benefits to the "control" areas, and conclusions are usually drawn before the evidence is in, much less evaluated. The decentralization law should be shaped by the politics of the experiment, not by any scientifically reviewed findings. In any event New York has been studied enough, the argument runs, and the crisis of confidence is already too acute. The system needs shaking up, and the potential benefits of decentralization are sufficient to make the gamble worth taking.

A more conservative approach would start with the proposition that the City's government is extraordinarily complex because its problems are complex and that, rightly or wrongly, the system cannot work if important interests refuse to cooperate. On that basis any decentralization law would be preceded by a substantial period of public discussion, negotiation with all interested groups, and probably experimentation and pilot projects. And no law would be passed until the concept were accepted by all major interest groups, either because they approved it or because they realized that its support from others was too great to overcome. Such an approach would avoid unnecessary mistakes and conflict, but it would also involve compromises. Given the opportunity, moreover, powerful opposing interests might well be able to veto decentralization entirely or to force so many compromises as to make it meaningless.

If the more cautious approach were adopted, experimentation could take many forms. The Lindsay Administration has already experimented with several forms of decentralized citizen participation with its UATF's, neighborhood city halls, and the community planning boards, as well as with the federally sponsored Community Action and Model Cities programs. None of these programs materially altered the form or content of continuing mainstream government services, at least in part because there were no decentralization services for local groups to influence. As a result, the City's Office of Neighborhood Government suggested in 1971 that political decentralization could not work until the City's service departments were reorganized. In other words administrative decentralization must precede political decentralization.

Operating on this assumption the City is mounting a series of experiments to see how control of important governmental services can be decentralized administratively to facilitate adapting services to local needs, to make integration of local services possible, to spur local management initiative, to stimulate local planning and establishment of local priorities, and ultimately perhaps to constitute a governmental apparatus for local political forces to control. The City has selected five community districts with differing socioeconomic characteristics to be pilot administrative decentralization districts. The service district boundaries of the major City departments that serve those areas are to be redrawn, so as to be congruent with each other and with the community district. Those same departments will also delegate as much responsibility as possible to their district supervisors. Finally, the mayor's Office of Neighborhood Government will appoint a coordinator for each district who will convene a neighborhood cabinet of district supervisors to develop joint program efforts and will intercede on their behalf with representatives of the City's principal overhead agencies.

One of the first efforts in the pilot districts will be to develop district information systems with data on current conditions and inventories of existing programs and activities. The City is developing performance criteria to judge program achievements in these districts. This information will be compiled into a budget for each district, though more a descriptive budget than a prescriptive one, at least at first. Later the information will be the basis for rudimentary district plans, which will seek to set priorities and suggest how City programs can be adapted to serve the special needs of each district.

During the early years of this experiment, no attempt will be made to organize any new district political bodies. There will be ample local political input from existing civic groups, political clubs, and special interest groups. Indeed, the accessibility of the City's coordinator and the district program supervisors is an essential part of the experiment. But the City hopes to avoid some of the problems of Community Action and Model Cities, which endowed local political organizations with great expectations but with no levers to affect any important administrative or program decisions. Indeed, none of the pilot districts overlaps the model neighborhoods, and the Community Corporations are not to be given any special role, as they do not deliver essential services.

If administrative decentralization proves feasible and worth the effort, it could pave the way for reorganization of the City's political structure. Hopefully, the experience gained in the administrative decentralization projects would be useful in designing a new political structure. And any such new decentralized political structure would start out with an administrative structure already in place and thus avoid some of the confusion and inefficiency that could cripple decentralization if the political reorganization came first.

But the administrative decentralization-first approach also has its problems. Administrative decentralization would not be a long-run solution, both because the central delegators of power would never give up real authority and because the critical element of shifting political power would be missing. The new administratively decentralized bureaucracy would soon become entrenched and would develop strong relationships within government and with local interest groups—such as, for example, the community boards. A whole new network of public and private interest groups would become just as committed to preserving the administratively decentralized status quo as existing groups are to preserving the present centralized system.

Furthermore, it could be argued that as long as all decisions continue to be subject to central review, decentralization will not be tested at all. And there will be no effort to experiment with new budgetary or fiscal approaches or with modifications of civil service or collective bargaining arrangements. Finally, the crucial element in the success or failure of multipurpose political decentralization will be the response of district residents, and this will not even be encouraged, much less tested.

If experimentation is to precede full-blown decentralization, then political and administrative decentralization should perhaps be tested together. Under a more ambitious scheme, then, the number of pilot districts would be increased, and provisional governments would be elected in some of them. As the tests progressed, some districts would develop their own budgets and begin to operate under some form of functional allocation grant system, as described in Chapter 5. At the same time those districts would form their own civil service commissions and begin to develop their own standards for employee classification, hiring, promoting, disciplining, and firing. They would also participate in negotiations with employee unions with regard to work rules, personnel practices, and professional policies.

Such pilot politically decentralized districts would provide a much fuller test of the utility of decentralization and should develop better guides for the framing of the ultimate system. But they would also create much more tension than the more modest administrative scheme and would be more vulnerable to the kind of political manipulation and bureaucratic and union undercutting that characterized the City's school decentralization experiments. Nevertheless, since the local political process would be a main subject of the test, political activity of all kinds should be expected, indeed, encouraged. All would not be smooth and rational at first, nor would participation be as widespread as hoped. One can only hope that the experiment would be permitted to last long enough to be a fair test. As far as the administrators, bureaucrats, public employees, and their unions are concerned, a main objective of the experiments would be to demonstrate that City officials and employees can do a better job under decentralization, without sacrifice of any essential rights or privileges. Tests should not be started until there is full understanding of the ground rules and a willingness at least to give them a try.

A more modest beginning would be the creation of a City-state commission to study decentralization and report to the City and to the state legislature. A principal purpose of any such commission should be to stimulate public discussion and careful analysis by the principal interest groups that would be affected. A legislative finding that multipurpose political decentralization deserved serious consideration would be a useful impetus to the development of the public understanding that should precede any decentralization effort.

Except for the decentralize-first-experiment-later scheme, there is no reason why all of the above approaches should not go forward simultaneously. Decentralization might have the best chance of succeeding if the City government and the state legislature both declared that multipurpose political decentralization deserved full consideration and if the state appropriated funds to pay for experimentation and evaluation. The City might then realign all service district boundaries to conform with community district boundaries, with appropriate adjustments, so as to create 30 to 40 comprehensive districts. A citywide, district-based information system could be developed and as much authority as possible delegated to all district supervisors. The City could pursue its broader administrative decentralization pilot projects in as many districts as feasible. And full-fledged political decentralization projects might be launched in perhaps three areas of widely different sociopolitical character.

Any period of experimentation should last a full five years. By the end of that time it should be possible to decide how far the City should go toward decentralization, and the effort would be extensive enough to ward off special interest obstructionism, unless the effort were going so badly that it should be stopped on the merits. While such experiments will not be scientific as a practical matter, or even controlled, unscientific experimentation is better than none, because there is no other way to learn. In New York City the stakes are high enough to make the attempt well worth making.

APPENDIX:
THE DELIVERY OF
SANITATION SERVICES IN
A DECENTRALIZED
NEW YORK CITY
Michael L. Schwartz

INTRODUCTION

A decision to decentralize the government of New York City along the lines summarized in Chapter 7 of the foregoing study would reflect a judgment that, over all, the result will be an improvement in City services. Yet such a move would clearly entail different adjustments and adaptations in different service areas and would affect the delivery of different services in different ways. The body of this study necessarily blurs some of these variations, but for several reasons it may be useful to consider decentralization in the context of a single municipal service. Analysis of the present performance of a particular City function and of the changes decentralization would bring should reveal some of the important interstitial problems that any effort at large-scale reform will have to confront. It may also provide a different perspective on the broader questions of policy and politics discussed in the preceding pages.

What follows is an account of the performance of the municipal sanitation function, with these objectives in view. Sanitation is an appropriate service to examine for these purposes because it is faced with many of the seemingly intractable problems that have beset City

---

This study is largely based on information obtained through interviews and could not have been written without the kind assistance of the more than two dozen people, officials of the Department of Sanitation and others, with whom the author talked. In addition a ground-breaking Ph.D dissertation on the department by Peter L. Shaw was very helpful on several points. All errors are the responsibility of the author.

government in recent years and which have stimulated discussion of
decentralization as a remedy: rapidly rising need for service, even
more rapidly rising demand for service, and inadequate response to
both the need and the demand. In metropolitan areas of the United
States, pounds of refuse production per day increased by more than
20 percent between 1960 and 1970, and in New York City the current
rate of increase is twice that figure—4 percent per year. Disposable
packaging and other new patterns of consumption produce vast amounts
of street litter.

Moreover, sanitation services have recently been the subject of
major political controversy. In the area of refuse collection, in particular, citizens and political leaders alike have charged that some parts
of the City receive better or more frequent service than others; anger
and bitterness over sanitation services have fomented situations just
this side of being riots. The City's three Model Cities areas have all
made sanitation an important program priority. And in some middle-
class areas, poor sanitation services are perceived—and resented—
as symbols of an indifferent government.

The City's sanitation service has not been able to meet the need
and the demand. It is widely agreed that the quality of service has
long been deteriorating; by 1969 the Department of Sanitation was in
a condition of crisis. Refuse collection schedules were never adhered
to in many parts of the City, nor were street-sweeping schedules.
Ill will between citizens and department personnel was rampant all
across the City. Sanitation became probably the most salient issue
in the 1969 mayoralty campaign.

Many proposals were made to ease the sanitation crisis, ranging
from the substitution of paper and plastic refuse containers for galvan-
ized steel cans—an approach now in limited use—to the automation of
the sanitation function by the construction of pneumatic refuse tubes
terminating in enormous incinerators or compactors. Taxes on certain forms of packaging and other incentives to reduce the waste
load were also suggested.

But for the City the chief issue was, and is, how to strengthen
and improve the department. Union chief John DeLury called for
more men and newer equipment. Aides to the mayor advised him that
the administration of the department was sloppy and unimaginative.
And there were demands from many quarters for decentralization and
community control. In the aftermath of the mayoralty campaign,
Mayor Lindsay authorized the hiring of 1,000 new sanitationmen and
the filling of 400 vacancies that had accrued. In early 1971 he appointed
a modern-management-minded commissioner. And he directed the
administrator of the EPA to give the department intensive personal
attention.

Perhaps as a result of these steps, the situation has significantly

improved since the dark days of 1969-70. Recent statistics of the
department show dramatic reduction in backlog and overtime and a
significant rise in productivity over the earlier period. But there
remains much room for improvement and some hope that decentralization of the department would bring it about.

PRESENT PERFORMANCE OF THE
SANITATION FUNCTION

The Department of Sanitation

Responsibilities

     The City of New York runs the world's largest sanitation
operation and gives its citizens a broader range of free sanitation
services than does any other unit of government in the world. The
New York City Charter vests in the EPA two chief functions under the
heading "sanitation"—an operational responsibility and an enforcement
responsibility.[1]
     As to the operational responsibility, the EPA is required to
provide for the following:

     1. The sweeping, cleaning, sprinkling, flushing, washing, and
sanding of the streets
     2. The removal and disposition of ashes, street sweepings,
garbage, refuse, rubbish, and waste
     3. The removal of ice and snow from the streets
     4. The removal of incumbrances from streets and the storage
or disposal of such incumbrances in accordance with regulations
adopted by the Board of Estimate, except that such board may provide
by regulation that the removal and storage of household effects or
other chattels shall be a responsibility of the general services administration
     5. The operation, maintenance, and use of incinerators or other
plants or equipment for the destruction or disposition of ashes, street
sweepings, garbage, refuse, rubbish, and waste.

     By contrast a 1964 survey of 984 communities with populations
of 5,000 or more, revealed that 55 percent of these communities did
not provide free municipal service; that in 95 percent of them, collections were made no more than twice a week; and that many other
kinds of service that New Yorkers receive from the department were
not publicly provided in many parts of the country.[2]

Although the City Charter provisions seem to require the Department of Sanitation to "remove and dispose" of garbage and refuse without distinction, it has never provided universal service; and since 1956 no commercial establishment has received City collection service, although the department annually accepts for disposal nearly 2.5 million tons of waste from private cartmen and demolition and construction sites.

The City Charter gives the EPA administrator authority to determine what types of refuse the department will collect, from whom it will be collected, and all other matters concerning the kind and manner of collection service. It is not clear how broad the administrator's discretion is under this provision. At the present time ashes, garbage, and rubbish are collected from the following:

1. All residential buildings, except for commercial tenants in such buildings
2. All "public buildings" owned by, or housing agencies of, the City or state, but not federal or interstate agency buildings
3. "special use buildings," meaning those exempt from City real estate taxation.

In addition to regular collection service, bulk pickups are made from these classes of buildings.

It is crucial to understand, however, that other provisions of law cast upon property owners and citizens a major share of sanitation activities. Thus, provisions of the City Housing Maintenance Code, which is enforced by employees of the Department of Housing, require the landlord of an apartment house to do the following: (a) provide janitorial services, (b) provide for regular refuse collection within his property, and (c) provide an adequate number of metal containers to store the refuse within his property and impose correlative obligations on tenants. Sections of the Health Code, which the department enforces jointly with the Department of Health, prohibit landlords and citizens alike from maintaining specified unsanitary conditions.[3]

Many sections of the Health Code overlap with provisions of the City Charter and Administrative Code that are enforced by the department in the exercise of its enforcement responsibilities, the other of the two chief functions mentioned above. Section 1403(1)(d) of the City Charter provides that the EPA "may adopt regulations controlling the use of sidewalks and gutters by abutting owners and occupants for the disposition of sweepings, garbage, refuse or rubbish, and may provide that the violation thereof shall be punishable by civil penalty, fine or imprisonment." Also, in connection with its refuse collection responsibilities, the Administration is empowered to prescribe civil penalties for violations of the regulations concerning

placement of refuse for collection. Such regulations are in effect.
Sections of the Administrative Code also prohibit "littering" and
"dumping."

City agencies other than the Department of Sanitation have
operational as well as enforcement responsibilities in the general
area of sanitation. The most important case is the Department of
Parks, which is solely responsible for collecting refuse in the City's
hundreds of large and small parks. Moreover, many of the vacant
lots located around the City are owned by the City and are under the
responsibility of the Department of Real Estate; it can, but rarely
does, contract privately or with the Department of Sanitation to have
them cleaned.

In sum, the Department of Sanitation's jurisdiction under present
law reaches from building line to building line: Its operational responsibility is limited to the removal of properly placed refuse of certain
kinds and the cleaning of the "streets," which are defined not to include
sidewalks; it has a broader enforcement power over the conduct of
private persons in the discharge of the sanitation responsibilities
committed to them. It is important to bear these legal points in mind
in assessing the department's operations, since they mean that the
dirtiness of New York reflects not only deficiencies in these operations
but also conditions resulting from the City's housing problems—in
particular the collapse of building services in many parts of the City—
and the problems of code enforcement as a mode of regulation.
General ignorance of this "public-private mix" of sanitation responsibilities may account for much of the bitterness with which the
sanitation issue has been debated; citizens—and some elected officials—
berate the department for the fact that the City is filthy, without
acknowledging that the department does not really have a mandate to
keep the City clean, but only to perform certain parts of that job.

The structure of sanitation services in New York City came in
for major criticism in a report prepared in late 1970 by the deputy
mayor-City administrator's office. As its title—Refuse Collection:
Department of Sanitation vs. Private Carting—suggests, the report
compares the activities and costs of the department and the City's
private cartmen, who collect refuse from commercial establishments,
construction sites, and the like. The study on which it was based
found that the department's collection costs per ton were nearly three
times those of the private sanitation companies and that, in general,
the latter provided more efficient and reliable service than does the
department. "The inefficiency of the latter," it asserted, "is due to
its monopoly position with respect to residential collection. Because
of this monopoly, technological and managerial improvements are
likely to yield only modest improvements in present operations. The
effective remedy is to make structural changes in the entire system

by weakening the monopoly and increasing competition. Accordingly,"
the report concluded, "the general recommendation emerging from
this study is that the Department of Sanitation should gradually be
reduced in size and scope, and that the private cartage industry should
be given the opportunity to expand and provide some of the refuse
collection service now offered by the Department."

Both the findings and recommendations of the report—which
are further discussed below (page 227)—were disputed by many inside
and outside the department.[4] Less controversial, and perhaps more
interesting, was the reminder in the report that New York City attempts
to do a very great deal indeed—much more than most American cities—
through the department.

Organization

To fulfill its many responsibilities the department employs over
14,000 people and spends more than $185 million a year. In these
terms it is among the largest operations conducted by the City.
Though it is by no means an organization on the scale of the Board of
Education, and although its budget is less than one-tenth that of the
Department of Social Services, its activities—in contrast to those
agencies just mentioned—are financed almost exclusively out of City
revenues, like those of the Police and Fire departments, and are
therefore subject in fact as well as law to virtually exclusive City
control.

The department is run by a commissioner. This job has seen
a very rapid turnover in the last few years; prior to the recent
appointment of Herbert Elish, there had been one full-time and four
acting commissioners since 1967. As a result management of the
department was largely in the hands of the deputy commissioners, in
charge of the two staff bureaus (administration and engineering) and
four line bureaus (motor equipment, plant maintenance, cleaning and
collection, and waste disposal) of the department. It was during this
period that the department fell into the conditions of the crisis described
above.

Of the six bureaus, the most important for present purposes is
the Bureau of Cleaning and Collection, which directs, supervises,
and coordinates the department's street-cleaning, waste collection,
and snow removal operations within the five boroughs. The bureau
assigns by far the largest part of the department's manpower (roughly
11,300 men of the total of 14,000) and accounts for about 70 percent
of the department's budget; it is also the arm of the department that
has most contact with the public and whose work is most readily
judged by the public.

The bureau is run from the headquarters Office of the Director, who is known within the department, in conformity with the old custom, as chief of staff, or "chief." He is assisted by seven assistant chiefs and a field organization divided into eleven "borough commands," and further into 58 "sanitation districts," each containing an average of five "sections." The most recently created borough commands, Queens North and South, were formed in October 1969, during the mayoralty campaign, from the old Queens East zone. In 1967 the number of borough commands was increased from eight to ten, to reduce the span of control between borough and district offices. In the same year the department revised district boundaries for the first time since 1951.

The basic limit on the number of districts and hence on district size is the number of officers available for assignment, since the department attempts to have two officers on the day shift and one on the night shift in every section. In other words the districting process is chiefly a matter of distributing supervisory personnel around the City. At the present time, and for the past few years, the department is and has been suffering a marked shortage of experienced men in the lower supervisory titles—section foreman and assistant foreman— largely because of the effects of a liberal retirement option enacted in the same year as the most recent redistricting; thus it is hard to assess the wisdom of that districting.

The sizes of the districts seem at first glance to vary widely: population ranges from 20,000 to 300,000 and area from a low of 1.2 square miles to a high of 21.5 square miles. The department apparently has not attempted to make districts in any sense "equal" all across the City. However within each (political) borough, there is a rough equality. The department study on which the 1967 redistricting was based explicitly rejected sole reliance on either district population or physical area; an effort was made instead to develop factors to provide a reliable gauge of work load. The factor is known as the population-ton-mile factor (PTMF), and is obtained by multiplying population by average monthly tonnage by the number of curb-miles. Operating experience of the department in the old districts was also taken into account, by examining records of average loads per shift, men and trucks assigned, and so on. The basic principle of the redistricting was then that the PTMF for any district should be "within range of" the average PTMF for the borough command.

But district size does not determine the assignment of men and equipment. Since the measure of service need that is employed in districting is only an estimate and since, in any event, the need varies from time to time, assignments are modified at frequent intervals, both through permanent transfers of men and equipment and, more often, by temporary shifts in resources from district to district. The details of these processes are discussed below.

The Sanitation District—Powers
and Constraints

Powers

Sanitation districts are intended to be autonomous operating
units. Within the constraints discussed below, a district superintendent
is free to make daily determinations as to whether all the routes
normally scheduled for a given day and shift should be run or whether
certain of the sections within his district require an especially large
commitment of men and equipment. However, absolute priority is
given to the collection function; the number of collections per week is
set for every section by a schedule prepared at headquarters, and the
superintendent is not free to vary the mix of collection, sweeping and
flushing, and bulk pickup. Perhaps for this reason, when the waste
collection work load grows rapidly, the street-cleaning, lot-cleaning,
and bulk collection effort—the latter two not being conducted according
to a schedule—are reduced. For example between 1965 and 1969, annual man-days spent on street cleaning declined from about 275,000
to fewer than 200,000.

If a collection must be omitted, it is initially the district superintendent's responsibility to try to make it up, using the resources
under his command. These resources include on the average 15 to 20
officers, 180 sanitationmen, 25 to 30 collection trucks, 5 to 10 pieces
of other equipment (flushers, power sweepers, snow plows) and, of
course, a garage where the equipment is housed and where minor
repairs can be performed (an average of three mechanics are on
duty during the day shift). These figures are averages in two senses:
first, the number of sections per district varies from four to six;
second, and far more significantly, the number of men and machines
actually available to a superintendent fluctuates because of absences,
vacancies, withdrawals, breakdowns, and other causes.

If the district superintendent is unable, with his own resources,
to meet his collection schedule or to reschedule missed collections
without depriving other areas of adequate service, he can turn to the
borough command superintendent for assistance. The eleven borough
superintendents have plenary power to shift men and equipment among
the districts in their commands. They also have the power to overrule the determination of a district superintendent as to how to deal
with backlog, or even as to whether a backlog exists; the borough
commands regularly dispatch officers to inspect districts under their
authority. If neither a change in intradistrict operations nor temporary
interdistrict assignments are adequate, a borough superintendent can
request the following from headquarters: (a) resources from other
borough commands; (b) the assignment of the Night Mobile Task Force

to the troubled district; or (c) an authorization to assign men to over-time work.

The district superintendent has the primary responsibility for seeing to it that the sanitationmen perform their duties well and thoroughly. In discharging this vital function, the superintendent relies heavily on his section foremen. They supervise the actual conduct of operations and do the paperwork that provides the only complete record of operations that the department maintains. The chief records of operations are the section and district operations records books. The section book is compiled from the collection load tickets (D.S. 350) on which an assistant foreman enters for each shift the start and finish time of each collection crew; the time spent on each collection trip (exclusive of time spent at, and traveling to and from, the disposal location; the weight load as recorded at the disposal site; information about the truck (including breakdowns); and so on. By tallying these tickets the foreman or assistant foreman can tell whether or not the collection operation is being conducted at a steady, sustained level. If irregularities appear, he can either make route adjustments himself or refer the problem to the district superintendent's office.

In addition the section foreman is responsible for maintaining payroll and personnel records and for making home visits to men reporting in sick.

Discipline of the men is theoretically also in the hands of the superintendent and his foremen. The Bureau of Cleaning and Collection is in some respects organized on military lines; like the Police and Fire departments, the bureau is a uniformed force, and the uniforms of officers bear bars of rank. Sanitationmen are subject to a detailed code of discipline, some provisions of which are obviously modeled on standard codes of military justice. Violations of the code are in the first instance subject to reprimand by the officer in charge, normally the assistant foreman or foreman. In theory no other sanctions can be summarily imposed; in case of any serious violation, charges must be prepared (any officer can prefer charges) and a hearing had thereon. Moreover, if any exercise of authority is disputed, the aggrieved Sanitationman may invoke the hearing process, the thrust of which is to remove the dispute from the district level; in three forty-eight-hour stages, it can be taken to the borough office, bureau headquarters, and finally the commissioner's hearings deputy, who conducts well over 1,000 complaint proceedings a year. Informally, more summary discipline is imposed; senior officers can and do order suspensions for serious irregularities without much fear of challenge, since the union is reluctant to defend real recalcitrance. Some officers—especially the older ones—assert the same prerogatives, but many are hesitant to confront local union representatives.

Constraints on the District Superintendent

While many aspects of the present organization of the bureau vest in the district superintendent substantial responsibility, a wide variety of contraints impairs his ability to exercise it.

Administrative Constraints. The administrative organization of the bureau is far from being consistent in the role it assigns to the district superintendent. A number of important functions are not in his hands, although it could be persuasively argued that they belong there.

Chief among these is the responsibility for determining the mix of services delivered in the district. The department's policy of placing an absolute priority on meeting collection schedules means that a superintendent cannot decide that over some period of time he will use more of his resources for, say, bulk collection or manual street sweeping—critical needs in low-income communities—and lessen collection. Collection and sweeping schedules are established at headquarters. Of course, the superintendent is consulted, and his advice taken into account, in the scheduling process. But when, for example, in the spring of 1971, collections in middle-class areas of the City were reduced from three to two per week, the decision was made by the commissioner in consultation with the chief of staff; indeed, the Mayor himself played a large role in this decision. More-over, "Worth Street"—department headquarters, located at 125 Worth Street in Manhattan—not infrequently transfers men and equipment from one borough to remedy a situation in another that is not satis-factory to the top brass. For example, interborough detachments have been employed to meet the new twice-a-week schedules unfailingly. Over the past 18 months, Worth Street has also adopted a con-scious policy of scrutinizing reports from the districts far more searchingly and critically than had been its practice.

Actions of the borough superintendent also limit the district superintendent's range of options. He too has the right to overrule a district superintendent to determine both that one of his districts is adequately clean (so that men and equipment can be withdrawn from it) and that another is inadequately clean (so that additional resources should be assigned to it). Indeed, this power of the borough super-intendent represents the major day-to-day incursion on the district superintendent's planning and activities.

Of course, this is by design. The initial assignment of men to districts is based upon only a rough estimate of service need, and these shifts—or "temporary detachments," as they are called in the lexicon of the department—can be made without consulting the union or the seniority lists, as would be necessary if men were permanently reassigned—"transferred"—from one district to another. Moreover, headquarters and the borough commands are staffed by officers of superior ability, whose judgments of need are presumptively sounder than those made at the district level. Their ability to make these detachments is presumably indispensable in the event of a sanitation crisis—when the Mets win the pennant and parade up Broadway or the Young Lords throw garbage in the street of East Harlem—or of a major snowfall. But the department defends these incursions, and those of the chief of staff's office, more broadly, arguing that the department's responsibility is not to see that district superintendents do as well as they can but to assure the maintenance of an acceptable average sanitation condition citywide.

Yet it seems clear that the power of a headquarters official or borough superintendent to overrule a district superintendent so readily entails a major cost, by depriving the district superintendent of any genuine sense of responsibility for his district and of any freedom to innovate in his operations. The men resent it too; they have little incentive to work quickly or efficiently, since they know that unusually good performance will mean that they will be sent into another district. But the unflattering opinion of the competence of the district super- intendents, which in part explains the practice, is probably more nearly warranted at the present time in light of the department's retirement crisis than it was in years past. And if the department supply of manpower is as inadequate as is claimed, then these transfers represent an alternative to the extensive use of overtime. While the department reported using 110,065 hours of overtime for refuse collection in the year ending June 30, 1969, it seems likely that this figure would be doubled or trebled if the practice of making temporary detachments was abandoned. Of course there is a third possibility—a roving squad to supplement the efforts of regularly scheduled crews.

In the summer of 1969 Mayor Lindsay authorized the creation of such a body, the "Night Mobile Task Force." There are 100 men presently assigned to the force, which is dispatched to areas that in the bureau director's judgment require services over and above what the borough superintendent can provide. But its activities are of marginal importance in the department's work. The force is too small to represent an alternative to intraborough command transfers as a source of operational flexibility. Moreover, it operates only at night, presumably in part because of the great difficulty that any mobile force would have in maneuvering through traffic in daytime hours.

The second area, closely related to the first, in which the district superintendent has little real responsibility is community relations. It is a striking feature of department operations—and a depressing commentary on the state of the City—that district super- intendents were at one time virtually under orders not to act upon citizen complaints or meet with community groups on their own initiative, and they still refer many communications from the public to the Office of Citizen Involvement (OCI) in the EPA. Indeed, such communications are not encouraged; for example, district office telephone numbers are not publicized. Moreover, all innovative programs for improving sanitation conditions are conducted under the direct supervision of OCI and, indeed, either originate there or are put into operation from this office, though conceived in the mayor's office or in an EPA office. The department's commitment to central control of community relations is justified on the grounds that, at least in poorer neighborhoods, district superintendents would otherwise be overwhelmed by requests—or demands—for various special services.

However, the OCI has some local offices of its own. In 1967 Mayor Lindsay inaugurated three sanitation self-help offices in New York "to provide local groups with a base from which to conduct community improvement activities." The offices, now increased somewhat in number, are located in each of five boroughs. Office space is provided by other city agencies or community groups in the area. This close tie to other groups or agencies was designed as an economy measure and, also, to keep assistance readily available.

The self-help offices are usually staffed by two sanitationmen, carefully screened so that they can act as effective public relations men for the department. They are viewed as a buffer between irate citizens and the department. They attend community meetings, Urban Task Force meetings, block organization meetings, church meetings, and so forth, outlining the programs that such groups can utilize through the offices, explaining deficiencies in service, distributing literature, and so forth. In addition, the offices assist groups interested in sponsoring lot cleanups, block cleanups, bulk pick-up drives, and the like to plan the effort and obtain department equipment for disposal. But the self-help offices are not part of the district structure. And the need to forward a request from an office to the OCI to the director of the bureau, and then back down the ladder through the borough command to the district superintendent is extraordinarily burdensome.

In 1968 an attempt was begun to bring the district offices themselves closer to the neighborhoods they serve; a plan was prepared to designate a community service officer in each district. These men would have provided district liaison for the self-help offices where they operate and would have enabled the district office to be more responsive to community groups. But the community service officer program was never implemented, apparently because of budgetary constraints.

The OCI has also conducted some very limited experimentation with new ideas in the collection and containerization of refuse.

Thirty-gallon-capacity plastic and treated paper bags with wall brackets were distributed by the self-help offices and evaluated. One-cubic-yard containers were installed in high-density areas at curbside to eliminate use of cans, and were serviced daily. But again these efforts are wholly in lieu of any experimentation at the district level.

The third major function that is practically out of the superintendent's hands is inspection and code enforcement. Although this activity, in collaboration with similar work performed by police officers of the Health and Housing departments, is expected to enforce the public-private "mix" of sanitation services that the City has adopted, it is the stepchild of the department. Only 191 sanitation patrolmen were budgeted in 1970, and because it is apparently the department's routine practice to raid these positions for other work deemed more urgent, only 128 were assigned to the inspectional force, and all but 25 were given duties other than field enforcement.

While the number of patrolmen has substantially increased in the past year, the major effect of the existence of this miniscule force is to perpetuate the departmental tradition that enforcement is a "headquarters" activity. Thus, while all sanitation officers are legally empowered to issue summonses for violations of the code provisions within the department's jurisdiction, they do not consider it an important part of their jobs, and little more than one-seventh of all summonses issued by the department in 1969 were issued by district officers.

Fourth, district superintendents do not have the authority to determine whether and when to clean vacant lots in their districts. The department's responsibility for lot cleaning depends on whether the property is owned privately or by the City. In the latter case the property is cleaned and the Department of Real Estate is billed. In the case of a privately owned lot, the department can act only if the Department of Health declares the lot a health hazard or the Fire Department certifies a fire hazard; in theory, the owner is then billed.

But in both cases the responsibility lies with the borough superintendents, each of whom has a special lot-cleaning detail. In the case of privately owned lots this assignment has some reason, because of the necessity for consultation with another agency and the complex legal steps that must be gone through before cleaning can proceed. But, once again, the effect of this assignment is to deprive the district office of responsibility for a problem that is of the utmost concern in low-income neighborhoods.

Finally, the district superintendent has no formal authority over the mechanics assigned to the district garage; although his garage foreman plays some role in scheduling repair work, the mechanics are under the control of the Motor Equipment Bureau, and responsible to the foreman of mechanics in their borough. Considering the

importance of fleet maintenance, this lack of authority is most unfortunate.

Resource Constraints. As important as the impact of these administrative arrangements may be, the performance of the sanitation
function is influenced even more seriously by fundamental resource
decisions made far above the district level. The superintendent's
ability to meet collection schedules and sweeping schedules depends
on having enough men and trucks. But he has no control over the
supply of these resources.

     Taking manpower first, in terms both of total assigned manpower
and of available manpower per shift and/or per route, the district
superintendent is at the mercy of actions and policies within the
authority of the bureau director or the commissioner. Starting at the
top, the number of sanitationmen to be hired is decided by and among
the commissioner, the Bureau of the Budget, and the mayor. And
until very recently the department fared poorly in the budget wars.
Between 1954 and 1964 its share of the City's expense budget fell
from 4 to 3 percent, and since the creation of the EPA it has declined
further. The result is that the department has consistently complained
that it does not have enough men to meet its growing responsibilities.
It is hard to settle on a reliable measure of manpower adequacy, but
many indicators substantiate the department's complaint. The total
force of sanitationmen, even including the 1,000 new sanitationman
positions authorized in the 1971 (fiscal year) budget, is smaller than
the force was 35 years ago (as union chief DeLury is fond of pointing
out). And the department is rarely up to authorized strength; because
of budgetary accruals—of which the department has historically gotten
a large number—the force is currently about 500 men short.

     The shortage is most acute in the supervisory titles, but vacan-
cies—and the resulting availability of accruals—have occurred at a
fantastically high rate throughout the force because of the liberal
retirement options authorized by the state legislature in 1967 in an
amendment to the Administrative Code. In the past three years a
number of supervisors equal to more than 100 percent of the 1968
supervisory force have retired! The reason given for enacting the
retirement law was that sanitation work is so dangerous that the life
expectancy of sanitationmen—about 55 years—made the prior pension
arrangement, keyed to retirement at 65, wholly inappropriate. It is
sure that the accident rate among sanitationmen is appallingly high;
the accident rate for sanitationmen is more than twice that of policemen or firemen and considerably in excess of that of lumberjacks. But
it is clear that the massive retirement of officers has forced the
bureau to promote men of lesser caliber, about whose performance
old hands in the department shake their heads.

The determinations of manpower quotas are made in the bureau director's office. The factor that now governs these determinations is that each district should have enough men to be able to complete waste collection on Mondays—the peak load day—without leaving any backup; the theory is that if manpower is adequate for this task, it is adequate for any. While district records are employed in making the determination that a larger complement is needed, there seems to be little probing as to why the district superintendent found the prior force assigned inadequate. This is probably explained by the frequency with which men are "temporarily detached" from one district to another and, more generally, the lack of final control over his men enjoyed by the district superintendent. This transiency was especially marked in the recent years of crisis. With the increase in authorized strength of 1,000 positions, the work force in each district has become more permanent.

However, men are free to transfer from one district to another whenever an assignment in the receiving district is available. Transfer rights are spelled out in the collective agreement and are governed by seniority. Although it has often been charged that men initially assigned to poorer neighborhoods seek transfer out as soon as their seniority is sufficient—leaving these areas with the most junior men— because of prejudice, all of the people to whom we spoke said that the chief reason for transfers was a desire to be assigned to a district near one's home, since the working day begins at 7:00 a.m. In any event the exercise of transfer rights obviously impairs the stability of a district's work force.

And the shortage of supervisory personnel continues. As a result section offices are woefully understaffed, and section foremen are detached as a matter of course. The district superintendent is thus powerless to build up an effective intradistrict organization.

Within the ceiling represented by the total work force, many administrative procedures in which the district superintendent plays no role further constrict his supply of manpower. First, and again citywide, a monthly average of about 500 sanitationmen per day (not including officers) are detailed to duties other than refuse collection and sweeping, mostly in district offices borough command offices, or at headquarters. And this figure does not include the loss in actual field manpower caused by the department's practice of using sanitation- men for clerical, janitorial, and other "civilian" functions ("limited duty men"—mostly injury victims—fill many of these posts). Moreover, the department is still considered a source of chauffeurs for high City officials.

Second, and no less important, is the impact of labor contract and work rules provisions on the available force. The department must negotiate with a total of 17 unions about terms and conditions of employment, but only two—the Uniformed Sanitationmen's Association, a local of the International Brotherhood of Teamsters, and the Association of Classified Employees (representing uniformed officers), a local of the Service Employees International Union—negotiate for all uniformed employees, the vast majority of bureau personnel.

The contracts provide for two days off per week—Sundays and one other, known as "chart day," which the contracts require to be scheduled regularly throughout the week. The result of this schedule is that the same number of men are available on each of the six weekdays, which is extremely undesirable, since the workload on Monday is heavier throughout the City than it is on any other day. In addition the contract contains provisions for 25 days of vacation a year, 11 paid holidays, and liberal rules concerning leave for illness—the Administrative Code guarantees unlimited sick leave, jury duty, and so on.

The impact of these provisions on the work force actually available is devastating. In the period from July 1970 to June 1971, for example, the total force averaged 11,412; but the average daily attendance (excluding Sundays) was a mere 6,656.

The other major constraint on performance is the frequent unavailability of equipment. The department orders all trucks, sweepers, flushers, and other equipment used in the field through a central office at headquarters. But the purchasing process is a far cry from a carefully planned and administered capital acquisition program. For example, although the department has, over the past 15 years, regularly operated between 1,600 and 1,800 trucks, the rate of replacement of old equipment has fluctuated widely, obviously in response to extrinsic budgetary pressures rather than any rational pattern of managerial decisions. Thus, in 1967 no new trucks were received, and in 1965, only 11, although 189 and 87 trucks were retired in those years; on the other hand in 1966, 175 trucks were received and only 60 retired.

Beginning in 1968 the Lindsay Administration began a three-year program to replace almost the entire fleet, and in 1969, 644 trucks were received and 468 retired. However, there is no indication as to whether the haphazard replacement cycle of past years will revive when the current crash acquisition program is completed or whether a more orderly process will be adopted.

Moreover, as in the case of manpower, the total size of the fleet is no measure of the resources actually available to a district. This is because of the astonishingly high rate of accidents and breakdowns experienced by the department fleet. The regular statistical records of the department show that the percentage of trucks "down" at any one time has recently averaged about 35 percent. By comparison the Railway Express Agency fleet has a "down" factor of about 7 to 8 percent and the Post Office a factor of about 10 percent; the

Los Angeles Department of Sanitation reports a figure of between
12 and 15 percent. And private cartmen in New York report a "down"
factor of only 5 percent. While other aspects of the department's
performance have improved in the last year and one-half, little progress
has been made in reducing the "down" rate.

The "down" rate is explained in part by the failure in the past
to replace trucks as regularly as they should have been. This has
had two important consequences: the fleet has been overage, and many
trucks have been overused (it is common for trucks to be used on two
successive shifts). Moreover, the trucks are of course driven under
extremely arduous conditions. But there are other reasons as well.
First, trucks that "go down" stay "down" for too long a time. Until
recently all major repairs were made at a single garage facility
located in Maspeth, Queens, and disabled trucks had to be towed there.
In the last several months a number of other major repair facilities
have been opened, and this may improve matters. However, at least
at Maspeth, spare parts are frequently unavailable. And there are
frequent complaints that work habits of mechanics there are poor—slow
and careless. In addition, some observers have suggested that the
men in the field are not sufficiently careful with the equipment they
use. In part this may reflect the fact that crews are not regularly
assigned to the same pieces of equipment and that more generally
there seems to be no incentive for the men to use care in handling
equipment. Finally, it should be noted that, while there are mechanics
assigned to the district garages, the City saves money by almost never
calling these highly paid men for weekend duty, so that there is almost
always a somewhat larger "down" factor on Mondays, one of the two
peak load days.

Work Patterns as Constraints on the District Superintendent. The
district superintendent's theoretical autonomy is also, and in a sense
most basically, limited by a network of formal and informal rules that
play a large role in determining the actual work patterns of the men
and officers.

The most important of the formal rules is the strict definition
of the working day contained in the collective agreement between the
Uniformed Sanitationmen's Association and the department. According
to its provisions the eight-hour day for which the men are paid includes
fewer than six hours of actual field work. The men are entitled to
30 minutes for lunch, two 10-minute work breaks during the day, 15
minutes for washup at the end of the day and the traveling time (often
as much as an hour) necessary to reach the section office for shift-end
check-out. Moreover, from the time available for refuse collection,
there must also be subtracted the time spent going to and from the
disposal site, as well as the time (often considerable) spent waiting

at the site before dumping. While some planners have discussed the possibility of reducing the travel time by building intermediate transfer stations all around the City, both the high cost and the inevitability of strong political opposition make adoption of this plan unlikely. Nonetheless, it is clear that disposal operations have an important impact on the level of collection services provided.

The "working day" of the men is now more significantly determined by the availability of equipment than by contract provisions or department procedures. Ordinarily, men pick a regular tour, by seniority; but the equipment problem discussed above has forced the department to schedule a large number of special night shifts to make up the collections missed during the day—there simply are not enough trucks available for any other schedule.

The informal work patterns of the force are difficult to document, but our interviews and conversations left a strong impression that these patterns include a significant amount of lack of discipline and carelessness. For example, there is little doubt of the accuracy of reports that some sanitationmen "keep back a part" of their loads at the disposal site, so that they will not have to make as many collection stops on their next route. Moreover, there is a widespread belief that the men do a goodly amount of "slacking off" while they are in the field. And the younger men, accustomed by their union (and the temper of the times) to think chiefly of their rights, resist discipline to a disturbing degree.

These practices are clearly symptoms of a serious erosion of morale among the force. The frequent changes in tours of duty to which they have been subjected, the lack of public cooperation, and the equipment problems discussed above have combined to produce a mood of bitterness and discouragement among the men. The rapid turnover at supervisory and management levels and the difficulties of integrating the department into EPA—a favorite target of union chief DeLury— have contributed to this state of affairs.

Some of these practices would seem to be subject to more effective control. To take the examples mentioned above, it seems clear, first, that the practice of "keeping back a part" is possible only because the department weighs trucks only when they arrive at a disposal site and not when they leave; and second that "slacking off" could be reduced if, as is done in some cities, all officers were supplied with scooters so they could inspect operations more closely.

But the problem of men doing what their union representative tells them to do rather than what their superior tells them is more difficult and, indeed, goes to the heart of the difficulty experienced by district superintendents and their subordinate officers. A total of 600 shop stewards and 20 business agents represent the men's interest at the many locations of the department. And since there is a growing tendency to define the rights and duties of the men not only in labor agreements but in highly detailed work rules, the areas of discretion enjoyed by the officers are shrinking; a vigilant union representative stands ready to challenge any exercise of discretion that appears to infringe the men's rights and to carry it to a higher level for resolution. The officers have themselves recently unionized, but their union relies heavily on the skill and experience of DeLury, and officers probably feel some hesitation therefore to assert themselves as supervisors. Moreover, since all officers have risen through the ranks, their sympathies may be more strongly with the sanitationmen than with the policies and problems of higher echelons in the administration; this is almost certainly true of the flood of newly promoted officers.

Yet on balance, one must be impressed by the commitment of the men and officers to their arduous, dangerous, and unglamorous work. If they feel little loyalty to their district and supervisors, they express loyalty to the department and its tradition of getting a dirty but necessary job done; some men are the second or third generation of their families to work in the department. This solidarity is a distinct asset of the department and may account for the fact that its work has gotten done at all during the recent years of personnel and equipment crises. It has kept the men going during the period when the consequences of years of shortchanging the department became visible to the City as a whole. And loyalty to the union is an aspect of this commitment to the job; the men feel they can count on DeLury as they cannot count on the "politicians" and "snobs" who run the City. A tour of the incredibly dingy and neglect-ridden facilities of the department makes it hard to blame them.

It has frequently been suggested that the responsiveness of the sanitation force would be substantially enhanced if more "local residents" were employed by the department. Particularly in the case of black and Puerto Rican neighborhoods, ethnic hostility between the sanitationmen and citizens is alleged to account for the inadequate performance of both groups, and especially the sanitationmen.

It is true that more and more sanitationmen live outside not only their assigned districts but beyond the City, in the suburban counties—a state law governing residence of public officers was amended in 1961 to permit this. Moreover, neither the sanitationmen nor the officers receive any but the most cursory training in "sensitivity" and "community relations"—which might or might not make any useful difference in their behavior. And there is evidence of a great deal of hostility between sanitationmen and citizens—not only in poor communities, but perhaps most intensely there. At the present time the ethnic composition of the uniformed force is about 75 percent Italo-American, 10 percent black, and a tiny percentage Puerto Rican. These figures (apart from the recent small influx of Puerto Ricans) have not changed much in the past 35 years. However, serious efforts have been made to increase the number of blacks and Puerto Ricans in the past several years, and the response has not been encouraging. Despite intensive recruitment by the department and the union and easing of various civil service rules in connection with an examination in January 1970, very few minority group members completed the application process. Apparently, the job was thought to be so lacking in status and opportunity that, despite the high pay and security it offers, blacks and Puerto Ricans were not interested. Moreover, the list that resulted from this exam was 13,000 names long, and may remain in force until 1974. Thus, it seems unlikely that a better-motivated sanitation force could be produced by changing the department's hiring practices in this regard.

Conclusions

The undoubted tendency of district superintendents not to command is probably strengthened—albeit unwittingly—by the absence of genuine responsibility for their districts. The facts that they have little or no role in program development, that their relations with the residents of the areas they serve must go up a line of command and through a central "community relations office," that even their day-to-day decisions about manpower deployment are subject to peremptory over-ruling by the borough superintendent—these facts combine to make of them only the agents of a system that must be characterized as highly centralized, and not the relatively independent administrative officers that they might appear on an organization chart.

It is difficult to evaluate the relative importance of the administrative centralization on the one hand and the resource and morale problems of the department on the other. But it can confidently be said that the ability of the current generation of supervisors to deal with those problems is doubtful, if only for the reason of their inexperience and consequent lack of command skill and judgment. This probably accounts for the fact that while the new commissioner is taking tentative steps at administrative decentralization, these do not seem to be a priority for him. On the contrary, as of this writing, the efforts of the commissioner are chiefly taking the form of a searching scrutiny of district and borough operations by himself and his top aides, notably including the bureau director. The commissioner has to date hired about 35 industrial engineers to assist headquarters planners. He has also sent out "collection productivity teams" to assist field officers in planning more efficient schedules and routes; current practices are being reviewed district by district at headquarters. Moreover, headquarters officials are taking a larger role in enforcing discipline in the ranks and among the officers. And consideration is being given to changing collection frequencies in some areas.

Some of this is a matter of expediency; both the mayor and EPA Administrator Jerome Kretchmer are determined to establish that they can achieve at least short-term improvements over the situation that prevailed in the darkest days of the 1968-70 period. For the longer run there is considerable attention being given to reducing the oversight exercised at least by headquarters officers, giving greater discretion to the borough commanders. The industrial engineers have been spending some of their time in the district offices, side by side with the superintendents, and it is hoped that there will eventually be one permanently assigned to each superintendent. But experienced men in the department wonder whether the growing lack of discipline in the field does not require a tighter rather than a looser rein over the long term. Though in the next breath they may add that that probably would not work either.

THE POLITICS OF SANITATION

The Past

Over the years the performance of the sanitation functions of the City has been deeply affected by problems of the sort discussed above, but never—until recently—by the presence of strong public concern.

Although the department was a highly political organization in the days before it was brought wholly under civil service, sanitation work itself is not traditionally an important political issue in New York. In the past there have been few voluntary organizations especially concerned with sanitation; the Citizens Committee To Keep New York Clean, incorporated in 1955, is apparently the only one still in existence. While block associations and general purpose civic groups would from time to time conduct or sponsor "cleanup" campaigns, there were no groups who monitored the department's activities and programs. Moreover, the City Administration traditionally neglected the department; as Wallace S. Sayre and Herbert Kaufman wrote more than seven years ago:

> Sanitation Commissioners, in their aspirations to control their department, derive little help from Mayors or the Board of Estimate. The agency provides few opportunities for Mayors to develop public policy. Higher priorities tend to crowd it off the Mayor's agenda, even if he were convinced that this assistance to the Commissioner would be decisive. . . .

> The Sanitation Commissioner exercises his main
> opportunities for leadership in close bargaining with the
> leaders of the largely autonomous union organization of
> his own employees.[5]

Presumably this public disinterest reflected aversion to the
unglamorous nature of the "garbageman's" work. It probably also
stemmed from general public indifference to the broad range of problems that are today thought of as comprising the "environmental
crisis."

The Present

In the past two years the mayor's office and several other outside
agencies have initiated a number of programs to improve department
performance. The Lindsay Administration's interest in sanitation
problems dates from the eight-day strike of sanitationmen in February
1968, when the mayor got a vivid demonstration of the importance of
this service. A year later an unexpectedly heavy snowstorm caught
many borough commands unprepared, with nearly disastrous political
consequences for Lindsay. Thereafter, the mayor embarked on a
major effort to woo union President DeLury, with much greater success
than he has had with other municipal union leaders. In the last general
election DeLury endorsed the mayor; the budget for 1971 (fiscal year)
contained an authorization for 1,000 additional sanitationman positions,
and the department was for a time the only City agency exempted from
the current hiring freeze, so that a total of 1,400 lines were filled at
a time when other agencies were not permitted to replace vacancies.

One result of these events is that the operations of the department
have come under intense scrutiny from members of the mayor's staff
and from a new Office of Program Planning in the EPA. The long
history of political isolation of the department seems to be ending.

The Administration's activities in sanitation have included
several initiatives to foster more productive relations between the
department and residents in some of the areas it serves. These
programs reflect the Lindsay Administration's strong across-the-board
concern for community involvement in the operation of government
programs; but there is also a recognition that, in light of the joint
public-private responsibility for sanitation, citizen performance
needs to be improved as well. And the growth of citizen concern
about the environment—sanitation was probably the most important
substantive issue in the 1969 mayoral campaign—suggests that citizen
involvement might be productive.

For these reasons, several of the UATF's have established

permanent subcommittees, called "sanitation task forces" (STF's),
to promote better sanitation practices on the part of citizens and to
oversee the operations of department personnel. The STF's have
recently negotiated arrangements with the department to facilitate
their watchdog roles: they have an assurance of access to the superintendents of the sanitation districts contained in the UATF districts
(the two districts' boundaries are not congruent), including their attendance at STF's meetings. It is unclear what the relation is to be
between the STF's and the borough superintendents. Moreover, it
seems that no formal changes are contemplated in the relation between
the borough commands and the district offices in the areas having
STF's. More generally, the plan does not contemplate changing the
administrative structure of the department in any respect; it seems
to be the hope that independent citizen group pressure will bring about
improved department performance. In some measure this decision
grows not out of hope but out of administration reluctance—underlying
many of its programs—to tamper with the internal arrangements and
procedures of a long-established agency; there is a pervasive mistrust
and apprehensiveness about the department itself among many of the
"mayor's people." It is perhaps for this reason that the numerous
other efforts of the administration in sanitation—the activities of the
Neighborhood Stabilization Program in "transition" neighborhoods,
the sanitation work of the EPA Office of Program Planning—all are
conducted through bodies outside the department.

The administration has also given assistance and encouragement
to the efforts of the City's three Model Cities areas to improve both
department performance and sanitation conditions. The most advanced
of these—the Community Clean-Up Program in the Central Brooklyn
Model Cities area—was implemented during 1969. Office space was
provided by the department as in the case of a self-help office, although
unlike other self-help offices, the Model Cities office has its own
equipment. The program is directed by Whitten McNeil, a sanitationman, with the title of field coordinator and rank of special investigator.
There are two groups of employees under his command: (a) from the
Sanitation Department, five assistant foremen and 51 sanitationmen
who operate all the equipment (with the exception of sidewalk power
brooms called "sidewalk vacs"); and (b) from the community, nine
program supervisors, or crew chiefs, and 130 EPA aides.

The projects undertaken are cleanups of areas not usually
serviced by the department—abandoned buildings, open lots, alleys,
and so on. The Model Cities offices also manage a program to
encourage property owners and shopkeepers to care for their neighborhood, and the EPA aides sweep the upkept walks regularly. Also,
the Model Cities Program includes some experimentation with new
techniques and equipment. The day-to-day garbage collection is done

by the sanitation district personnel in the districts within the Model
Cities area.

Conclusion

These experiments in improving department-community relations
have been in effect for too short a time to permit any final judgment
about them. Moreover, none of them amounts to decentralization in
any sense; they do not modify the administrative structure of the
department or redistribute decision-making power. Instead, they
represent a modest expansion of department activities in sanitation
problems that the department has either neglected or considered a
private responsibility and a first step in exposing an historically
isolated City agency to the pressures and problems of City government
in the 1970's. Moreover, it must be made clear that these community-
oriented efforts are far from being the major part—or even a significant part—of the City's current effort to improve sanitation service.

DECENTRALIZATION AND SANITATION:
THE COMMUNITY CONFRONTS SCARCITY

Introduction

The division of the City into 30 to 60 semiautonomous local
government districts, as proposed in the foregoing study, would give
sanitation district superintendents a great deal more discretion than
they possess at present. At a minimum superintendents would be free
to shift resources among different sanitation functions, undertake
various special projects—intensive City-owned lot cleaning, assistance
to neighborhood cleanup drives, and so forth—and experiment with
new techniques and (if funds are available) new equipment. To the
considerable degree that their inability to do so now stems from the
control exercised by headquarters and borough command offices,
decentralization would untie their hands.

But how much more discretion would the districts enjoy? For
it is more to the point to observe that decentralization would vest in
district superintendents the responsibility for dealing with the condition
of nearly perpetual scarcity in which the department operates. If there
is a single theme that emerges from the discussion in the section of
this appendix concerned with the present performance of the sanitation
function, it is that, in light of the demands on it, the department has
been for at least a decade—and probably will continue to be—short of

men, and equipment, and effective supervisory personnel. While the
waste load rises relentlessly at a rate of 4 percent a year; while
the City's population is composed of more and more lower-class
individuals unwilling or unable to assume legal or civic responsibility
for dealing with refuse; while the housing stock is increasingly
neglected—while these and other factors add to the department's
responsibilities, the City cannot afford to hire more men, cannot afford
to maintain its equipment adequately, and is increasingly staffed by
inexperienced supervisors. Under the present "centralized" administration it has tried to cope with this situation by a number of techniques, the chief of which exploit precisely the centralized nature of
that administration: large-scale "detachments" of men and equipment
from district to district, searching operations reviews by a concentration of talented officers in department headquarters, and a major
political effort at winning the goodwill of union leader John DeLury.

Presumably, none of these expedients would be available to
the political and administrative leadership of a semiautonomous
neighborhood government, and, assuming adoption of a "functional
allocation model" for financing local governments, a vastly increased
share of the budget is unlikely. Hence, decentralization would deprive
officials of some tools presently employed for dealing with a condition
of inexorable scarcity and would confront them with the challenge of
developing new administrative and political techniques for doing so.

What might these alternatives be? What new problems might
they create? Would the net result be an improvement in sanitation
services? The rest of this appendix attempts to answer these, and
related, questions.

Patterns of District Autonomy

The first question that must be resolved is whether decentralization means only giving local districts the responsibility of providing
presently offered services or whether it means that the power to
redefine "sanitation services" is also vested locally. The likely
consequences of each alternative are sketched below.

Strengthening Performance of the Sanitation
Function as Presently Defined

Assuming that the local districts were not permitted to change
substantially the kinds and variety of services provided under the
present system, the local sanitation officer would presumably possess
at least those powers that are denied him under the present administrative structure, as discussed above. Three of these merit a special

look: (a) the power to schedule and deploy his resources; (b) responsibility for community relations; and (c) responsibility for enforcing sanitation laws. What effects would his exercise of these powers have on service delivery?

Scheduling and Deployment. Some of the basic decisions that a sanitation officer must make are inextricably connected with fundamental resource determinations. The number of officers, men, and machines available to him sets limits on the number of collections he can schedule, the frequency with which streets can be swept, and so on. Hence, the local district officer in charge of sanitation can be expected to lobby for a larger share of the district's fiscal equalization grant or, in some kind of association with fellow officers from other districts, for a larger central allocation to the functional grant for sanitation. It is doubtful that under either fiscal system, he (or they) would be more effective than senior officers of the department are now. The necessary skills for such budgetary bargaining are not likely to be widely distributed among the individuals who will fill these jobs.

And the various other devices by which district superintendents now acquire additional resources—detachments, transfers, hidden appropriations—would not be available to the head of the local sanitation agency. Thus, the initial allocation of resources would take on heightened importance.

Indeed, the intial allocation would become so important, by contrast with the practice under the present system, as to call into question the appropriateness of the present district boundaries. As explained above these are considered not chiefly as units for the assignment of men as for assignment of officers; it is more nearly true that the eleven borough commands are the "districts," to which more or less permanent assignments of men and equipment are now made.

On the other hand it is almost self-evident that the district superintendent, through his own observation and the observation and records of his junior officers, is in the best position to know what are the sanitation needs of streets and buildings neighborhood by neighborhood, and what the possible response is, given the capacity of the men, traffic conditions, and so on. It is for this reason he is now consulted, and his advice taken into account, when manpower quotas are being made up for his district and when schedules are being revised.

But while the district superintendents have the most ready access to the information on which local scheduling and deployment decisions must be based, once again it is unlikely that many of them have the skills and judgment to make the best possible use of it. The work of analysis and planning is complex, and it is far from clear that even the present headquarters staff is equal to it, much less the incumbent district officers. At a minimum, and despite the considerable expense involved, a competent technical staff would have to be available to the district officer, either in his office or in the form of some remnant of the present bureau headquarters staff functioning as a citywide technical assistance agency. The alternative would be frequent interruptions in service in many districts and, in some areas, near chaos.

However, even if planning were of a very high order, it may well be that work load and job conditions vary too often to justify full confidence in the schedules and assignments that result from it. If so (and still assuming that there is no citywide backup force to compensate for the elimination of interdistrict detachments and transfers) the prudent district officer will not commit all his resources to planned activities, but will provide in effect his own backup force. It follows that, with more or less the same resources he has today, schedules are likely to be contracted compared to those now in force, though, assuming better planning, they should be more reliable.

This result may not be unsatisfactory in large areas of the City. When many districts went from "three to two" last spring, residents who were consulted about the move expressed a willingness to trade planned frequency for reliable infrequency. But in poorer neighborhoods the result would presumably be wholly unacceptable. Yet it is hard to see how decentralizing the scheduling and deployment power could lead to any other result.

It might be possible in some districts to reduce truck crews from three to two or even one. This would free men for extra collections if the supply of equipment were increased. But in poor, crime-ridden neighborhoods, the three-man crew is considered as much a necessity for safety as for efficient collection, and one can anticipate strong union opposition to crew reduction in such neighborhoods.

In sum decentralizing these powers means a net reduction in resources actually available to a district and an amplification of the importance of initial budgetary decisions. Any increase in local discretion to transfer resources from one sanitation service to another seems a small gain by comparison.

Community Relations. In a decentralized system the local sanitation officer might have to respond to complaints, participate in community affairs, and so on much more regularly than does the district superintendent at present. This is another reason for the reserve force, which, as argued above, he will almost certainly wish to establish. Clearly, this prospect offers both the opportunity of enhancing vital public cooperation with the sanitation force and the danger that the necessary routine functioning of the agency will be impaired. Which is the more likely result?

In a situation of resource shortage, the officer's participation in public meetings and the like may very often take the form of explaining why he cannot do something. In other words he will be on the line in the process of exposing citizens to the facts of life about the capacities of City government. In the early stages at least, someone is going to have to perform this disagreeable but necessary task, and the elected officials of the district may be inclined to leave it to the service officers, such as the local sanitation head. But this would be most unfortunate; it would probably both impair routine service and do little to promote an atmosphere of public understanding—since there is no reason to expect that the service chief will have any particular political skills. Therefore, either the elected officials will have to accept this responsibility or the service heads will have to have a staff officer for community relations.

The former seems by far the more desirable approach. Current personnel of the department, who are likely to staff the sanitation service during the period of transition and for a time thereafter, have not shown any great willingness or ability to deal effectively with the public. Moreover, they are unlikely to be able to distinguish important public spokesmen from spurious, headline-seeking "community leaders." Finally, local elected officials will have to assume responsibility for the quality of service vis-à-vis the public in order to establish and strengthen the importance of their offices. This will be in their own personal interest and will also be critical if the whole decentralization venture is to achieve what must be a major goal: to create a coherent local structure through which public wishes are made known and policy decisions arrived at.

In short the problem of "community relations" is more an aspect of the broad political challenge that the decentralization venture must confront than a problem for the service delivery organization. If it is important that people do not litter, that they stop failing to store garbage properly, and all the rest—and, of course, these changes in citizen behavior are critical—it is the immediate responsibility of elected officials to bring them about. It is almost certainly undesirable to make a service organization such as the sanitation agency respond willy-nilly to public demands; it must function by and large according to a fixed and finite agenda of particular responsibilities and succeed or fail in terms of that. It can and should provide assistance to the elected officials in their performance of their role; for example, it is to be hoped that the local sanitation agencies will do a much better job of keeping reliable records and generating trustworthy and comprehensible statistics than the department historically has done.[6] But it seems likely, even if paradoxical, that in a decentralized New York, "community relations" will and should become a less, rather than more, important part of agency activities.

This conclusion prompts one further observation. It may well be that a movement toward administrative as opposed to political decentralization would land the agency in the worst of both worlds: the district offices would appear to the public to have the capacity to respond to their wishes, but there would be no mediating structure through which careful and reasonable expression of these wishes could occur and through which thoughtful responses to them could be formulated. The district officer would be at the mercy of the loudest voices and the most unscrupulous tacticians.

Enforcement. One of the most potentially fruitful opportunities that decentralization would create is the chance to strengthen enforcement of the laws that prohibit unsanitary conduct. The present trivial enforcement effort has already been described, but it is worth reiterating at this point that a major improvement in it is essential if delivery of sanitation services is to improve. Although it is possible to imagine public assumption of some of the sanitation responsibilities now committed to private citizens (see below), this not only would be expensive, but in any event could be only partially effective; there is an irreducible minimum of private cooperation in any successful sanitation program. For example cars must be moved if streets are to be swept; yet EPA Administrator Kretchmer recently declared that "improperly or illegally parked cars impede us from cleaning 60 percent of the curbspace we cover," and a comic strip printed in Our Daily Planet, a newspaper published by the mayor's Council on the Environment, depicted Superman flying such cars away, but commenting, "This isn't a job for Superman! It's a job for every New Yorker!"

It is naïve to think that enforcement will not be necessary to obtain this cooperation, even in a decentralized New York. Habits of sloppiness and uncleanliness are not going to vanish because there is a local district government, nor is it likely that community-mindedness will sweep apathetic neighborhoods because the City has been decentralized. (Indeed, since at least some segments of some communities are likely to view the local district derisively and since community politics is likely to become more contentious, what might be called "demonstrative dirtiness" may even worsen the sanitation problem.)

However, the environment for enforcement may well change more or less directly as a result of governmental reorganization. Enforcement officers may be much less reticent in issuing summonses if the district government makes a strong public commitment to neighborbood cleanliness; the local government is less likely to be cowed by fears of violent reactions to a tough enforcement program than the City has been. Assuming that most serious crime control responsibilities continue to rest with the central government, sanitation violations would almost automatically assume a higher spot on the enforcement agenda than they now have.

Moreover, decentralization would set the stage for accomplishment of an administrative reform that has long been urged: consolidation of inspectional and enforcement activities over the broad range of environmental matters subject to code regulation—housing, fire, health, sanitation, and the rest. A corps of local sanitation patrolmen with responsibility for all these areas would be less costly and probably more efficient than the present system of divided responsibilities. From the sanitation point of view, one desirable effect of such a consolidation might be that the link between housing conditions and sanitation problems in poor neighborhoods would have to be acknowledged; this would lighten the burden of reproach that the sanitation agency would inherit from the departments in these areas.

However, the success of any enforcement effort depends as much on the courts as on the enforcing agency, and the citywide courts have not been effective forums for sanitation violations in the past. Hence, it might be desirable to establish local tribunals for the resolution of routine sanitation cases—or all code violation cases. Even if it were constitutionally necessary to preserve a right of appeal into the state courts—even if a right to trial de novo in those courts were preserved— this step might do much to strengthen the hand of local political officials in pursuing the goal of a cleaner district.

Redefining the Sanitation Function

In the close analysis of the present legal definition of public sanitation functions that would necessarily precede decentralization, it might be decided either to enlarge or contract these at the time of decentralization or to give local districts the power to do so as they see fit. Changes in the extent of these functions might be desirable, even if the City were not decentralized; but decentralization might well be accompanied by much greater pressure for reforms of this order than now seems to exist. If the power to make such decisions as the following were given to the districts, it would substantially broaden their range of options in meeting sanitation problems.

"Load Shedding." As explained above, the administrator of the EPA presently is vested by the City Charter with authority to determine who will receive department refuse collection service. The categories of buildings from which collections are made have stayed constant since 1956. But, as discussed above, a recent report by the City administrator urged that the department "shed" some of its commitments as a means both of reducing the cost of sanitation operations, improving efficiency, and even generating a little additional revenue.

Would—or should—this option be available to local governmental
units? Would it be especially appropriate to have decisions about
categories of services be made district by district?

The City administrator's report recommended, first, termination
of municipal refuse collection from almost all public buildings and
private institutions that are tax exempt. If local governments had the
power to make similar decisions, the benefits would accrue unevenly
across the City, since the distribution of such properties is uneven.
Conversely, in the cases of buildings such as schools, which are part
of a citywide system, different local rules about refuse collection
might create budgetary and administrative difficulties. Finally, it
might be that a uniform City policy would be desirable with respect
at least to state and federal government buildings, embassies and
consulates, and other facilities that are located in New York City
because of its special status as the major American metropolis.

Consideration might also be given to ending municipal collection
from certain classes of residential property. For example, the City
administrator's report notes that one- and two-family dwellings are
currently very expensive for the department to service and might be
"shed." In Chicago, by contrast, free municipal service is provided
only to private homes and apartment buildings no larger then four
dwelling units. Giving local districts the power to make decisions
to "shed" residential customers would create a risk of intradistrict
discrimination; but there would probably exist a judicial remedy
against any really invidious decision. It might also be objected that
this power would not be of much use in poor neighborhoods, where
residents and landlords could not afford to contract for private hauling.
However, if the report's cost figures are even remotely accurate,
local districts could achieve savings, even if they contracted with private carters on behalf of classes of buildings being "shed." (This
might be a bit complicated if the distribution of buildings in the class
did not lend itself to the construction of an efficient collection route
or routes.)

Contracting Out. Any suggestion of contracting out is likely to alarm
the union, at least if it threatens a loss of jobs or even if it means
that men would be transferred from collection duties to others—bulk
collection, manual street sweeping—which are less favored. In the
body of the book (Chapter 6), it is suggested that a strike is not a
danger if a district has contracted out all its sanitation work. However,
it is more likely that, at least at the outset, districts would want to
contract out only a part of the responsibilities that the City now assumes.
Simple prudence might well dictate this, since private cartmen might
prove unequal to the task of residential collection. The union might
settle for displacement by attrition, but if many districts moved

towards substantial reliance on private cartmen, the threat to the
union's viability would probably evoke a major response that could
not be contained within district boundaries.

While the City's private cartage industry is by no means insubstantial, it would clearly not be able to absorb even a significant fraction of the department's present waste collection business. Hence, if
a large number of districts opted for contracting out, prices in the
private sector might rise significantly. On the other hand this new
demand might stimulate the creation of new carting companies, many
perhaps in minority neighborhoods. This might be the means by which
minorities could win a larger role in the performance of the City's
sanitation function, on terms more acceptable to them than seems to
be possible within the department.

Changing the "Public/Private Mix." As indicated above, present law
imposes substantial sanitation responsibilities on building owners
and private citizens, but at least in the poorer neighborhoods, it is
perfectly clear that this private portion of the "public/private mix."
of sanitation responsibilities is now simply not being performed.
Garbage is not properly stored to await collection, littering is epidemic,
sidewalks are not swept, and so on. Moreover, in areas where buildings
have been demolished, lots are not kept clean.

In some districts it may be desired to assume some of these
private responsibilities. At the present time the department does not
have the authority to enter private buildings without a certification
of a fire or health hazard from the Fire or Health Department or a
judicial finding of nuisance, and there might be constitutional obstacles
to conferring such authority on the local sanitation agency. Hence,
in neighborhoods where building services are grossly inadequate, it
may be necessary to organize the tenants to perform the janitorial
work of preparing the garbage for collection. Modest but sustained
expenditures for containers or paper and plastic bags may also be
necessary.

Abandoned and tenantless, but still privately owned, buildings
present more difficult problems, as do privately owned lots, since
not only can they not be entered and cleaned without a judicial finding
of nuisance or a fire or health hazard certification, but the expedient
suggested above is not possible either. In these circumstances local
districts might usefully initiate litigation to establish a broader public
power to enter and clean such properties than is presently thought to
exist; it might well be that the public interest in enhancing the cleanliness of the environment would weigh more heavily when asserted by
a unit of government with respect to a small geographic area under
its jurisdiction than would a comparable claim asserted as to the
City as a whole. Finally, local districts may also prove more willing

and able than the City to ignore legal niceties, move in, clean up, and run the risk of having to defend trespass suits.

In the event a district took any of these steps with respect to private property, it would be to its advantage to coordinate these activities with inspectional and enforcement activities in related areas, such as housing maintenance and fire prevention. The additional costs that would be incurred by an expansion of cleaning work might appropriately be in part offset by such coordination.

There would not seem to be any legal obstacles to the assumption of sidewalk-cleaning responsibility by local sanitation agencies, although the current City Charter provisions would have to be modified to authorize it. Sidewalk sweeping is one of the ongoing programs of the sanitation aide force in the Central Brooklyn Model Cities area. However, at least if the effort is conducted on the lines of the Model Cities Program, it could prove quite expensive, requiring both a substantial commitment of manpower and the purchase and maintance of special equipment. The Model Cities Program finances its effort with 100 percent federal dollars, but since this source of funds is not likely to be available to the local districts, they will be faced with a hard budgetary choice. And a sidewalk-sweeping program could not, of course, be directly financed through user charges.

In middle-class areas the district governments might wish to place more responsibility on private persons. What has been described as "load-shedding" would, of course, be the polar case; but short of this, the district could, for example, tighten rules about private container placement or require segregation of different types of waste to facilitate disposal or recycling activities.

Interfunctional Coordination

Regardless of which of these models, or variants of them, is adopted, decentralization may create a number of opportunities for more efficient and effective service delivery. One suggested in the body of the book is that decentralization may make it easier to co-ordinate the delivery of related or interdependent City services than it is at present. Since service delivery districts will have common boundaries and since administrative arrangements that now create incentives for departmental loyalty will be displaced by incentives to district loyalty, it seems a reasonable hope that interfunctional cooperation will be more common than it now is. This result is obviously much more likely if districts have discretion to redefine the sanitation function.

In the context of sanitation services, there are at least two areas where such cooperation might be fruitful—in addition to the possibility of coordinated code inspection discussed above. First, it may be possible to coordinate more effectively sanitation-sweeping and collection schedules with parking schedules of the department of highways, as well as with activities of the traffic division of the police department. This would have two advantages: (a) more or less regular street sweeping might become possible in neighborhoods where, at the present time, curbs can rarely be reached because of illegal parking; and (b) traffic could be more readily diverted from side streets, where it now impedes collection.

Second, the division of responsibilities for cleaning streets in the vicinity of parks between sanitation and parks department personnel could be clarified or even renegotiated. At the present time these areas are often unusually dirty because of the uncertainty of responsibility, and it is perhaps especially unfortunate that recreational areas should be unattractive or even dangerous because of poor sanitation service.

Control of Men and Equipment

Regardless of the extent of the powers confided to the local districts, the most critical issue is whether the district sanitation chiefs will be able to exercise better control of their men and equipment than they do at present. It is also the most nearly imponderable. Much will depend on their personal qualities of leadership and acumen and on the manner in which labor relations are structured in the decentralized City, and many of the department's policies are now defined in collective bargaining. For these and other reasons there is little that can usefully be added here to what is said in Chapter 6 of the preceding study. But a few more or less concrete observations responsive to current problems in the Department of Sanitation can be offered.

First, and virtually as a matter of definition, decentralization will mean that the district head will have under his command a stable and (at least numerically) dependable force of men, trucks, and junior officers. Except in emergencies he will not be subject to detachments of these resources. (The negative impact of this fact on poorer districts is discussed above. Over some period of time he should be able to establish closer, more productive relations with the work force as a result. To the imponderable extent that current lack of discipline and low morale among the force can be explained by the absence of a field hierarchy to which the men can form a commitment, these problems may ease.

Second, both the administrative and political officers of the new districts can anticipate that any proposal to expand the discretion of local supervisors to discipline the men will meet with strenuous union resistance. Conversations with current union leaders make it clear that the current grievance procedures are not negotiable.

Third, decentralization will have to be accompanied by a major overhauling of the fleet maintenance operations of the department, probably entailing significant capital expenditures to improve district maintenance facilities. As described above inadequate maintenance has a devastating effect on the operations of the department, and the limited capacity of the district superintendents to affect the availability of equipment is a major weakness in the current maintenance operation. Thus, the district garages must be upgraded, their tools and parts inventories enlarged, and their staff brought under the control of district officers, if the districts are to enjoy more than paper discretion. (Alternatively, districts might contract out maintenance.)

Finally, it should be emphasized that a much improved training program will have to be instituted to fit district chiefs and their subordinates for their responsibilities. The rapid turnover in supervisory titles in past years means that many current, and almost all future, officers will have inadequate field experience; present training practices, geared to a less mobile and rebellious age, will have to be drastically revised. And this too will cost money.

Central Functions in a Decentralized Sanitation Operation

It has been assumed in this appendix, as in the preceding study, that, of the major divisions of the department, only the Bureau of Cleaning and Collection will be decentralized; waste disposal, routine equipment acquisition, and major equipment maintenance will be kept as central responsibilities. There are good reasons for this assumption, but since these activities have an important impact on the delivery of services at the district level, a brief, closer look is desirable.

As to waste disposal it is widely recognized that the City is fast approaching a crisis, as land-fill sites reach their capacity and incinerators conflict with air pollution control programs. Here, if in any area of sanitation services, the need for innovation has become desperate and the necessity for "waste avoidance" dramatically apparent. And if the crisis is not surmounted, scheduling and operations in the district will become very difficult. These considerations suggest that it might not be a bad idea to impose at least part of the disposal burden on the districts; perhaps they could be denied the right to dispose amounts in excess of some figure at City-owned disposal locations or, at least, charged stiff fees for such excess disposal. Indeed, districts could be required to maintain local dumps or local incinerators or to contract for all disposal, either with the

City or with private land-owners, as private cartmen do now.   And
some districts—especially if they required segregation of kinds of
garbage—might be able to sell some of it for recycling.

But these ideas—or at least the most extreme of them—are
probably not feasible. The health hazards associated with all forms of
disposal argue for a small number of disposal sites under careful supervision. They should be located in undeveloped areas and out of the
path of development, since they ruin their surroundings for all other
uses. However, some means should be adopted to force upon the districts an appreciation of their stake in a sound, long-term resolution
of the disposal dilemma.

Department vehicles are bought out of capital budget funds, and
the plan proposal (in the preceding study) contemplates that the capital
budget will be raised and spent centrally. However, local district
officials will have to play a major advisory role in the equipment
acquisition process. Only they will have the operating experience
needed to choose among different kinds and models of equipment.
Moreover, there is a growing variety of new refuse-loading equipment
coming into the market, and the various districts may want to experiment with them. Finally, the districts will have much greater maintenance responsibilities than at present, and their officials will be in
the best position to know what sorts of guarantees, design modifications,
and so on to negotiate for in order to reduce "down" time.

There will have to be some large central maintenance facilities.
It might be, however, that districts should not have unlimited free
access to them, that they should have to pay for excessive service
requirements in order to give them an incentive to careful handling
of the equipment and to give local citizens a monetary measurement
of official care or carelessness.

Conclusions: A Personal Statement

In the preceding study it is suggested that the chief goal of a
decentralization of New York City would be to improve the delivery
of municipal services, or, at least, to increase public acceptance of
and responsibility for the level of services provided. Obviously,
only the interaction of many factors would determine if this goal were
achieved. My examination of the sanitation function suggests to me
that, in terms of those factors most readily analyzed and assessed,
failure is at least as likely as success.

On the other hand the factors to which I have given the most
attention may not be the critical ones. In particular, my treatment
of the possible impact of decentralization on citizen behavior is perhaps
too skimpy. But I have had reasons for limiting the discussion of

what I consider an inherently imponderable factor that ought to be made explicit here.

First, in my view too much writing on this subject has been vague and rhetorical, emphasizing just those points least subject to reasoned discussion. This is unfortunate for several reasons. If decentralization comes, it would be well if it were preceded by careful definition of the likely results and problems to avoid further inflaming the politics of New York. Moreover, for decentralization to happen, many people not initially sympathetic to it will have to be won over—or at least negotiated with. The municipal employee unions are, of course, the prime example. I assume that they will not be persuaded by rhetoric. But the unions are not the only ones: my work has taught me that commissioners and other top-level bureaucrats— even though nominally allies of the mayor—may be less than enthusiastic; they will want to know just what's in it for them and their departments.

I don't believe that my research is by any means as complete and detailed as may be necessary for these purposes, but I do dare to hope that it succeeds in suggesting the complex and intricate outlines of the problems. From my work in these, I know that they are extraordinarily difficult and elusive.

Finally, it may be that in the last analysis, decentralization should come not because of the improvements in service it will bring but in spite of a possible decline in service. If so, we ought to be candid about this. In the long run—and the not so very long run at that—disingenuousness in politics serves no cause other than that of discord and despair.

CHAPTER 1
    1. Section 101, Demonstration Cities and Metropolitan Development Act of 1966, 42 U.S.C. 3301.

CHAPTER 2
    1. Wallace S. Sayre and Herbert Kaufman, Governing New York City: Politics in the Metropolis (New York: W. W. Norton, 1965); Lyle C. Fitch and Annmarie Hauck Walsh, eds., Agenda for a City: Issues Confronting New York (Beverly Hills, Calif.: Sage Publications, 1970).
    2. For comparison of wages of New York City employees with employees of other major cities and of private industry, see Wages and Benefits of Municipal Government Workers in New York City, Regional Labor Statistics Bulletin No. 29, Bureau of Labor Statistics, Middle Atlantic Region (June 1971). For comparison of pensions of New York City employees and those of auto, steel, and electrical workers, see New York Times, June 7, 1971, p. 19, col. 7.
    3. Joseph J. Monan and Anthony Downs, "Public Goods and Private Status," The Public Interest (Spring 1971).
    4. Maurice R. Berube and Marilyn Gittell, eds., Confrontation at Ocean Hill-Brownsville (New York: Praeger Publishers, 1969); Mario Fantini, Marilyn Gittell, and Richard Magat, Community Control and the Urban School (New York: Praeger Publishers, 1970).

CHAPTER 3
    1. For development of this argument in analogous situations, see Gerson Green and Geoffrey Faux, "The Social Utility of Black Enterprise," in Black Economic Development, William F. Haddad and Douglas G. Pugh, eds. (Englewood Cliffs, N.J.: Prentice Hall, 1969).
    2. See, e.g., Royal Commission on Local Government in England, John P. Redcliffe-Maud, chm., Report (London: H.M. Stationery Office, 1969), Chaps. IV and V.
    3. See, e.g., Richland, "Constitutional City Home Rule in New York," 54 Col. L. Rev. 311 (1954), 55 Col. L. Rev. 598 (1955).
    4. See, e.g., Frank Smallwood, Metro Toronto: A Decade Later (Toronto: Bureau of Municipal Research, 1963), p. 30, and H. Kaplan, Urban Political Systems: A Functional Analysis of Metro Toronto (New York: Columbia University Press, 1967),

pp. 83, 218-20. For an analysis of similar problems of metropolitan councils of government, see Bernard Michelman and Terrance Sandalow, Materials on Government in Urban Areas (St. Paul, Minn.: West Publishing, 1970), pp. 815-23.

5. For a perceptive and still valid discussion of the tone and procedures of the Board of Estimate, see Wallace S. Sayre and Herbert Kaufman, Governing New York City: Politics in the Metropolis (New York: W. W. Norton, 1965), pp. 626-56.

CHAPTER 4

1. For other discussions of the allocation of service delivery responsibilities between tiers of municipal government, see Advisory Commission on Intergovernmental Relations, Performance of Urban Functions: Local and Areawide (Washington, D.C., 1963), p. 281; Committee for Economic Development, Reshaping Government in Metropolitan Areas (New York, 1970), p. 83; Royal Commission on Local Government in London, Report (London: H.M. Stationery Office, 1960), p. 371.

2. Report of Commission on the Delivery of Personal Health Services, Gerald Piel, chm., Comprehensive Community Health Services for New York City (1967).

3. 42 U.S.C. Sec. 1402 (11).

4. Two studies delivered to the City in 1969 both suggest that the combination of aging housing, increasing costs, low tenant incomes, and rent control has a greater impact upon the rate of housing deterioration in the City than does simple landlord rapacity. George Sternlieb, The Urban Housing Dilemma: The Dynamics of New York City's Rent Controlled Housing, prepared for the Department of Rent and Housing Maintenance, released on April 27, 1970; New York City Rand Institute, Rental Housing in New York City (New York, 1970).

5. See studies of New York's "Neighborhood Conservation" Program, Harris, An Interim Report on Neighborhood Conservation in New York City (New York: Housing and Redevelopment Board, 1963); Abeles, Schwartz & Associates, Chelsea: A Decade of Change (New York, 1969) (prepared for the Lower West Side Community Corporation).

6. See Roger Starr, "Immobilism in Housing," The Public Interest (Summer 1969).

7. Royal Commission on Local Government in England, The L.S.E. Greater London Group: Lessons of the London Government Reforms, 7 Research Report No. 2 (London: H.M. Stationery Office, 1968).

8. Gerald Rhodes and F. K. Ruck, The Government of Greater London (London: H.M. Stationery Office, 1970).

9. Royal Commission on Local Government in England, John
P. Redcliffe-Maud, chm., Report (London: H.M. Stationery Office,
1969), Annex 4.

10. This is the approach suggested in Babcock and Bosselman,
"Citizen Participation in Zoning, A Suburban Alternative for the
Central City," 32 L. & Contemp. Prob. 220 (1967). They advocate
similar placement of zoning powers at a decentralized level within
large cities. They are more optimistic than we, however, about
the ability of such local units to meet the needs of the city as a whole
without the exercise of central City override powers.

11. See President's Commission on Law Enforcement and the
Administration of Justice, Task Force Report, Courts (1967), Chap.
VIII, pp. 97-107; Sanford H. Kadish, "The Crisis of Overcrim-
inalization," The Annals of the American Academy of Political and
Social Science, CCCLXXIV (November 1967), 157-70; Herbert
Packer, The Limits of the Criminal Sanction (1968); and Norval
Morris and Gordon Hawkins, The Honest Politician's Guide to Crime
Control (Oxford University Press, 1964).

12. Testimony of David Hardy of New York Daily News, in
Report of the National Advisory Committee on Civil Disorders
(New York: Bantam, 1968), p. 305; Joseph Goldstein, "Police
Discretion Not To Invoke the Criminal Process: Low-Visibility
Decisions in the Administration of Justice," 69 Yale L. J. 543, 575
(1960).

13. See 19 Correctional Research Bulletin, "What is the Role
of the Community in the Development of Police Systems?" (November
1969), p. 8.

14. See Waskow, "Community Control of the Police," Trans-
action (December 1969), p. 4., and "Neighborhood Police Districts:
A Constitutional Analysis," 57 Calif. L. Rev. 907 (1969). Both of
these plans recommend the election of a neighborhood commission
empowered to appoint and remove the precinct commander.

15. See the arguments advanced by Philadelphia's Fraternal
Order of Police in its decade of battling that city's Civilian Review
Board, as compiled in Loman and Miswer, "The Police and the
Community," Field Surveys IV, A Research Study Submitted to the
President's Commission on Law Enforcement and Justice (1966),
pp. 261-70. Ultimately, the order was successful in having the board
abolished. See New York Times, December 28, 1969.

16. A brief summary of the project may be found in Criminal
Justice Coordinating Council of New York City and the Vera Institute
of Justice, "In Lieu of Arrest, the Manhattan Bowery Project," p. 1.
(Date of publication missing.) A more detailed account is in Vera
Institute of Justice, "First Annual Report of the Manhattan Bowery
Project" (1969). A comparable program is evaluated in St. Louis

Metropolitan Police Department, "The St. Louis Detoxification and Diagnostic Evaluation Center," report submitted to the Law Enforcement Administration under Grant #284.

17. The most comprehensive review of the project may be found in "Training Police as Specialists in Family Crisis Intervention," Final Report to the Office of Law Enforcement Administration, Grant #157 (1970). More conveniently accessible descriptions are presented in Bard and Berkowitz, "Training Police as Specialists in Family Crisis Intervention: A Community Psychological Action Program," Community Mental Health Journal, III, 315 (1967), and Bard, "Family Intervention Police Teams as a Mental Health Resource," 60 Journal of Criminal Law, Criminology and Police Science (1969), p. 247.

18. See Family Court Act, 29A McKinney's Consolidated Laws of New York (Judiciary Court Acts), 1969 and Supplement. An Association of the Bar of the City of New York study, Children and Families in the Courts of New York City (1954), describes the operation of the New York system prior to 1962. The report prompted the 1962 Family Court Act. And see Directors of Administration of the Courts, First and Second Judicial Departments, "A Study of the Family Court of the State of New York Within the City of New York and Related Agencies and Recommendations Concerning Their Administration" (July 1969); and State of New York, "Family Court, Unfulfilled Mission," Report of the Administrative Board of the Judicial Conference of the State of New York for the Judicial Year July 1, 1968 to June 30, 1969 (1970), pp. 287-325. Recommendations accepted from the former report and planned changes are described in "Annual Report of the First Judicial Department," in Report of the . . . Judicial Conference, pp. 63-70.

19. The Family Court's failure as an instrument of conciliation is suggested by the fact that of the 44,675 new cases it received in 1968-69, exactly 10 were for conciliation in an effort to avoid divorce or separation. Report of the . . . Judicial Conference, p. 319.

20. A National Opinion Research Center survey of 10,000 households in 1965 revealed that only about 50 percent of all crimes were reported to the law enforcement authorities; 34 percent of those who did not report an incident explained that they did not want the matter treated as a criminal affair or the offender harmed. Ennis, "Crime, Victims and Police," in James F. Short, Jr., ed., Law and Order: Modern Criminals (Trans-action Books, 1970), p. 94.

21. Department of Corrections, Daily Inmate Census (August 24, 1970).

22. Such a program is described in Vera Institute of Justice, "The Manhattan Court Employment Project," Report to the Manpower Administration of the U.S. Department of Labor (1970).

CHAPTER 5
    1. Section 123a of the New York City Charter (1961).
    2. The New York State Commission on the Quality, Cost, and
Financing of Elementary and Secondary Education has developed
a different kind of formula for allocating educational funds—in that
case state funds. See Chap. II, pp. 2.12 of the commission's report
of January 1972.
    3. McKinsey & Company, Inc., Allocating Educational Funds to
the Community School Districts (November 1970), Exhibit 25, facing
page 3-6.
    4. See 20 U.S.C., Sec. 241(a) ff.
    5. John E. Coons, William H. Clune, and Stephen Sugarman,
Educational Opportunity: A Workable Constitutional Trust for State
Financial Structures, 57 Cal. L. Rev. 309 (1969), pp. 319-22.
    6. McKinsey & Company, Inc., Allocating Educational Funds,
pp. 3-9.
    7. Ibid.
    8. Ibid., pp. 3-11.

CHAPTER 6
    1. 9 McKinney's Consolidated Laws of New York (Civil Service
Law), Sec. 200 ff.
    2. Executive Order 52 (September 29, 1967).
    3. Local Laws of the City of New York, No. 1 (1972), The City
Record (January 20, 1972), p. 218.
    4. Executive Order 52, Sec. 8.
    5. Executive Order 52, Sec. 5(c).
    6. New York City Health and Hospital Corporation Act of 1969,
Sec. 9; McKinney's Unconsolidated Laws, Sec. 7390.
    7. New York Times, June 8, 1971, p. 19. col. 7, and May 27,
1971, p. 12, col. 7.
    8. See, e.g., Schiller v. Bd. of Examiners, 72 N.Y. Dept. R.
148, 149 (three-tier grading standard).
    9. Commission on Organization of the Executive Branch of the
Government, Personnel and the Civil Service: A Report to the
Congress (February 1955), p. 61.
    10. Griggs v. Duke Power Co., 401 U.S. 424 (1971).

APPENDIX
    1. Chapter 57 of the City Charter, added in 1968, created EPA
and recodified the earlier charter provisions relating to performance
of the municipal sanitation function. These are now found in Chap.
57, Sec. 1403. Chapter 31 of the Administrative Code imposes
additional responsibilities on the department. See, e.g., Administrative Code, Sec. 755(2)-2.0 (night offal to be removed).

2. The data can be found in American Public Works Association, Refuse Collection Practice (3d. ed.; 1966), App. B, pp. 449-72.

3. In the case of the Housing Code, Administrative Code, Sec. D26-22.03, requires provision of "adequate janitorial services" by landlords; Sec. D26-14.05 requires regular garbage collection within a multiple dwelling; and Sec. D26-14.03 requires the provision of receptacles to contain waste accumulated during 72 hours and their placement in front of the building for collection by the department. Tenants' responsibilities are covered in Sec. D26-14.05(d) and (e). The prohibitions against littering and dumping are found in Administrative Code, Sec. 755(2)-7.0 and -7.1. The relevant sections of the Health Code are those relating to nuisances. Administrative Code, Secs. 565-15.0 ff.

4. The report provoked a detailed rebuttal from EPA Administrator Kretchmer and Commissioner Elish, Private Cartmen and the Department of Sanitation (January 1972), which generally argued (a) that the City administrator's figures were inaccurate, and (b) that in any event it is not appropriate to compare the operations of the private cartmen and the City. A month later the Citizens Budge Commission published a study called Reducing Refuse Collection Costs in New York City, which generally agreed with the City administrator's findings and recommendations. For the code provisions relating to regulation of private cartmen, see Administrative Code, Secs. B32.267 ff.

5. Wallace S. Sayre and Herbert Kaufman, Governing New York City: Politics in the Metropolis (New York: W. W. Norton, 1965), pp. 300-301.

6. It has often been asserted that the department's statistics are not reliable, and the incumbent commissioner is taking steps to create a dependable management information system. A separate but related question is what the appropriate measures of adequate performance would be. For one set of suggestions, see L. Blair, H. Hartny, and P. Don Vito, Measuring the Effectiveness of Local Government Services: Solid Waste Collection (Urban Institute, 1970).

The books and articles listed below are ones the authors found particularly relevant. More extensive bibliographies of publications about New York City's government and about decentralization and community control may be found in Wallace S. Sayre and Herbert Kaufman, Governing New York City; in Robert H. Connery and Demetrios Caraley, Governing the City; and in Donna E. Shalala, Neighborhood Governance: Issues and Proposals.

BOOKS AND PAMPHLETS

Advisory Commission on Intergovernmental Relations. Performance of Area Functions: Local and Area Wide. Washington, D.C., 1963.

Altshuler, Alan A. Community Control: The Black Demand for Participation in Large American Cities. New York: Western Publishing, Pegasus, 1970.

Childs, Richard S. Civic Victories. New York: Harper & Bros., 1952.

Committee for Economic Development. Reshaping Governing in Metropolitan Areas. New York: The Committee, 1970.

Connery, Robert H., and Demetrios Caraley, eds. Governing The City: Challenges and Options for New York. New York: Praeger Publishers, 1969.

Fitch, Lyle C., and Annmarie Hauck Walsh, eds. Agenda for A City: Issues Confronting New York. Beverly Hills, Calif.: Sage Publications, 1970.

Graduate School of Public Administration, New York University. Financing Government in New York City. Final Research Report to the Temporary Commission on City Finances. New York, 1966.

Michelman, Bernard, and Terrance Sandalow. Materials on Government in Urban Areas. St. Paul, Minn.: West Publishing, 1970

Netzer, Dick. Economics and Urban Problems. New York: Basic Books, 1970.

Office of the Mayor. A Plan for Neighborhood Government. New York, 1970.

Office of the Mayor. Program for the Decentralized Administration of Municipal Services in New York City Communities. New York, 1971.

Royal Commission on Local Government in England. Report. London: H. M. Stationery Office, 1969.

Royal Commission on Local Government in Greater London. Report. London: H. M. Stationery Office, 1960.

Sayre, Wallace S., and Herbert Kaufman. Governing New York City: Politics in the Metropolis. New York: W. W. Norton, 1965.

Shalala, Donna E. Neighborhood Governance: Issues and Proposals. New York: American Jewish Committee, 1971.

Walsh, Annmarie Hauck. The Urban Challenge to Government: An International Comparison of Thirteen Cities. New York: Praeger Publishers, 1969.

ARTICLES

Kaufman, Herbert "Administrative Decentralization and Political Power," Public Administration Review XXXIX (January-February 1969).

Meltsner, Arnold J., and Aaron Wldavsky. "Leave City Budgeting Alone." In Financing the Metropolis, edited by John P. Crecine. Beverly Hills, Calif.: Sage Publications, 1970, pp. 311-58.

Wellington, Harry H., and Ralph K. Winter. "Structuring Collective Bargaining in Public Employment," 79 Yale L. J. 803-70 (1970).

WALTER G. FARR is Professor of Law at New York University and has been the Director of a study of decentralization of New York City's government, sponsored by the Association of the Bar of the City of New York.

After 10 years of private practice, he joined the Agency for International Development, where he was Deputy Regional Administrator for the Near East and South Asia. In 1967 he became the first Director of the Model Cities Administration in the Department of Housing and Urban Development. Professor Farr has been a consultant to the Task Force on Jurisdiction and Structure of the New York State Study Commission for New York City. He has also consulted with the Ford Foundation in the area of minority economic development and was Director of the Ford Urban Law Fellowship Program.

Professor Farr received his B.S. degree from Yale and his LL.B. from Yale Law School.

LANCE LIEBMAN is Assistant Professor of Law at Harvard and a member of the faculty of the Kennedy School of Government.

Professor Liebman was law clerk to Justice Byron White of the U.S. Supreme Court during the Court's 1967 Term. From 1968 to 1970 he was on the staff of Mayor John Lindsay of New York City as Assistant to the Mayor, as Secretary to the Mayor's Cabinet, and as Executive Director of the Mayor's Urban Action Task Force. Working on problems of transportation and economic development, during 1969 and part of 1970 he was in charge of the city's activities and experiments in the field of neighborhood government.

Since 1970 Professor Liebman has been teaching at Harvard and researching the problems of land-use control, in particular the problem of integrating the suburbs both racially and economically, and of dispute settlement and law-making by consent, including devices for third-party intervention. With Professor Graham Allison of the Kennedy School, he has been directing an on-going investigation of the Model Cities experience. He is a successor trustee of the Yale Corporation and a member of the board of the Center for Conflict Resolution, and he has been a consultant to the Sloan Foundation, the Ford Foundation, and the National Academy of Sciences.

Professor Liebman received his B.A. from Yale, his M.A. in English history from Cambridge, and his LL.B. from Harvard Law School.

JEFFREY WOOD, currently associated with a large New York City law firm, has worked in low-income housing and urban development law. Prior to serving as Associate Director for this study, he was with the General Counsel's Office of the Department of Housing and Urban Development in Washington, D.C., where he dealt with the Model Cities Program and with the low- and moderate-income housing construction subsidiary of one of the country's major manufacturing companies. He has also been a Lecturer in Law at the Columbia Law School.

Mr. Wood was an undergraduate in the Woodrow Wilson School of Princeton University, and spent two years studying economics at Cambridge University before he obtained his law degree from Yale University.